DOLLARS AND VOTES

DOLLARS AND VOTES

How
Business Campaign Contributions
Subvert Democracy

DAN CLAWSON
ALAN NEUSTADTL
MARK WELLER

Temple University Press
Philadelphia

Temple University Press, Philadelphia 19122
Copyright © 1998 by Temple University
All rights reserved
Published 1998
Printed in the United States of America

♾The paper used in this publication meets the requirements of the American
National Standard for Information Sciences—Permanence of Paper for Printed
Library Materials, ANSI z39.48-1984

TEXT DESIGN: Judith Martin Waterman

LIBRARY OF CONGRESS CATALOGING-IN-PUBLICATION DATA

Clawson, Dan.
    Dollars and votes : how business campaign contributions subvert
democracy / Dan Clawson, Alan Neustadtl, Mark Weller.
        p.   cm.
    Includes index.
    ISBN 1-56639-625-5 (cloth : alk. paper). — ISBN 1-56639-626-3 (pbk. :
alk. paper)
        1. Business and politics—United States.   2. Corporations—United
States—Political activity.   3. Campaign funds—United
States.   4. Political action committees—United States.   I. Neustadtl,
Alan, 1957–   .   II. Weller, Mark, 1962–   . III. Title.
JK467.C52 1998   98-11172
322'.3'0973—dc21   CIP

CONTENTS

DEDICATED TO
STEPHEN SHRAISON
1959–1997

PREFACE

CAMPAIGN FINANCE IS IN TURMOIL, DESPITE THE FACT (IN PART BECAUSE of the fact) that little is changing. Each day brings new instances of scandal, and even though this book is being rushed into production, with as short a gap as possible between our final revisions and its appearance in print, inevitably much will have happened in the interval. But whenever you are reading this, and whatever the headlines of the day say, we can be sure that:

- Money continues to exercise a disproportionate influence.
- The distribution of wealth is wildly unequal.
- Most of the campaign contributions come, directly or indirectly, from business.
- The media stories, which focus on the latest scandal, don't explain the operation of the *system* of campaign finance.
- Many politicians sound like Claude Rains in *Casablanca*: These politicians are "shocked, deeply shocked" to discover the president and vice president actively worked at fundraising and, in doing so, granted privileged access to donors; the implication is that Mr. (or Ms.) Deeply Shocked does not engage in such activities.

Media accounts are partial and misleading for a variety of reasons: Sometimes the reporters—and to a significant degree the participants themselves—do not understand the system; in other cases, the journalistic conventions or the press of daily events make it difficult to provide the background needed to make sense of the bare (and scattered) facts. But the fundamental problem is that, in order for decent people to participate in a thoroughly corrupt system, they must maintain a conspiracy of silence and a hypocrisy so deep and thoroughgoing that it often deceives the participants themselves.

Most of the writing about campaign finance—certainly most of the academic work—is based on analyses of official records. Some people have talked to the politicians involved, but we are among the very few who have interviewed the people who give them the money. This book draws heavily on our interviews with corporate "government relations" officials about what they do and why they do it; they provide some of the most damning evidence imaginable. Because those who dish out the money don't have to run for office, because few people scrutinize their activities, and because past experience tells them that they rarely feature in media accounts, they were surprisingly candid, revealing to us perhaps more than they intended.

The corporate executives quoted in this book generously shared with us their time, wit, and insights. We appreciate their willingness to talk honestly, but we don't acknowledge them by name because we promised them confidentiality. They are charming, shrewd, and perceptive about politics, but they are key participants in a system we strongly oppose. We regret that they probably won't be happy with what we have to say, even when—perhaps especially when—we use their words to make our case.

For fifteen years, most of our research has focused on campaign finance. This book is based on and incorporates substantial material from an earlier book, *Money Talks: Corporate PACs and Political Influence*. About half the material here is new, including not only new chapters (4 on soft money and 7 on the 1996 scandals), but also changes on virtually every page and substantial alterations to most chapters (especially 1, 3, and 5; 2 and 6 were less extensively reworked). Some of those changes update the analysis or introduce new examples, others improve the presentation of the ideas, and some involve reconceptualizations of basic points. Soft money—the principal focus of the current controversy—was far less important in 1991, when we finished the writing of *Money Talks*, than it is today. We now talk about soft money in every chapter, and in Chapter 4 we've undertaken the most sustained analysis yet done of key aspects of soft money, moving beyond simply presenting lists of the biggest donors.

Money Talks was coauthored with Denise Scott. Though she is not a co-author of *Dollars and Votes*, her ideas and contributions are present in every chapter. Denise's work on the earlier book as well as her solo research on gender in government relations have shaped our own thinking fundamentally and introduced much of what is valuable here.

We will not thank again the people and institutions acknowledged in *Money Talks*, but their contributions at that time are reflected in this book as well.

Michael Ames, of Temple University Press, took an interest in the project, made numerous helpful suggestions, and provided enthusiastic support that encouraged us to undertake this new work. Mary Capouya clarified and sharpened our prose; every page bears her imprint. Judith Martin Waterman helped turn a manuscript into a book. Michael Dickerson of the Federal Election Commission assisted us in tracking down the last few oddball cases; some people complain about government bureaucrats, but we are repeatedly impressed by the number of civil servants who regularly do more than the job requires.

DAN CLAWSON: For the past three years my primary activity has been editing *Contemporary Sociology*. In many ways this has been the most stimulating intellectual enterprise I've ever engaged in. Although I can't specify exactly how that has contributed to this book, there's no doubt in my mind that the ideas here owe much to the seventy-five hundred books I looked at, the two thousand reviews I read, and especially, the hundreds of suggestions from board members and dozens of board meetings that now inform the way I think about the world.

Helen Smith's editing was one key part of the *Contemporary Sociology* experience. While my own writing benefited from her editing, I learned even more from noting the changes she made in hundreds of reviews and the extent to which these (often small) changes made the prose more readable. My writing may have improved, but I am not so foolhardy as to think I can now do without an editor; on the contrary, I more than ever appreciate the need for one. Helen Smith has edited this work, and although I haven't always taken her advice, she has significantly increased its liveliness.

Mary Ann and Laura Clawson not only put up with the hassles involved in any book. They did more: serving as a sounding board and offering their own ideas and comments, many of them now incorporated here. Mary Ann also called numerous readings to my attention, suggested revisions, and edited parts of the manuscript.

I have been energized and inspired by the revival of the labor movement. Campaign finance is often a bleak area; over and over again, the bad guys win. In the labor movement, however, away from those with wealth and power, large numbers of unrecognized people demonstrate a level of heroism and dedication that raises the prospect of a better world, one shaped by democracy and votes, not business and dollars.

ALAN NEUSTADTL: Writing a book like this takes enormous time and energy, which necessarily takes away from time spent with family and friends. I thank those who gave me the time to work on this book and apologize for my absence. I thank those who helped me laugh through the work. The short list includes my "best friends" Aidan and Betty, and my sailing buddies Bill Falk and Tim Moran. Finally, I thank my coauthors for their sacrifices and efforts to make this a great book. As usual, the soundtrack for this effort, as well as for my life, was provided by the Grateful Dead.

MARK WELLER: My family, Linda and Dayan, gave loving support, despite my neglect while I worked on this project. I owe them most of all. Our parents, Gail and Paul Weller and Harriet and Ray Goulet, rescued us many times with their generosity. Tom and Kate Winans, Paula Donnelly, and Burr Brown in New England, and Pat Burger, Derek Dykman, and Carmen Gagne in California gave us emergency child care, lots of laughs, and two places to call home. I blame Bill Monning for first involving me in campaign finance reform. Bruce Grube and the sociology faculties at San Jose State University and the University of Massachusetts at Amherst encouraged me, sometimes prodded me, and gave me a chance. My heartfelt thanks to all of them.

DOLLARS AND VOTES

FOLLOW THE MONEY

THE MONEY PRIMARY

IMAGINE THE NOVEMBER ELECTION IS JUST A FEW WEEKS AWAY, AND YOUR friend Sally Robeson is seriously considering running for Congress two years from now. This year the incumbent in your district, E. Chauncey DeWitt III, will (again!) be reelected by a substantial margin, but you and Sally hate Chauncey's positions on the issues and are convinced that with the right campaign he can be beaten. Sally is capable, articulate, well informed, respected in the community, politically and socially connected, charming, good at talking to many kinds of people, and highly telegenic. She has invited you and several other politically active friends to meet with her immediately after the election to determine what she would need to do to become a viable candidate.

The meeting that takes place covers a host of topics: What are the key issues? On which of these are Sally's stands popular, and on which unpopular? What attacks, and from what quarters, will be launched against her? What individuals or groups can she count on for support? How, why, and where is the incumbent vulnerable? But lurking in the background is the question that cannot be ignored: *Can Sally (with the help of her friends and backers) raise enough money to be a contender?*

This is the *money primary, the first, and, in many instances, the most important round of the contest.* It eliminates more candidates than any other hurdle. Because it eliminates them so early and so quietly, its impact is often unobserved. To make it through, candidates don't have to come in first, but they do need to raise enough money to be credible contenders. Although having the most money is no guarantee of victory, candidates who don't do well in the money primary are no longer serious contenders. Certainly, plenty of well-funded candidates lose—Michael Huffington spent $25 million of his own money in an unsuccessful 1994 race for the Senate. But in order to be viable, a candidate needs to raise a substantial minimum.

How much is needed? If Sally hopes to win, rather than just put up a good fight, she, you, and the rest of her supporters will need to raise staggering amounts. (At least they are staggering from the perspective of most Americans; Ross Perot, Steve Forbes, or Michael Huffington may view the matter differently.) In order to accumulate the *average* amount for major-party congressional candidates in the general election, you will collectively need to raise $4,800 next week. And the week after. And *every* week for the next two years.

But even that is not enough. The average amount includes many candidates who were never "serious"; that is, they didn't raise enough to have a realistic hope of winning. If you and your friends want to raise the average amount spent by a *winning* candidate for the House, you'll have to come up with $6,730 next week and every single week until the election, two years away.

Well, you say, your candidate is hardly average. She is stronger, smarter, more politically appealing, and more viable than the "average" challenger. You think she can win even if she doesn't raise $6,730 a week. Let's use past experience—the results of the 1996 elections—to consider the likelihood of winning for challengers, based on how much money they raised. In 1996 more than 360 House incumbents were running for reelection; only 23 of them were beaten by their challengers. The average successful challenger spent $1,045,361—that is, he or she raised an average of over $10,000 every week for two years. What were the chances of winning without big money? Only one winning challenger spent less than $500,000, 12 spent between a half-a-million and a million dollars, and 10 spent more than a million dollars. Furthermore, 13 of the 23 winning challengers outspent the incumbent. A House challenger who can't raise at least a half-million dollars doesn't have a one percent chance of winning; the key primary is the money primary. The *Boston Globe* reported that "House candidates who headed into the final three weeks with the most in combined spending and cash on hand won 93 percent of the time."[1] What about that one low-spending winner? She is Carolyn Cheeks Kilpatrick, who won election by beating an incumbent in the primary and then having a walkover in the general election; the district, in Detroit, is the fourth poorest in the nation and consistently votes more than 80 percent Democratic. Although Kilpatrick spent only $174,457, few other districts make possible a similar election strategy.

In the Senate, even more money is needed. Suppose your candidate were going to run for the Senate, and started fundraising immediately after an election, giving her six years to prepare for the next election. How much money would she need to raise each and every week for those *six* years? The average winning Senate candidate raised approximately $15,000 per week.

For presidential candidates, the stakes are, of course, much higher: "The prevailing view is that for a politician to be considered legitimate, he or she must collect at least $20 million by the first of January 2000."[2] Presumably any candidate who does not do so is "illegitimate" and does not belong in the race.

If you collectively decide that the candidate you plan to back will need to raise $7,000 per week (for the House; $15,000 per week for the Senate), how will you do it? Suppose you hold a $10-per-person fundraiser—a barbecue in the park on Memorial Day or Labor Day. Even if 500 people attend, the affair will gross only $5,000, and net considerably less, no matter how cheap the hot dogs and hamburgers. And that takes no account of the problems of persuading 500 people to attend—just notifying them of the event is a major undertaking—or what it would mean to hold such an event every week, not just on Labor Day. In order to get through the money primary, an alternative strategy is needed, so candidates, especially incumbents, increasingly prefer to raise money at "big ticket" events.[3] Selling 10 tickets for a $1,000-per-person fundraiser brings in more than twice as much as the 500-person barbecue in the park.

Who is likely to cough up a thousand bucks to attend a fundraiser? Although practically anyone *could* come up with a thousand dollars (witness Oseola McCarty, a domestic worker in Mississippi, who saved $150,000 from wages that were never more than a few dollars per week), a disproportionate number of such contributors are corporate political action committees (PACs), executives, and lobbyists. One typical version of the $1,000-per-person fundraiser is a breakfast: The candidate and 10 to 30 PAC officers and lobbyists from a particular industry (trucking, banking, oil and gas exploration). Even with a lavish breakfast, the candidate's net take is substantial. If enough lobbyists and corporate executives can be persuaded to come, perhaps the candidate could get by on one fundraiser every couple of weeks.

Coming up with the money is a major hassle; even for incumbents, it requires constant effort. *National Journal*, probably the single most authoritative source on the Washington scene, reports that "there is widespread agreement that the congressional money chase has become an unending marathon, as wearying to participants as it is disturbing to spectators," and quoted an aide to a Democratic senator as observing, "During hearings of Senate committees, you can watch senators go to phone booths in the committee rooms to dial for dollars." Just a few years ago—in 1990, the date of this statement—soliciting funds from federal property, whether Congress or the White House, was routine, openly discussed, and not regarded as problematic. The activity had always been technically illegal, but only in 1997 did it become an issue, with President Clinton and (especially) Vice President Gore singled out as if they were the only offenders.

But long before the 1996 election, politicians felt that they had no choice: The Senate majority leader reported that "public officials are consumed with the unending pursuit of money to run election campaigns."[4] Senators not only leave committee hearings for the more crucial task of calling people to beg for money. They also chase all over the country, because their re-election is more dependent on meeting rich people two thousand miles from home than on meeting their own constituents. Thomas Daschle, the current Democratic leader in the Senate, reports that, in the two years prior to his election to the Senate, he "flew to California more than 20 times to meet with prospective contributors," going there almost as often as he went to the largest city in his home state of South Dakota.[5] This process is sometimes carried to an extreme: Representative John Murtha, Democrat of Pennsylvania, was criticized because at one point he had raised nearly $200,000, of which only $1,000 came from his district. The same processes operate at the presidential level, where donors hold the key to success at the polls. The day after the 1996 Iowa caucuses propelled Lamar Alexander's candidacy into the first tier, he took time off from campaigning in New Hampshire for a phone conference call to tell 250 supporters that he needed each of them to raise $5,000 by the end of the week "to help keep his campaign afloat."[6] The *New York Times* headlined one 1996 story, "In New Jersey, Meeting the Voters Is a Luxury," and declared that "the real campaign" was "raising money for a barrage of television ads," with both major party candidates admitting that they spent "at least half a day, two or three days a week, on the telephone asking for money."[7]

Not only is it necessary to raise lots of money; it is important—for both incumbents and challengers—to raise it early. Senator Rudy Boschwitz, Republican of Minnesota, was clear about this as a strategy. He spent $6 million getting reelected in 1984, and had raised $1.5 million of it by the beginning of the year, effectively discouraging the most promising Democratic challengers. After the election he wrote, and typed up himself, a secret evaluation of his campaign strategy:

"Nobody in politics (except me!) likes to raise money, so I thought the best way of discouraging the toughest opponents from running was to have a few dollars in the sock. *I believe it worked. . . . From all forms of fundraising I raised $6 million plus and got 3 or 4 (maybe even 5) stories and cartoons* that irked me," he said. "In retrospect, I'm glad I had the money."[8]

Similarly, in March 1996 Bill Paxon, chair of the House Republican campaign committee, said, "We've been pounding on members[9] to raise more money by the filing deadline; if they show a good balance, that could ward off opponents."[10]

THE CONTRIBUTORS' PERSPECTIVE

Candidates need money, lots of it, if they are to have any chance of winning. The obvious next question, and in some sense the focus of this book, is who gives, why, and what they expect for it.

Contributions are made for many different reasons. The candidate's family and friends chip in out of loyalty and affection. Others contribute because they are asked to do so by someone who has done favors for them. People give because they agree with the candidate's stand on the issues, either on a broad ideological basis or on a specific issue. Sometimes these donations are portrayed as a form of voting—people show that they care by putting their money where their mouth is, anyone can contribute, and the money raised reflects the wishes of the people. Even for these contributions, however, if voting with dollars replaces voting at the ballot box, then the votes will be very unequally distributed: the top 1 percent of the population by wealth will have more "votes" than the bottom 90 percent of the population. In the 1996 elections, less than one-fourth of one percent of the population gave contributions of $200 or more to a federal candidate.[11] PACs and large contributors provide most of the money, however; small contributors accounted for under one-third of candidate receipts.[12]

It is not just that contributions come from the well-to-do. Most contributors have a direct material interest in what the government does or does not do. Their contributions, most of them made directly or indirectly by business, provide certain people a form of leverage and "access" not available to the rest of us. The chair of the political action committee at one of the twenty-five largest manufacturing companies in the United States explained to us why his corporation has a PAC:

The PAC gives you access. It makes you a player. These congressmen, in particular, are constantly fundraising. Their elections are very expensive, and getting increasingly expensive each year. So they have an ongoing need for funds.

It profits us in a sense to be able to provide some funds because in the provision of it you get to know people, you help them out. There's no real quid pro quo. There is nobody whose vote you can count on, not with the kind of money we are talking about here. But the PAC gives you access. Puts you in the game.

You know, some congressman has got X number of ergs of energy and here's a person or a company who wants to come see him and give him a thousand dollars, and here's another one who wants to just stop by and say hello. And he only has time to see one. Which one? So the PAC's an attention getter.

So-called soft money, where the amount of the contribution is unlimited, might appear to be an exception: Isn't $100,000 enough to buy a guaranteed outcome? We will argue that it is *not*, at least not in any simple and straightforward way. PAC contributions are primarily for members of Congress; they are for comparatively small amounts, but enough to gain access to individual members of Congress. The individual member, however, has limited power. Soft money donations are best thought of as a way of gaining access to the president, top party leaders, and the executive branch. These individuals are more powerful than ordinary members of Congress, so access to them comes at a higher price. That privileged access is invaluable, but, as we will try to show, it does not—and is not expected to—*guarantee* a quid pro quo. The following example illustrates how corporations benefit from this "access" and how they use it to manipulate the system.

WHY DOES THE AIR STINK?

Everybody wants clean air. Who could oppose it? "I spent seven years of my life trying to stop the Clean Air Act," explained the vice president of a major corporation that is a heavy-duty polluter. Nonetheless, he was perfectly willing to make campaign contributions to members who voted for the act:

How a person votes on the final piece of legislation often is not representative of what they have done. Somebody will do a lot of things during the process. How many guys voted against the Clean Air Act? But during the process some of them were very sympathetic to some of our concerns.

In the world of Congress and political action committees things are not always what they seem. Members of Congress all want to vote for clean air, but they also want to get campaign contributions from corporations, and they want to pass a law that business will accept as "reasonable." The compromise solution is to gut the bill by crafting dozens of loopholes. These are inserted in private meetings or in subcommittee hearings that don't get much (if any) attention in the press. Then the public vote on the final bill can be nearly unanimous. Members of Congress can reassure both their constituents and their corporate contributors: constituents, that they voted for the final bill; corporations, that they helped weaken it in private. *Dollars and Votes* analyzes how this happens; clean air, and especially the Clean Air Act of 1990, can serve as an introduction to the kind of process we try to expose.

The public strongly supports clean air, and is unimpressed when corporate officials and apologists trot out their normal arguments—"corporations are already doing all they reasonably can to improve environmental quality," "we need to balance the costs against the benefits," "people will lose their jobs if we make controls any stricter." The original Clean Air Act was passed in 1970, revised in 1977, and not revised again until 1990. Although the initial goal was to have us breathing clean air by 1975, the deadline has been repeatedly extended—and the 1990 legislation provides a new set of deadlines to be reached sometime in the distant future.

Corporations control the production process unless the government specifically intervenes. Therefore, any delay in government action leaves corporations free to do as they choose; business often prefers a weak, ineffective, and unenforceable law. The laws have not only been slow to come, but corporations have also fought to delay or subvert implementation. The 1970 law ordered the Environmental Protection Agency (EPA) to regulate the hundreds of poisonous chemicals that are emitted by corporations, but, as William Greider notes, "In twenty years of stalling, dodging, and fighting off court orders, the EPA has managed to issue regulatory standards for a total of seven toxics."[13]

Corporations have done exceptionally well politically, given the problem they face: The interests of business are diametrically opposed to those of the public. Clean air laws and amendments have been few and far between, enforcement is ineffective, and the penalties minimal. On the one hand, corporations *have* had to pay *billions* for cleanups; on the other, the costs to date are a small fraction of what would be needed to actually clean up the environment.

This corporate struggle for the right to pollute has taken place on many fronts. The most visible is public relations: the Chemical Manufacturers Association took out a two-page Earth Day ad in the *Washington Post* to demonstrate its concern; coincidentally, the names of many of the corporate signers of this ad appear on the EPA's list of high-risk producers.[14] Another front is expert studies that delay action while more information is gathered. The federally funded National Acid Precipitation Assessment Program took ten years and $600 million to figure out whether acid rain was in fact a problem. Both business and the Reagan administration argued that nothing should be done until the study was completed.[15] Ultimately, the study was discredited: The "summary of findings" minimized the impact of acid rain, even though this did not accurately represent the expert research in the report. But the key site of struggle was Congress. For years, corporations successfully defeated legislation. In 1987 utility companies were offered a compromise bill on acid rain, but they "were very adamant that they had beat the thing since 1981 and they could always beat it," according to Representative Edward Madigan (Republican–Illinois).[16] The utilities beat back all efforts at reform through the 1980s, but their intransigence probably hurt them when revisions finally came to be made.

The stage was set for a revision of the Clean Air Act when George Bush, "the environmental president," was elected, and George Mitchell, a strong supporter of environmentalism, became the Senate majority leader.[17] But what sort of clean air bill would it be? "What we wanted," said Richard Ayres, head of the environmentalists' Clean Air Coalition, "is a health based standard—one-in-1-million cancer risk," a standard that would require corporations to clean up their plants until the cancer risk from their operations was reduced to 1 in a million. "The Senate bill still has the requirement," Ayres said, "but there are forty pages of extensions and exceptions and qualifications and loopholes that largely render the health standard a nullity."[18] Greider reports, for example, "According to the EPA, there are now twenty-six coke ovens that pose a cancer risk greater than 1 in 1000 and six where the risk is greater than 1 in 100. Yet the new clean-air bill will give the steel industry another thirty years to deal with the problem."[19]

This change from what the bill was supposed to do to what it did do came about through what corporate executives like to call the "access" process. The principal aim of most corporate campaign contributions is to help corporate executives gain "access" to key members of Congress and their staffs. In these meetings, corporate executives (and corporate PAC money) work to persuade the member of Congress to accept a predesigned loophole that will sound innocent but effectively undercut the stated intention of the bill. Representative John D. Dingell (Democrat–Michigan), who was chair of the House committee, is a strong industry supporter; one of the people we interviewed called him "the point man for the Business

Roundtable on clean air." Representative Henry A. Waxman (Democrat–California), chair of the subcommittee, is an environmentalist. Observers had expected a confrontation and contested votes on the floor of the Congress.

The problem for corporations was that, as one Republican staff aide said, "If any bill has the blessing of Waxman and the environmental groups, unless it is totally in outer space, who's going to vote against it?"[20] But corporations successfully minimized public votes. Somehow, Waxman was persuaded to make behind-the-scenes compromises with Dingell so members, during an election year, didn't have to side publicly with business against the environment.[21] Often the access process leads to loopholes that protect a single corporation, but for "clean" air most of the special deals targeted not specific companies but entire industries. The initial bill, for example, required cars to be able to use carefully specified, cleaner fuels. But the auto industry wanted the rules loosened, and Congress eventually incorporated a variant of a formula suggested by the head of General Motors' fuels and lubricants department.[22]

Nor did corporations stop fighting even after they gutted the bill through amendments. Business pressed the EPA for favorable regulations to implement the law: "The cost of this legislation could vary dramatically, depending on how EPA interprets it," said William D. Fay, vice president of the National Coal Association, who headed the hilariously misnamed Clean Air Working Group, an industry coalition that fought to weaken the legislation.[23] As one EPA aide working on acid rain regulations reported, "We're having a hard time getting our work done because of the number of phone calls we're getting" from corporations and their lawyers.

Corporations trying to get federal regulators to adopt the "right" regulations don't rely exclusively on the cogency of their arguments. They often exert pressure on a member of Congress to intervene for them at the EPA or other agency. Senators and representatives regularly intervene on behalf of constituents and contributors by doing everything from straightening out a social security problem to asking a regulatory agency to explain why it is pressuring a company. This process—like campaign finance—usually follows rules of etiquette. In addressing a regulatory agency, the senator does not say: "Lay off my campaign contributors or I'll cut your budget." One standard phrasing for letters asks regulators to resolve the problem "as quickly as possible within applicable rules and regulations."[24] No matter how mild and careful the inquiry, the agency receiving the request is certain to give it extra attention; only after careful consideration will they refuse to make any accommodation.

Soft money—unregulated megabuck contributions—also shaped what happened to air quality. Archer Daniels Midland argued that increased use of ethanol would reduce pollution from gasoline; coincidentally, ADM controls a majority of the ethanol market. To reinforce its arguments, in the 1992 election ADM gave $90,000 to Democrats and $600,000 to Republicans, the latter supplemented with an additional $200,000 as an individual contribution from the company head, Dwayne Andreas. Many environmentalists were skeptical about ethanol's value in a clean air strategy, but President Bush issued regulations promoting wider use of ethanol; we presume he was impressed by the force of ADM's 800,000 Republican arguments. Bob Dole, the 1996 Republican presidential candidate, helped pass and defend special breaks for the ethanol industry; he not only appreciated ADM's Republican contributions, but presumably approved of the more than $1 million they gave to the American Red Cross during the period when it was headed by his wife, Elizabeth Dole.[25] What about the post-1994 Republican-controlled Congress, defenders of the free market and opponents of government giveaways? Were they ready to end this subsidy program, cracking down on corporate welfare as they did on people welfare? Not a chance. In 1997, the Republican chair of the House Ways and Means Committee actually attempted to eliminate the special tax breaks for ethanol. Needless to say, he was immediately put in his place by other members of the Republican leadership, including Speaker Newt Gingrich and most of the Senate, with the subsidy locked in place for years to come,[26] in spite of a General Accounting Office report that "found that the ethanol subsidy justifies none of its political boasts."[27] The Center for Responsive Politics calculated that ADM, its executives and PAC, made more than $1 million in campaign contributions of various types; the only thing that had changed was that in 1996, with a Democratic president, this money was "divided more or less evenly between Republicans and Democrats."[28]

The disparity in power between business and environmentalists looms large during the legislative process, but it is enormous afterward. When the Clean Air Act passed, corporations and industry groups offered positions, typically with large pay increases, to congressional staff members who wrote the law. The former congressional staff members who now work for corporations both know how to evade the law and can persuasively claim to EPA that they know what Congress intended. Environmental organizations pay substantially less than Congress and can't afford large staffs. They are seldom able to become involved in the details of the administrative process or to influence implementation and enforcement.[29]

Having pushed Congress and the Environmental Protection Agency to allow as much pollution as possible, business then went to the Quayle council for rules allowing even more pollution. Vice President J. Danforth Quayle's council, technically known as the "Council on Competitiveness," was created by President Bush specifically to help reduce regulations on business. Quayle told the *Boston Globe* "that his council has an 'open door' to business groups and that he has a bias against regulations."[30] During the Bush administration, this council reviewed, and could override, all regulations, including those by the EPA setting the limits at which a chemical was subject to regulation. The council also recommended that corporations be allowed to increase their polluting emissions if a state did not object within seven days of the proposed increase. Corporations thus have multiple opportunities to win. If they lose in Congress, they can win at the regulatory agency; if they lose there, they can try again at the Quayle council (or later equivalent). If they lose there, they can try to reduce the money available to enforce regulations, or tie the issue up in the courts, or plan on accepting a minimal fine.

The operation of the Quayle council would probably have received little publicity, but reporters discovered that the executive director of the council, Allan Hubbard, had a clear conflict of interest. Hubbard chaired the biweekly White House meetings on the Clean Air Act. He owned half of World Wide Chemical, received an average of more than $1 million a year in profits from it while directing the Quayle council, and continued to attend quarterly stockholder meetings. According to the *Boston Globe*, "Records on file with the Indianapolis Air Pollution Control Board show that World Wide Chemical emitted 17,000 to 19,000 pounds of chemicals into the air" in 1991.[31] At that time the company did "not have the permit required to release the emissions," was "putting out nearly four times the allowable emissions without a permit, and could be subject to a $2,500-a-day penalty" according to David Jordan, director of the Indianapolis Air Pollution Board.[32]

This does not, however, mean that business always gets exactly what it wants. In 1997, the Environmental Protection Agency proposed tough new rules for soot and smog. Business fought hard to weaken or eliminate the rules: hiring experts (from pro-business think tanks) to attack the scientific studies supporting the regulations and putting a raft of lobbyists ("many of them former congressional staffers," the *Washington Post* reported[33]) to work securing the signatures of 250 members of Congress questioning the standards. But the late 1990s version of these industry mobilizations adds a new twist—creating a pseudo-grassroots campaign. For example, business, operating under a suitably disguised name (Foundation for Clean Air Progress), paid for television ads telling farmers that the EPA rules would prohibit them from plowing on dry windy days, with other ads predicting the EPA rules "would lead to forced carpooling or bans on outdoor barbecues— claims the EPA dismisses as ridiculous."[34] Along with the ads, industry worked to mobilize local politicians and business executives in what business groups called a "grass tops" campaign.

Despite a massive industry campaign, EPA head Carol Browner remained firm, and President Clinton was persuaded to go along. Of course, industry immediately began working on ways to undercut the regulations with congressional loopholes and exceptions—but business had suffered a defeat, and proponents of clean air (that is, most of the rest of us) had won at least a temporary and partial victory. And who leads the struggles to overturn or uphold these regulations? Just as before, Dingell and Waxman; Republicans "are skittish about challenging" the rules publicly, "so they gladly defer to Dingell as their surrogate."[35] Dingell's forces have more than 130 cosponsors (about one-third of them Democrats) for a bill to, in effect, override the EPA standards.

In business–government relations most attention becomes focused on instances of scandal. The real issue, however, is not one or another scandal or conflict of interest, but rather the *system* of business–government relations, and especially of campaign finance, that offers business so many opportunities to craft loopholes, undermine regulations, and subvert enforcement. Still worse, many of these actions take place beyond public scrutiny. *Dollars and Votes* analyzes not just the exceptional cases, but the day-to-day reality of corporate government relations.

WHY BUSINESS?

Dollars and Votes focuses on business and the way it uses money and power to subvert the democratic process. This runs counter to the conventional wisdom, which treats all campaign contributions as equally problematic. A "balanced" and "objective" approach would, we are told, condemn both business and labor; each reform that primarily restricts business should be matched by one that restricts labor. We've heard these arguments, thought them over, and rejected them. They assume that what we have now is "balance" and that all changes should reinforce the existing relations of power. We see no reason to accept that as an a priori assumption.

Why are business campaign contributions more of a problem than contributions by labor (or women, or environmentalists)? First, because business contributes far more money. According to a study by the Center for

Responsive Politics,[36], in the last election business outspent labor by an 11 to 1 margin. Most reports about campaign finance give the impression that labor contributes roughly as much as business—a distortion of the reality.

Second, as we argue in Chapter 6, beyond the world of campaign finance, business has far more power than labor, women's groups, or environmentalists.

Third, business uses campaign contributions in a way few other groups do, as part of an "access" process that provides corporations a chance to shape the details of legislation, crafting loopholes that undercut the stated purpose of the law. Other groups do this on rare occasions; business does so routinely. Businesses are far more likely than other donors to give to *both* sides in a race; nearly all the soft money donors who gave to both sides were corporations (see Chapter 4).

Fourth, there is a fundamental difference between corporate and labor PAC contributions. That difference is democracy; unions have it, corporations don't. This overwhelmingly important distinction is concealed by almost all public discussion. No one talks about it, no one seems to take it seriously. There is a virtual embargo on any mention of this fact, but it merits serious consideration.

The original legislation ratifying the creation of PACs, passed in 1971 and amended in 1974 after Watergate, intended that corporations and labor unions be treated in parallel fashion. In each case, the organization was permitted a special relationship to the group that democratically controlled it—stockholders in the case of corporations, members in the case of labor unions. The organization was permitted to communicate with those individuals and their families on any issue (including political issues), to conduct registration and get-out-the-vote campaigns, and to ask those people for voluntary contributions to a political action committee.

In the 1975 SUN–PAC decision, the Federal Election Commission, for almost the only time in its existence, took a bold step. In fact, it essentially threw out a key part of the law and then rewrote it, permitting corporations to solicit PAC contributions not just from their stockholders but also from their managerial employees. This had two consequences. First, corporate PACs—but no others—are able to coerce people to contribute. Second, corporate PACs are not, even in theory, democratically controlled. Each of these consequences needs to be examined.

Neither stockholders nor union members can be coerced to contribute—the organization doesn't have power over them, they have power over the organization. Managers, however, can be coerced. As a result, virtually all corporate PAC money comes from employees rather than stockholders.

If your boss comes to you and asks for a contribution, saying he or she hopes that all team players will be generous, it's not easy for you, an ambitious young manager, to say no. Some companies apparently do not pressure employees to contribute, but others do. For example, at one company we studied, the head of government relations told us that each year he and the company's lobbyist go to each work unit and hold an employee meeting: "We talk about the PAC and what it means to the company and what it means to them as individuals, and we solicit their membership; if they are members, we solicit an increase in their gift." Then the employees' boss is asked "to get up and say why they are members and why they think it's important for an employee to be a member." The upper-level manager clearly has no confidentiality, which in itself sends a key message to others. A number of coercive elements converge in this solicitation: The meeting is public, employees are to commit themselves then and there in the public meeting, the boss recommends that subordinates contribute, and an impression is probably conveyed that the boss will be evaluated on the basis of his or her employees' participation rate. The PAC chair insists there is no pressure, but admits employees feel differently:

> And yet regardless of how many times you say that, there's always going to be some employees who feel that you got them into that meeting to put pressure on. But if they feel pressure it's self-imposed from the standpoint of the solicitation. Because there will be several of us, including myself, who will get up and say, we want you to be a member and here's why.

However, even his definition of "no pressure" is cause for concern: "But as far as a manager or anybody getting up and telling you that if you don't participate we're going to fire you, . . . there's no pressure." No one is told they will be fired for failing to contribute, but it seems probable that they will assume their boss will be disappointed and that their contribution or noncontribution will be remembered at promotion time.

The second consequence of the 1975 SUN–PAC decision is even more important. Corporate PACs are *not* democratic. Many corporations have steering committees that vote to decide to whom the PAC will contribute, but the committees are appointed, the corporate hierarchy selects individuals who are expected to take the corporate purpose as their own, and managers know that they will be evaluated on their performance on the committee. As one senior vice president explained: "Policy is made by the top of the company, and it filters down. They tell you what they want, and you do it."

The internal functioning of corporate PACs suggests how they relate to and value democracy. Most aspects of the political system are beyond the *direct* control of corporations, but they *can* determine how their PACs operate and make decisions. As a result, in all but a handful of corporate PACs democratic control is not even a theoretical possibility. The PAC raises its money from employees, but employees do not and cannot vote on the leadership or direction of either the PAC or the corporation. The PAC officer who is responsible for the day-to-day details of running the PAC is appointed. *No* corporation elects its PAC officer—any more than corporate employees elect any other official. While PACs do sometimes change political direction, this happens because the corporation is acquired or because a new CEO takes office, not because contributors are dissatisfied.[37]

Not only the PAC officer is appointed. Virtually all PAC steering committees are appointed, not elected. The chair of one of the handful with elections explained:

> We have a steering committee that's elected by the members. We send out ballots for the steering committee. It's a Russian election[38] admittedly—there is a slate of nominees and there is an opportunity for people to write in but as a practical matter it's almost impossible for a write-in to win.

The only corporation that reported having *some* contested elections agreed that, in general: "It is an elected-appointive; it's kind of a pseudo-election I guess is what it amounts to."

We might expect those ideological corporations that stress general principles of support for democracy and the "free" enterprise system to be exceptions to the undemocratic organization of corporate PACs. Not at all. At one corporation that boasted about its wholehearted support of the "free enterprise system," the chair of the PAC Committee matter-of-factly noted: "If our [company] chairman said we are going to have a certain kind of PAC, then we'd have an option of resigning or doing it the way he wanted". At another ideological corporation, *all* members of the PAC committee are among the top ten corporate officers. In PAC committee deliberations, we were told, "It's never heated because it's not a very democratic system."

The nondemocratic character of corporate PACs is consistent with the principles guiding the corporation as a whole. Corporations are not run on democratic principles; employees don't vote on corporate leadership or policies. Many corporate executives are dubious about democracy in general. Leonard Silk and David Vogel attended a set of meetings organized by the Conference Board for top executives. They concluded:

> While critics of business worry about the atrophy of American democracy, the concern in the nation's boardrooms is precisely the opposite.

For an executive, democracy in America is working all too well—*that is the problem.*[39]

Campaign contributions are (part of) the solution to the "problem" of democracy.

OUR RESEARCH

Because of business's uniquely important role, because corporate PACs are nondemocratic in a way that other PACs are not, and because business is by far the most important factor in the "access" process, most of our research focuses on corporations. We have been studying campaign finance for fifteen years, and this book draws on at least five sources of information. First and foremost, we draw on 38 in-depth interviews with corporate executives, most of them conducted in 1988 and 1989, each roughly an hour long; 79 percent of them were tape-recorded and transcribed, yielding hundreds of pages of transcripts. The corporations we interviewed are a representative sample; their PACs are similar to those of all large corporate PACs in terms of contributions to Democrats versus Republicans and incumbents versus challengers.[40]

To encourage candor, we promised our informants that we would maintain the confidentiality of both the individuals and the corporations involved. The most common question we were asked while arranging the interviews, a question repeated again at the beginning of the interview itself, concerned confidentiality. People emphasized they were willing to talk either with or without confidentiality, but made it clear they would be more forthcoming with a promise of confidentiality. The main question was some version of: "Am I going to be seeing this on *60 Minutes* or reading it on the front page of the *Washington Post?*"[41] Informant confidentiality is appropriate in this study because our focus is not on one or another specific instance of abuse, but rather on the systematic abuses that are inherent in the everyday operation of the campaign finance system. The corporate executives we interviewed made some revealing statements; we were impressed by the extent to which they were willing to be candid and honest. Did they tell us everything? No way. In our interviews, people rarely named names or revealed specifics. We're sure that, if some PAC officer switched sides and *really* told all, the material would be much juicier. But we wouldn't advise you to hold your breath waiting for that to happen, and it's amazing what corporate officials *did* tell us.

A second source of information is our analysis of all the "soft money" donations for 1992, 1994, and 1996 (the only years for which the data are publicly available). We analyzed not only donations by corporations, but also by labor unions, individuals, trade associations, women's groups, environmentalists, single-issue organizations—you name it. These are the donations that have attracted the most attention of late, and have been the focus in Clinton's campaign finance scandals. For a variety of reasons, above all, the difficulty of working with the data, far less systematic attention has been paid to these contributions than to PACs; what little attention has been given to soft money has focused on a handful of the largest donors. Although they are important, that focus distorts the larger picture.

Third, we have analyzed the PAC donations of the largest corporate PACs for every election from 1976 through 1996, an average of more than 20,000 donations per election.[42] Fourth, we occasionally draw on a mail survey of a random sample of corporate PAC directors, conducted in 1986, with a response rate of 58 percent (much higher than most surveys of PACs). Finally, we read everything we can get our hands on, search the Web, and in general collect every miscellaneous piece of information we can find on campaign finance.

Dollars and Votes uses corporate executives' own words to explain how business uses campaign finance and the access process to influence and subvert— our word, emphatically not theirs—the democratic system. The remainder of this chapter reviews the current state of campaign finance law, briefly sets out what will be covered in the remainder of the book, and introduces three theoretical issues that are important to our argument.

THE CURRENT LAW

The most provocative and also probably the most accurate beginning point is that there is, in effect, no law. Or, rather, an untold number of laws and regulations exist, but a determined donor can get around them. The morass of regulations creates enormous hassles for both candidates and donors, makes life more difficult for those attempting to use money to dominate the system, and provides a significant measure of public disclosure. But it does not prevent outrageous abuses, and it sanctions a system whose normal operation involves exchanging money for special influence. In practice, campaign finance is today *less* regulated than it has been at any time since 1907 (when the Tillman Act was passed). That is the starting point for any discussion of the law; the rest should be thought of as a map showing the obstacles placed in the way of smart lawyers, candidates, and donors.

We won't try to cover all the technicalities of the current law; the out-lines are confusing enough. *Individuals* may contribute $1,000 per candi-date per election. But since most candidates face both a primary and a general election, that limit doubles; the creative use of family members can further expand it. No individual may contribute more than $25,000 in total (to all candidates) per year, though people may also contribute $5,000 per year to a PAC.

Political action committees, or PACs, are entities that collect money from many contributors, pool it, and then make donations to candidates. Cor-porations, unions, and trade associations may sponsor PACs, paying all of their operating expenses (rent, phone, mailings, the salaries of individuals who work only on the PAC), but they can't put their own money directly into the PAC, because all PAC money must come from voluntary donations. PACs may contribute up to $5,000 per candidate per election (with prima-ries again doubling the limit), and may give an unlimited total amount.

Candidates must *disclose* all PAC donations (of any size), the names of all individuals who donate $200 or more, and the total amount spent and received (including the amounts received from donations of less than $200). PACs must disclose all donations, and report the names of all individuals who contribute $200 or more.

By far the most important recent change in campaign finance is the explosion of so-called soft money (analyzed in Chapter 4). "Hard money" refers to donations made (more or less) within the framework of the law as it was originally intended; "soft money"—which could equally well be called "loophole money"—is money that escapes the requirements of federal law. Like most such distinctions, it's less clear than it seems—for example, a 1991 federal regulation requires that soft money contributions be reported: That reporting is itself a (minimal) form of regulation.

Soft money differs from hard money in two critical ways. First, there is absolutely no limit on the amount of the contribution. A corporation can give one hundred thousand dollars, a million dollars, or more. Second, corporations, unions, and other organizations can take the money directly from their central treasuries. PACs must get their money from (at least sup-posedly) voluntary donations by individuals to the PAC. That placed some limit on corporate giving. Stockholders contributed very little, and although corporations could successfully coerce the money out of their managers, doing so became, at least, a problem. Now corporations may take the money directly out of their treasuries—and they have astonishingly deep pockets.

The Federal Election Commission (FEC) is supposed to monitor candi-dates and contributors and enforce the rules, but it is underfunded and takes—literally—years to reach decisions. In terms of action, the FEC is paralyzed on most important issues, since by law its commissioners are evenly balanced—three Democrats and three Republicans—but it requires a majority vote to act. Typically, the FEC takes (roughly) forever to official-ly consider a violation. Then it either fails to reach any decision or imposes a minimal fine. In one typical case, Republican Conrad Burns's 1988 election victory involved apparent campaign finance violations. His six-year Senate term was nearly over before the FEC managed to consider the case.

> The FEC commissioners eventually agreed that tens of thousands of dollars had improperly poured into the race in violation of federal stat-utes. But there the matter stalled as the commissioners deadlocked along party lines through 15 inconclusive votes on how to proceed.[43]

In the end, of course, the FEC did what it usually does—nothing. Burns is now well into his second term. He probably doesn't lie awake nights wor-rying about some fearsome punishment he might face for his campaign finance violations.

OVERVIEW

Chapter 2 analyzes the campaign contribution itself—how it should be understood, the criteria corporations use in deciding on donations, what corporations give over and beyond reported donations. We argue that PAC contributions—and even huge soft money donations—are best understood as gifts, not bribes. They create a generalized sense of obligation and an expectation of mutual back-scratching. We also look at the way corpora-tions present money to candidates: What really goes on at a fundraiser?

In Chapter 3, we investigate the "access" process. These are the dona-tions observers find most troubling. A corporation plays on a member's sense of indebtedness for past contributions in order to gain access to that member. In committee hearings and private meetings, the corporation then persuades the member to make "minor" changes in a bill—changes, say, that exempt a particular company or industry from some specific provi-sion.

Chapter 4 looks at soft money, the unregulated area whose megabuck donations are at the center of recent campaign finance scandals. We argue these are another form of "access" donations, but here the access is to the president or to party leaders, so the entry cost increases dramatically. Busi-ness dominates this form of giving.

Even some corporations are troubled by this "access" approach, and

Chapter 5 considers the alternative: donations to close races intended to change the ideological composition of the Congress. In the 1980 election a substantial group of corporations pursued an ideological strategy. We argue this was one of the reasons for the conservative successes of that period, and we examine why many of these corporations changed to access-oriented behavior. Thereafter, however, only a small number of corporations used this as their primary strategy, though most corporations make some such donations. Corporate mobilization was *not*, however, the key to 1994 Republican congressional victories. This is a paradox we explore.

Chapter 6 investigates the degree of political unity among corporations. Do competing firms or industries oppose each other in Washington, so that one business's political donations cancel out those of another corporation or industry? More generally, how much power does business have in our society, and how does its political power relate to its economic activity?

The book concludes with an examination of the Clinton scandals, the incidents that have renewed interest in campaign contributions and spawned a host of investigations, and of the possibilities for reform. Corporate executives are not worried about reform. They don't expect any meaningful changes, and they assume that if "reforms" are enacted, they will be easily evaded. We use the analysis developed throughout the book to indicate briefly why most reform proposals would be ineffective. We end by sketching a proposal that we believe would lead to meaningful and enduring reform. It won't be easy to enact such a reform, but we hope that if people understand how the current system operates and what would be needed to clean it up, they will demand significant change. One promising development is a movement to place real reform proposals on state ballot initiatives, thus appealing directly to voters and circumventing Congress's usual strategy of burying reforms in committee.

In developing our analysis, in the remainder of this chapter and in most chapters in this book, we further explore three points. First, power is exercised in many loose and subtle ways, not simply through the visible use of force and threats. Power may, in fact, be most effective, and most limiting, when it structures the conditions for action—even though in these circumstances it may be hard to recognize. Thus campaign contributions can and do exercise enormous influence by creating a sense of obligation, even if there is no explicit agreement to perform a specific service in return for a donation. Second, business is different from, and more powerful than, other groups in society. As a result, corporations and their campaign contributions frequently produce effects that other groups could not match simply by raising equivalent amounts of money. Third, this does not mean that business always wins, or that it wins automatically. If it did, corporate PACs and soft money contributions would be unnecessary. Business must engage in a constant struggle to maintain its dominance. This is a class struggle just as surely as are strikes and mass mobilizations, even though it is rarely thought of in these terms.

WHAT IS POWER?

Our analysis is based on an understanding of power that differs from that usually articulated by both business and politicians. The corporate PAC directors we interviewed insisted that they have no power.

> If you were to ask me what kind of access and influence do we have, being roughly the 150th largest PAC, I would have to tell you that on the basis of our money we have zero. . . . If you look at the level of our contributions, we know we're not going to buy anybody's vote, we're not going to rent anybody, or whatever the clichés have been over the years. We know that.

The executives who expressed these views clearly meant these words sincerely.[44] Their statements are based on roughly the same understanding of "power" that is current within political science, which is also the way the term was defined by Max Weber, the classical sociological theorist. Power, in this common conception, is the ability to make someone do something against their will. If that is what power means, then corporations rarely have any in relation to members of Congress, nor does soft money give the donor power over presidents. As one senior vice president said to us: "You certainly aren't going to be able to buy anybody for $500 or $1,000 or $10,000—it's a joke." Soft money donations of a million dollars might seem to change the equation, but we will argue they do not: Just as $10,000 won't buy a member of Congress, $1,000,000 won't buy a president. In this regard we agree with the corporate officials we interviewed: A corporation is not in a position to say to a member of Congress, "Either you vote for this bill or we will defeat your bid for reelection." Rarely do they even say: "You vote for this bill or you won't get any money from us." (These points are discussed in more detail in Chapter 3.)

The definition of power as the ability to make someone do something against their will is what Steven Lukes calls a "one-dimensional" view of power.[45] A two-dimensional view recognizes the existence of nondecisions: A potential issue never gets articulated or, if articulated by someone somewhere, never receives serious consideration. For example, in 1989 and 1990 one of the major political battles, and a focus of great effort by corporate

PACs, was the Clean Air Act. Yet twenty or thirty years earlier, before the rise of the environmental movement, pollution was a nonissue: it simply was not considered, although its effects were, in retrospect, of great importance. In one of the Sherlock Holmes stories, the key clue is that the dog didn't bark.[46] A two-dimensional view of power makes the same point: The most important clue in some situation may be that no one noticed power was exercised—because there was no overt conflict.

Even this model of power is too restrictive, however, because it still focuses on discrete decisions and nondecisions. Tom Wartenberg calls these "interventional" models of power, and notes that, in such models "the primary locus of power . . . is a specific social interaction between two social agents." Such models do not recognize "the idea that the most fundamental use of power in society is its use in structuring the basic manner in which social agents interact with one another."[47] Wartenberg argues, instead, for a "field theory" of power that analyzes social power as a force similar to a magnetic field. A magnetic field alters the motion of objects susceptible to magnetism. Similarly, the mere presence of a powerful social agent alters the social space for others and causes them to orient themselves toward the powerful agent.[48] For example, one of the executives we interviewed took it for granted that "if we go see the congressman who represents [a city where the company has a major plant], where 10,000 of our employees are also his constituents, we don't need a PAC to go see him." The corporation is so important in that area that the member has to orient himself in relation to the corporation and its concerns. In a different sense, the very act of accepting a campaign contribution changes the way a member relates to a PAC, creating a sense of obligation, a need to reciprocate. The PAC contribution has altered the member's social space, his or her awareness of the company and wish to help it, even if no explicit commitments have been made.

BUSINESS IS DIFFERENT

Power, we would argue, is not just the ability to force someone to do something against their will; it is most effective (and least recognized) when it shapes the field of action. Moreover, business's vast resources, influence on the economy, and general legitimacy place it on a different footing from other campaign contributors. Every day a member of Congress accepts a $1,000 donation from a corporate PAC, goes to a committee hearing, proposes "minor" changes in a bill's wording, and has those changes accepted without discussion or examination. The changes "clarify" the language of the bill, legalizing higher levels of pollution for a specific pollutant, or exempting the company from some tax. The media do not report this change and no one speaks against it. On the other hand, if a PAC were formed by Drug Lords for Cocaine Legalization, no member would take their money. If a member introduced a "minor" wording change to make it easier to sell crack without bothersome police interference, the proposed change would attract massive attention, the campaign contribution would be labeled a scandal, the member's political career would be ruined, and the changed wording would not be incorporated into the bill. Drug Lords may make an extreme example, but approximately the same holds true for many groups: At present, equal rights for gays and lesbians could never be a minor and unnoticed addition to a bill with a different purpose.

Even groups with great social legitimacy encounter more opposition and controversy than business faces for proposals that are virtually without public support. One example is the contrast between the largely unopposed commitment of tens or hundreds of billions of dollars for the savings and loan bailout, compared to the sharp debate, close votes, and defeats for the rights of men and women to take *unpaid* parental leaves. The classic term for something non-controversial that everyone must support is "a motherhood issue," and while it costs little to guarantee every woman the right to an *un*paid parental leave, this measure nonetheless generated intense scrutiny and controversy—going down to defeat under President Bush, passing under President Clinton, and then again becoming a focus of attack after the 1994 Republican takeover of Congress. Few indeed are the people publicly prepared to defend pollution or tax evasion. Nonetheless, business is routinely able to win pollution exemptions and tax loopholes. Although cumulatively some vague awareness of these provisions may trouble people, most are allowed individually to pass without scrutiny. *No* analysis of corporate political activity makes sense unless it begins with a recognition of this absolutely vital point. The PAC is a vital element of corporate power, but it does not operate by itself. The PAC donation is always backed by the wider power and influence of business.

Corporations are unlike other "special interest" groups not only because business has far more resources, but also because of its acceptance and legitimacy. When people feel that "the system" is screwing them, they tend to blame politicians, the government, the media—but rarely business. In terms of campaign finance, while much of the public is outraged at the way money influences elections and public policy, the issue is almost always posed in terms of politicians, what they do or don't do. This is part of a pervasive double standard that largely exempts business from criticism. We, however, believe it is vital to scrutinize business as well.

We did two dozen radio call-in shows after the appearance of our last book, *Money Talks*. On almost every show, at least one call came from someone outraged that members of Congress had recently raised their pay to $125,100. (For 1998, it will be about $137,000.) Not a single person even mentioned corporate executives' pay. *Business Week* calculated that in 1996 corporate CEOs were paid an average of $5.8 million (counting salary, bonuses, and stock option grants), or more than 200 times the average worker's pay, and more than 40 times what members of Congress are paid.[49] More anger is directed at Congress for delaying new environmental laws than at the companies that fight every step of the way to stall and subvert the legislation. When members of Congress do favors for large campaign contributors, anger is directed at the senators who went along, not at the business owner who paid the money (and usually initiated the pressure). The public focuses on the member's receipt of thousands of dollars, not on the business's receipt of millions (or hundreds of millions) in tax breaks or special treatment. It is a widely held belief that "politics is dirty." But little public comment and condemnation is generated when companies get away—quite literally—with murder. This disparity is evidence of business's success in shaping public perceptions. Lee Atwater, George Bush's 1988 campaign manager, saw this as a key to Republican success:

> In the 1980 campaign, we were able to make the establishment, insofar as it is bad, the government. In other words, big government was the enemy, not big business. If the people think the problem is that taxes are too high, and the government interferes too much, then we are doing our job. But, if they get to the point where they say that the real problem is that rich people aren't paying taxes, . . . then the Democrats are going to be in good shape.[50]

We argue that corporations are so different, and so dominant, that they exercise a special kind of power, what Antonio Gramsci called hegemony.[51] Hegemony can be regarded as the ultimate example of a field of power that structures what people and groups do. It is sometimes referred to as a worldview, a way of thinking about the world that influences every action, and makes it difficult to even consider alternatives. But in Gramsci's analysis it is much more than this, it is a culture and set of institutions that structure life patterns and coerce a particular way of life. Susan Harding[52] gives the example of relations between whites and blacks in the South prior to the 1960s. Black inferiority and subservience were not simply ideas ar-

ticulated by white racists, they were incorporated into a set of social practices: segregated schools, restrooms, swimming pools, restaurants; the black
obligation to refer to white men as "Mister"; the prohibition on referring
to black men as "Mister"; the use of the term "boy" for black males of any
age and social status; the white right to go to the front of any line or to take
the seat of any African American, and so on. Most blacks recognized the
injustice and absurdity of these rules, but this did not enable them to escape, much less defy, them. White hegemony could not be overthrown
simply by recognizing its existence or articulating an ideal of equality; black
people had to create a movement that transformed themselves, the South,
and the nation as a whole.

Hegemony is most successful, and most powerful, when it is unrecognized. White hegemony in the South was strong, but never unrecognized
and rarely uncontested. White southerners would have denied, probably in
all sincerity, that they exercised power: "Why our nigras are perfectly happy,
that's the way they want to be treated." But many black southerners would
have vigorously disputed this while talking to each other.[53] In some sense,
gender relations in the 1950s embodied a hegemony even more powerful
than that of race relations. Betty Friedan titled the first chapter of *The
Feminine Mystique* "The Problem That Has No Name," because women
literally did not have a name for, did not recognize the existence of, their
oppression.[54] Women as well as men denied the existence of inequality or
oppression, denied the systematic exercise of power to maintain unequal
relations.

We argue that today business has enormous power and exercises effective
hegemony, even though (perhaps because) this is largely undiscussed and
unrecognized. *Politically*, business power today is similar to white treatment of blacks in 1959—business may sincerely deny its power, but many
of the groups it exercises power over recognize it, feel dominated, resent
this, and fight the power as best they can. At least until very recently, *eco-
nomically*, business power was more like gender relations in 1959: Virtually
no one saw this power as problematic. The revived labor movement is beginning to change this, and there are signs that a movement is beginning to
contest corporate power. Nonetheless, if the issue is brought to people's
attention, many still don't see a problem: "Well, so what? how else could it
be? maybe we don't like it, but that's just the way things are." (This point
is further discussed in Chapter 6.)

Hegemony is never absolute. African Americans and women both were
(and are) forced to live in disadvantaged conditions, but they simultaneously
fought for dignity and respect. Unusual individuals always violated con-

ventions and tested limits. A hegemonic power is usually opposed by a counterhegemony. Thus, while children in our society are taught to compete with each other to earn the praise of authority figures, and while most children engage in this process much of the time, it is also true that the "teacher's pet" is likely to face ostracism. We hope this book makes a small contribution to weakening business hegemony and to developing a counterhegemony.

THE LIMITS TO BUSINESS POWER

We have argued that power is more than winning an open conflict, and that business is different from other groups because its pervasive influence on our society shapes the social space for all other actors. These two arguments, however, are joined with a third: a recognition—in fact an insistence—on the limits to business power. Though we stress the power of business, business does not feel powerful. As one executive said to us:

I really wish that our PAC in particular, and our lobbyists, had the influence that is generally perceived by the general population. If you see it written in the press, and you talk to people, they tell you about all that influence that you've got, and frankly I think that's far overplayed, as far as the influence goes. Certainly you can get access to a candidate, and certainly you can get your position known; but as far as influencing that decision, the only way you influence it is by the providing of information.

Executives believe that corporations are constantly under attack, primarily because government simply doesn't understand that business is crucial to everything the society does, but can easily be crippled by well-intentioned but unrealistic government policies. A widespread view among the people we interviewed is, "Far and away the vast majority of things that we do are literally to protect ourselves from public policy that is poorly crafted and nonresponsive to the needs and realities and circumstances of our company." These misguided policies, they feel, can come from many sources: labor unions, environmentalists, the pressure of unrealistic public interest groups, the government's constant need for money or the weight of its oppressive bureaucracy. Therefore, simply to stay even requires a pervasive effort. If attention slips for even a minute, an onerous regulation will be imposed or a precious resource taken away. To some extent such a view is an obvious consequence of the position of the people we interviewed: If business could be sure of always winning, the government relations unit (and thus the jobs of its members) would be unnecessary; if it is easy to win, PAC directors deserve little credit for company victories and much blame for defeats. But evidently the corporation agrees with them, since it devotes significant resources to political action of many kinds, including the awareness and involvement of top officials. Chief executive officers and members of the board of directors repeatedly express similar views.

Both the business view of their vulnerability, and our insistence on their power, are correct. A university analogy illustrates the contradictory reality. After six years of teaching, an assistant professor comes up for tenure; if awarded tenure, he or she is supposed to be guaranteed a job for life[55] and promoted to associate professor; if denied tenure, he or she is fired. Even in highly selective schools, 74 percent of all people who come up for tenure receive it.[56] To an outside observer this might suggest that untenured faculty don't have much to worry about and should relax. But the junior faculty under the gun are far more aware of the other side: There is a better than 1 in 4 chance they will be fired (under circumstances that would make it difficult ever again to get as good a job), even though they have been doing a fine job and no one has had any complaints.[57] More important, these high success percentages are only possible because the individuals with weak cases are pressured to leave before coming up for tenure, and the junior faculty who stay will spend six years with their nose to the computer, neglecting their families and personal lives in order to publish–publish–publish. Anyone who fails to do so, who tries simply to work a 40-hour week and live like a normal human being, is virtually certain to be denied tenure.[58] The "success" rates therefore ignore both the fact that the weakest candidates are dropped before they come to the test and that virtually every success is the result of years of hard work.

Business political successes are comparable. Like the rest of us, they can usually think of other things they'd like to have but know they can't get at this time, or could win but wouldn't consider worth the price that would have to be paid. More important, the odds may be very much in their favor, their opponents may be hobbled with one hand tied behind their backs, but it is still a contest requiring pervasive effort. Once upon a time, perhaps, business could simply make its wishes known and receive what it wanted; today, corporations must form PACs, give soft money, actively lobby, make their case to the public, run advocacy ads, and engage in a whole range of costly and degrading activities that they wish were unnecessary. From the outside, we are impressed with their high success rates over a wide range of issues and with the absence of a credible challenge to the general authority of business. From the inside, corporations are impressed with the serious consequences of their occasional losses and with the unremitting effort needed to maintain their privileged position.

We have stressed that business power does not rest *only* on campaign contributions. But campaign contributions remain crucial to business power. A football analogy may be appropriate: Business's vast resources and its influence on the economy may be thought of as equivalent to a powerful offensive line, able to clear the opposition out of the way and create huge openings. But someone then has to take the ball and run through that opening. The PAC and the government relations operation are, in this analogy, like a football running back. When they carry the ball, they have to move quickly, dodge attempts to tackle them, and, if necessary, fight off an opponent and keep going. The analogy breaks down, however, because it implies a contest between evenly matched opponents. Most of the time the business situation more closely approximates a contest between an NFL team and high school opponents. The opponents just don't have the same muscle. Often they are simply intimidated, or have learned through past experience the best thing to do is get out of the way. Occasionally, however, the outclassed opponents will have so much courage and determination that they will at least score—if not win.

◆ 2

GIFTS

NETWORKS OF OBLIGATION

E*VERYBODY* AGREES: BRIBERY IS ILLEGAL, UNETHICAL, AND SHOULD BE eliminated. Stopping outright bribery, however, will change our system only marginally. Recent Supreme Court rulings insist on a narrow and restrictive definition of bribery or extortion: "A public official, to be guilty of extortion under Federal law, must promise to do a specific favor in exchange for money or other compensation he received."[1] Out of 122,000 campaign contributions each year,[2] only a handful meet these strict conditions. The real problem is how we are to understand the other 99 percent of the contributions; they are the key to the way the campaign finance *system* operates and to devising a workable reform. In this chapter we explain the ordinary operation of the system and the way it corrupts even when—perhaps especially when—both donors and politicians are convinced that they have acted honorably.

Two main approaches, both deeply flawed, dominate the discussion of campaign finance. The first sees donations as a form of legalized bribery—in Will Rogers's famous phrase, "the best Congress money can buy."[3] This approach concentrates on those (relatively rare) instances where there is a direct, immediate, and explicit exchange. Such spectacular abuses are good for mobilizing anger, but they are only a small fraction of the *system* of campaign finance.[4] The principal alternative to the Will Rogers view argues that campaign contributions are like votes. Senator Mitch McConnell (Republican–Kentucky), the 1990s public spokesperson for opponents of any effort at reform, says, "If you are able to raise a lot of money it means you have a lot of support, and I think that should be applauded, not condemned."[5] A contribution is simply another way of expressing support, says one high executive:

What business PACs ought to be is a device by which business managers with similar political views can act together in support of those political views. Most businessmen don't have very much time to devote to understanding candidates and politics. They have a great interest in it; they don't have much time for it. The congressman from Nevada votes for the legislation that affects you in Massachusetts and Michigan just as much as the congressmen from Massachusetts and Michigan—that's a reality. Therefore, you have an interest in all of them. You don't have time to research it. Business PACs are a very convenient and effective device by which business managers with similar interests can voluntarily band together to support those political interests and values.

This view argues, in effect, that campaign contributions are a disinterested, and perhaps even a noble, means of participating in the democratic process. The executive who volunteered this view ran an ideological PAC; he felt that this was the way a corporate PAC "ought to be." And, he concluded, "If it were, that'd be a damn good thing." However, in his opinion most corporate PACs are engaged in a form of bribery.

This chapter, and this book as a whole, develops a third perspective. In our view most campaign contributions should be regarded as gifts. The aim of this particular kind of gift is to create a feeling of obligation. The gift is given in a way that will reinforce the politician's feeling of indebtedness to, and connection with, the corporation. At the same time, the fundraising events where these contributions are usually presented also provide a means for the corporation to begin the next step of the process: gaining access to a member in order to ask for a favor. Conceptualizing campaign contributions as gifts is not intended to let either politicians or donors off the hook.

Neither PAC officials nor members have a language or framework in which to understand or explain their own activity. Thus, during the course of an interview the same individual frequently switched back and forth, at times arguing that their contributions bought them absolutely nothing—

and therefore had no impact—and at times arguing that campaign contributions were necessary in order to gain access. It would be easy to attribute this vacillation to public relations or an attempt to deceive, but we think the confusion is real and that participants as well as ordinary voters lack a way to understand the meaning and effect of donations.

We begin with a theoretical analysis of gifts and the networks of obligation they create. Karl Marx thought that the key to *Capital* was the opening discussion of the commodity form. Similarly, although at a very different level, understanding the gift form is crucial to everything that follows. This theoretical point, which may seem abstract, is the necessary foundation for understanding the campaign finance system. Politicians and donors both insist that the money guarantees nothing, that no explicit agreements have been made—and they are (usually) right. Gifts do, however, ensnare participants, creating a sense of obligation and connection so strong that even those opposed to the system become compromised by it. As former Representative Peter Kostmayer (Democrat–Pennsylvania) noted: "You get invited to a dinner somewhere and someone gives you some money. And then you get a call a month later and he wants to see you. Are you going to say no?"[6] Campaign contributions may be gifts, but they are not given spontaneously; rather, they follow careful calculations and evaluations. Once the decision to contribute is made, the money must be delivered, and this provides a further means of creating a sense of connection and indebtedness. It also begins the next stage in the process, gaining access to advance the corporation's interests. Fundraising events thus serve two purposes, and form a bridge between the corporation's contribution and the politician's grant of access.

UNDERSTANDING GIFTS

Candidates can't legally offer to exchange money for favorable policy decisions, and corporations (or others with money) can't legally require a candidate to take a certain position in exchange for the money. The money that changes hands is a *gift*. Theoretically, it is freely given without the expectation of an equivalent being returned.[7]

Modern capitalist society is based on the market and market exchanges. In cash transactions some people are nice, some mean, most treat each other like nonpersons; but the personal relations have little effect on the transaction.[8] The market is so pervasive that its language, forms, and modes of thought come to dominate many aspects of life. Virtually all social phenomena can be purchased, even those, such as congressional votes, that should not be for sale. Can't find a date? Pay a dating service to arrange a match. Need someone to listen, sympathize, and lend you support? Pay a therapist. Do you treasure blue skies, sparkling streams, untouched forests? Some economist has calculated how much they are "worth" and recommended public policy based on these imputed values.[9]

The standard alternative to the market is relations based purely on selfless love or friendship—above all, the family. Friendships and families are not organized on market principles, for—the myth goes—friendships and families involve no rules, limits, or calculations. The family, for example, is said to be a unit where each is valued beyond price, where all work together for the common good with no consideration of who is doing more or less, and each is prepared to support the others "for better, for worse, for richer, for poorer, in sickness and in health, until death do us part." To a lesser degree, the same assumptions are said to govern friendships.

These two kinds of social relations—market exchange on the one side, and total: disregard of personal benefit on the other—are the primary models available in our society. People are uncomfortable thinking analytically about other kinds of social relations. This is as true for corporate government relations officials as for the rest of us: Their comments show they had difficulty escaping the bounds imposed by these categories.

Spurred especially by the women's movement, much recent social science attempts to show that this dualism oversimplifies reality. Arlie Hochschild pointed out that many market relations are based on *The Managed Heart*[10]: The stewardess is required to smile and be friendly, the bill collector to be stern and unforgiving. Even the automated and depersonalized fast-food industry emphasizes its friendly service. And a host of studies have shown that families involve economic relations and unequal power.[11]

We, too, question the dualism prevalent in many popular views of rules. Actions are often conceived as either enforced by state power in a legal bureaucratic system, or as unregulated. In fact, *social* regulatory processes can be more powerful and effective than *legal* enforcement. The most successful and pervasive rules may be precisely those that are not recognized as rules. People who violate unarticulated rules—who talk to themselves out loud in public, who turn their backs to people while talking to them, who stand facing the back of the elevator—may be labeled as "crazy."[12] One study of "Middletown" residents argued that such social rules influence conduct even if people do not think of them as rules and resent having them identified as such. Regarding one of these rules, Caplow argues:

> Few of the written laws that agents of the state attempt to enforce with endless paperwork and threats of violence are so well obeyed as this

unwritten rule that is promulgated by no identifiable authority and backed by no evident threat.[13]

Similarly, corporate officials frequently insist that their gifts are not necessarily reciprocated and that they do not expect them to be, and that campaign contributions have little or no impact on a member's behavior. It is obviously possible that such self-serving claims are knowingly deceptive. But it is also possible that PAC officials, like "Middletown" residents, do not recognize the rules they obey and resent having them articulated.

While we generally shy away from thinking about gifts systematically and analytically, gifts, whether in the United States or Samoa, follow *rules* that regulate what is and is not socially appropriate. The general principles regulating gift giving have been analyzed for "primitive" societies where gifts are the fundamental organizing principle of social exchange. The classic work is that of Marcel Mauss in *The Gift: Forms and Functions of Exchange in Archaic Societies*, originally published in French in 1925. Clearly Mauss couldn't have had any knowledge of corporate PACs, but his analysis often reads as if it were developed specifically for them. Mauss opens with a quote from the Scandinavian *Havamal*:

> "That friendship lasts longest . . . in which friends both give and receive gifts. A man ought to be a friend to his friend and repay gift with gift. . . . If you have a friend in whom you have sure confidence and wish to make use of him, you ought to exchange ideas and gifts with him and go to see him often. . . . A gift always looks for recompense."[14]

Mauss begins his own text by noting: "In Scandinavian and many other civilizations contracts are fulfilled and exchanges of goods are made by means of gifts." He says such gifts are supposedly "voluntary, disinterested and spontaneous," but in fact they are "obligatory and interested."[15]

In the campaign finance system, the process of giving and receiving money is fundamental to the creation of the social world shared by politicians and corporate government relations officials. Caplow finds that Christmas gifts are supposed to be wrapped and typically are opened at public occasions. Similarly, corporations don't simply drop their checks in the mail; they insist on delivering them personally and using this delivery to create a personal connection (see below). Caplow has noted that "ritualized gift giving, in any society, is a method of dealing with important but insecure relationships, whereby gifts are offered to persons or collectivities whose goodwill is needed but cannot be taken for granted."[16] In campaign finance, tremendous uncertainty, for both politicians and businesses, means that both sides feel vulnerable and want to find some way to give themselves an advantage. The company's very existence may depend on government action (or inaction). The politician's survival at the next election may depend on having enough money to buy extra television ads. A gift, either of political influence (by a member) or of cash (by a corporation) may at least reduce the degree of uncertainty about how the other will respond.

In markets each exchange involves its own reciprocal: I give you $15.98 and you give me the latest album by Ani DiFranco. Each accepts this as a fair and even trade; there is no expectation that one or the other of us will later do something additional in order to complete this exchange.[17] I may regard the album as a pearl beyond price or may find it terribly disappointing, but assuming the CD is in good physical condition, there won't be any further elements to this exchange. It is over and done with; we need never see each other again. A gift, however, creates a more enduring relationship. From the moment I receive your gift, until the time I am able to reciprocate it, we are bound to each other; me by the (implicit but very real) obligation to provide you with an object or service, you by the (unstated, but nonetheless real) expectation of receiving an equivalent. Thus gifts create more dense and enduring social relationships than market exchanges.

Gifts are governed by what Alvin Gouldner calls "the norm of reciprocity": If I do something for you, you are expected to reciprocate.[18] You probably do not respond to my gift with an exact equivalent; to do so would reduce the breadth and impact of the social relationship and create a sense of a forced and measured response rather than of one given freely and without calculation. If I unexpectedly need someone to watch my kids, and I ask my neighbor to do so, the appropriate response when I pick my kids up is simply to thank my neighbor, perhaps adding "Let me know if I can help you out sometime." To offer to pay them—or even to hand them a chit saying "Good for one hour of child care at an emergency time of your choosing"—would be an insult, implying that they helped you only in hope of a return, that you will compensate them exactly, and, thus, that this is a market exchange creating no bonds or claims to a future relationship. Nonetheless, over time, gift exchanges usually are roughly in balance; when they are not, both sides will probably be aware of this fact.

Relationships that are not in balance are likely to reflect a recognized difference in power and status. Thus employers regularly give their domestics old clothing and discarded objects. Judith Rollins reports the reactions of one domestic:

This woman was always giving me her old size five-and-a-half shoes. I wear an eight! But my mother always said, and she did domestic work for years, she said, "No matter what they give you, you take it." ... But if it was something I didn't want, I'd thank her, walk out of there, go around that corner and the first trash can I got to, I'd throw it in.[19]

The domestic is required to show effusive and eternal gratitude, even if the objects are worthless and totally unwanted. Almost universally, domestics express hostility to, and resentment at, a system that degrades them. They put up with this system because of the power differential in this relationship; were a domestic to offer an employer used clothing or equipment, the gift would be perceived as grossly insulting and probably lead to dismissal. Candidates for political office sometimes feel they are in a similar situation. "Hubert Humphrey described campaign fundraising as 'the most disgusting, demeaning, disenchanting, debilitating experience of a politician's life.' And he died before it got bad."[20] People "maintain ascendancy by regulating the indebtedness of others to them. . . . William F. Whyte, for instance, notes that the leader takes care not to fall into debt to his followers but to insure, on the contrary, that the benefits he renders unto others are never fully repaid."[21] Corporations want always to have contributed to a member prior to asking him or her for a favor.

Mauss's categorization of the Maori system in New Zealand is particularly appropriate to corporate PAC contributions to members of Congress: "In this system . . . one gives away what is in reality a part of one's nature and substance, while to receive something is to receive a part of someone's spiritual essence."[22] Corporations and politicians each give a part of their nature and substance—money from corporations, favors from politicians. The nature and substance of both politicians and corporations is public information, but at the same time "the presentation of a gift is an imposition of identity."[23] When politicians accept campaign contributions, they implicitly indicate that they view the donor as legitimate and will in the future be willing to discuss issues. Politicians return campaign contributions on occasion, though rarely, and then usually in response to media exposure.[24]

REQUESTS AND POLITICIANS' PRESSURE

To whom do individuals give gifts? To their friends, to those who invite them to special occasions, to those with whom they would like to be friends, and sometimes to those working for a worthy cause. Wedding gifts are almost never unsolicited; an invitation virtually demands a present, while an announcement makes a gift optional. Similarly, corporations rarely contribute except in response to requests. "We don't go out looking for people to give money to anymore. We are inundated with requests for money." This flood of invitations reduces the practical consequences of giving only in response to invitations:

I think any PAC administrator will tell you that we are just besieged with requests, both in Washington and the whole industry, for funding. It's horrendous. Whether they have campaigns or not, opponents or not.

However, it is significant that PACs felt they should only respond to requests and indicated that in many instances the reason a member did not receive a contribution was simply because he or she did not ask.

Donors coerce politicians, and politicians coerce donors. Mauss notes that to refuse to accept a gift, and sometimes even to refuse to give one, is "the equivalent of a declaration of war; it is a refusal of friendship and intercourse."[25] In the great majority of transactions a member of Congress's request for a contribution is low key, a simple invitation in the mail. At other times, however, the request has some of the character of the Godfather's "I'll make 'em an offer they can't refuse." One common experience of pressure beyond the mail invitation, but a very long way from any kind of threat, is:

You go into an audience with a member and his staff and somebody, usually a staff guy, is going to mention they have a fundraiser coming up. That's how it happens sometimes. Or if you're not a contributor, your people come to town, you'll get a young staff member; while if you're a contributor, particularly in the thousand up—oh, I don't know, strike that, even a contributor, 250, 500, or whatever, then you're going to get a more important staff member.

The congressional staff who mention a fundraiser are sending the PAC officer a gentle reminder that one good turn deserves another.

Member messages can be much stronger. One lobbyist told the *Wall Street Journal* that for Alfonse D'Amato, the New York Republican senator, "Nothing is enough. It's continuous pressure. If you don't contribute, they don't return your calls."[26] One of our corporations reported that in 1978, when they tried to schedule an appointment with a member, he wanted to know if they had a PAC before agreeing to the meeting. (They didn't, but they promptly formed one.) Others have gone even further:

Heavy-handed is a precise way of describing the tactics employed by South Dakota's Republican Senator James Abdnor in hitting up Washington lobbyists and PAC managers to buy $1,500 tickets to a fundraising dinner at which President Reagan was to be the star attraction. Abdnor sent the invitation around by messenger, with a reply card giving the invitee three choices: to make a $5,000 PAC contribution; to buy one or more tickets; or to say "No, our PAC does not wish to support the Salute to Jim Abdnor featuring President Reagan." What angered many PAC managers was Abdnor's instruction to the messenger not to leave the invitee's office without a response of some kind.[27]

These PAC officers were at least given the chance to say no without any stated consequences. While it is uncommon for members or staff to demand contributions as a quid pro quo for favors rendered, many corporations have experienced this at least occasionally:

> We just last year contributed to Lloyd Bentsen [Democrat–Texas, at the time chair of the Senate Finance Committee]. That was in the off year I think, the year preceding the election. And that was out of necessity. We contacted his office for something and were pretty much told point-blank that you don't contribute to us, why should we even help you. I know that to this day that makes one of our executives sick, that we contributed to Bentsen. Our executive was still gagging last fall because we had done that.

Another PAC officer reported that though John Kerry (Democrat–Massachusetts) makes a public issue of not accepting PAC contributions, his staff had nonetheless called the corporation to say that Kerry expected $5,000 in personal contributions from the company's executives.

What happens if the corporation does not contribute? No one really knows, but if the member is being aggressive about it, and it's someone the corporation has had or expects to have dealings with, what CEO would take the chance of refusing? The corporation cannot anticipate its future problems. Nor can it tell how long the member and staff will remember the refusal to contribute. Or what the member will (or won't) do if he or she does remember. In a situation where this member's support or opposition could change the company's bottom line by millions or even billions, is it worth incurring displeasure to save a measly $1,000 in PAC money? As one anonymous contributor noted about a call from Vice President Al Gore:

> For a vice president, particularly this vice president, who has real power and is the heir apparent, to ask for money gave me no choice. I have so much business that touches on the federal government—the telecommunications act, tax policy, regulations galore.[28]

Members and their staffs are prepared to accept an occasional refusal, especially if there is a prior history: "Some cases your relations with a guy go back so far, he might get upset and call you a cheap bastard but he would not end the relationship."

Corporate executives had many stories of members pressuring them to contribute. But how common is this? In the mail survey we conducted, 5 out of 6 (83.7 percent) corporations reported that candidates pressured them for a contribution at least occasionally; 1 in 5 (18.8 percent) said this happened frequently. Asked to assess the amount of pressure candidates place on PACs in general, not just on their own PAC, only 1 in 25 (3.6 percent) answered "none," almost a third (30.9 percent) said "a small amount," a majority (52.7 percent) answered "a moderate amount," and 1 in 10 (10.9 percent) said "a great deal." Candidate pressure is not a rare event, but neither is it a major problem for most corporations. At the same time, it sets the framework for day-to-day activity, and it is a factor that most corporations are conscious of much of the time. In the late 1980s, PAC officers used as evidence of increasing pressure the fact that they were receiving an increasing number of phone calls from members of Congress themselves, rather than from congressional staff. Today, big contributors are called by the president and vice president. Though PAC officers are partly responsible for this, many of them are nonetheless unhappy when it happens:

The other thing that makes me sad is when my phone rings and it's Senator So-and-So calling me on the phone to beg for money. And I say to myself, "Jesus Christ, the business of running this government is more important than you being on the phone all day calling PAC people!"

Requests for contributions do not come only from the members and their staffs. Some of the requests that are most likely to be honored come from officials of other corporations. These create networks of obligation between one corporation and another as well as between a corporation and a member (an important point that we will discuss in Chapter 6 on business unity).

PRAGMATIC AND IDEOLOGICAL APPROACHES

Corporations follow two very different strategies, pragmatic and ideological. Pragmatic donations are given specifically to advance the short-run interests of the donor, primarily to enable the corporation to gain a chance to meet with the member and argue its case. Because the aim of these donations is to gain "access" to the president, top party leaders, or members of Congress, the money is given without regard to whether or not the politician needs it and with little consideration of the politician's stance on large issues. The corporation's only concern is that the politician will be willing and able to help out. And, as we show in the next chapter, virtually all politicians, regardless of party, are willing to cooperate in this access process. Perhaps the most memorable characterization of this strategy was made by Jay Gould, nineteenth-century robber baron and owner of the Erie Railroad: "In a Republican district I was a Republican; in a Democratic district, a Democrat; in a doubtful district I was doubtful; but I was always for Erie."[29]

Ideological donations, on the other hand, are made to influence the political composition of the Congress or presidency. From this perspective, contributions need to meet two conditions: (1) they should be directed to politically congenial "pro–free enterprise" candidates (in practice, always conservatives)[30] who face opponents unsympathetic to business; and (2) they should be targeted to competitive races where the money has the potential to influence the election outcome. The member's willingness to do the company favors does not matter. Even a conservative "free enterprise" philosophy wouldn't be sufficient: If the two opponents' views were the same, then the election couldn't influence the ideological composition of Congress. Most incumbents—in some years as many as 98 percent of all House members—are reelected. Precisely because incumbents will probably be reelected even without PAC support, ideological corporations usually give to nonincumbents, either challengers or candidates for open seats.

Virtually all corporations use some combination of pragmatic and ideological strategies. The simplest method of classifying corporations is by the proportion of money they give to congressional incumbents: the higher this proportion, the more pragmatic the corporation.[31] In 1996, almost 4 out of 5 large corporate PACs gave at least 70 percent of their money to incumbents, and a majority gave at least 80 percent to incumbents.[32]

THE DECISION PROCESS

Pragmatic and ideological corporations make different kinds of contributions, and hence use different decision-making criteria. Better than 80 percent of corporate contributions are pragmatic. No corporation contributes to all candidates, so decisions must be made about which requests to honor. The initial screening is done by the government relations office and referred to the PAC steering committee, which is composed of middle- and upper-level managers from all parts of the corporation. The requests that are turned down by government relations are very unlikely ever again to be considered:

Seventy-five percent of the requests that come for contributions to federal candidates are processed through the Washington office and just get filed. They decide they don't want to recommend a contribution. So it just never shows up on the agenda.

In corporations where the steering committee is taken seriously, the PAC officer or government relations representatives fill out forms about the candidates they recommend for contributions. Forms are at most two pages long, so that committee members can quickly glance through each and check the factors that most concern them.[33] In a typical access PAC the government relations staff "gives us all the background and then gives us a little bit of a summary on what committees and subcommittees they're on and what things they have helped us on in the past." Ideological PACs include basic information about the candidate, but they do not supplement that with committee assignments but with "voting records, the recommendations of outside organizations, what the positions of the challenger are, how close the race is expected to be. I pick out key issues that are important to us and say, here's how they voted on these issues. Clean Air Act, product liability, plant closing, and there's one other [issue] I did last year."

PRAGMATIC CRITERIA

Pragmatic corporations focus primarily on the members' committee assignments, past relationship with the company, and willingness to help out. As a senior vice president at one utility company explained:

When people help you get a tax abatement or someone goes out of their way to make certain that rights of way are more easily procured or certain bureaucratic obstacles are removed, you tend to want them to be there if you ever need to come back again. So you will make those contributions in that situation.

Most of these decisions are fairly simple and non-problematic:

If we have a member in Congress that's on the energy committee or has helped us with acid rain or environmental issues, we don't question that a whole lot, because that's kind of what we're about.

On the other hand, some access-oriented corporations give even to members who have opposed their positions, in an attempt to create a sense of indebtedness even among adversaries:

We have operated our education program on the basis of not only getting to the people we know are sympathetic to our activities and what we think our needs might be, but also to help win over some of the folks who are presumed to be on the other side. And if you don't do anything with them, if you just leave them alone, they are bound to be on the other side. So we have helped some people who actually were negative on our issues. If you back off and leave it to the opposition, then for sure we'll lose their support. You might not be able to get that person's vote, but you might be able to neutralize them to the point that they would understand that there is another side to that issue, and might be willing to walk away from the issue rather than go in and do something that you may not like.

Much academic literature argues that members frequently do favors for companies not because they have received corporate campaign contributions but because the company and its employees are the member's constituents. Constituency relationship is thought to be more important than campaign contributions in explaining which companies get access to, and support from, which members. PAC directors often agree with the logic of this academic argument and argue that if the company had a large plant in a member's district, they didn't need a PAC to see the member. Nonetheless, corporations *do* contribute to such members, reinforcing the constituency relationship with a PAC contribution. In our mail survey of corporate PACs, 60 percent indicated that having company operations in a member's district makes "a great deal" of difference in their decision, and a further 25 percent indicated it makes "a moderate amount" of difference. Time after time, PACs took it for granted that they would contribute to races in the districts where they have employees or investments. It is therefore mistaken to contrast PAC contributions and constituency relationship.

Why would a company give donations if it already had a constituency relationship with a member? Wouldn't constituency by itself be enough to gain the company access? A corporate vice president explained the practical fallacy in the academic argument:

First, you have to remember if you have a plant with five hundred people, four hundred and fifty are labor or union or nonmanagement. And so if you look around on that basis, in theory the member normally is not going to vote with you, because normally the guy in the plant is not concerned with the same issues that our chairman of the board is.

Secondly, I find it's not unusual for a member of the House, or particularly a senator, to not be conversant with the fact that you are in his state or district. Until you get to one of the staffers and you remind him you are X, Y, and Z. "Oh yes, now I remember you." I think we also have a tendency to think the first thing they do when they wake up is think, "How is [our corporation] doing?" And that's not the first thing they do in the morning. They may never do that during the day. I think that most of the people that I talk to, constituency relationship is clearly one of the criteria.

In effect, these corporate executives are saying that the constituency relationship is not enough, that it needs to be reinforced by a campaign contribution. The public agrees: According to a 1997 Princeton Survey Research Associates poll, 67 percent of voters think their own congressional representative would pay more attention to the views of large outside donors than to a constituent's views. Members of Congress, in this instance former Senator Wyche Fowler, agree:

The brutal fact that we all agonize over is that if you get two calls and one is from a constituent who wants to complain about the Veterans Administration mistreating her father, for the tenth time, and one is from somebody who is going to give you a party and raise $10,000, you call back the contributor.[34]

Pragmatic corporations are also influenced by two largely apolitical considerations. First, general competence:

I think it is much more important to be able to get in and see even an opposition member that will work and pay attention to what you say, and when they realize their natural inclination is not what is correct, they've got your input, than it is to have some yo-yo out there who is with you all the time but doesn't understand. Because they are ineffective in influencing their colleagues. And you can't get a whole body that is going to do what you want to do. So the idea is that the smarter they are and the more access you have to them, the more useful they are in the process.

Second, some executives stressed that there were certain candidates with whom they simply "hit it off." One woman PAC officer had met a woman candidate (for an open seat) at a "meet and greet" sponsored by the Republican party and had enjoyed talking to her. Even though the company targeted the bulk of its money to incumbents, the PAC made a donation to this candidate, who went on to win, and the relationship has continued.[35]

IDEOLOGICAL CONTRIBUTIONS

Ideological PACs, or access PACs making one of their limited number of ideological contributions, have a somewhat harder time of it. Giving to challengers generally means the corporation cannot be guided by past giving, but has to research the candidates anew each year. Moreover, ideological contributions are targeted to close races, and it is generally difficult to predict in advance which races they will be. Some contributions are given as seed money to help a challenger become viable, and those decisions can be made ahead of time, but many decisions need to be compressed into the last few months of a campaign. Access-oriented contributions, on the other hand, can be made almost equally well at any time, since the issue is not the election, but the member's power and willingness to help.

Most *ideological* corporations rely in significant part on the recommendations of BIPAC (the Business–Industry Political Action Committee), the Chamber of Commerce, and in a perverse way on those of the ADA (Americans for Democratic Action) and the AFL–CIO's COPE (Committee on Political Education). This simplifies their decision making.

We use the Americans for Democratic Action, and we use its mirror image, the ACA [Americans for Constitutional Action]. You can take a look at those five numbers and you know what he is. He can sit and make speeches to you all day, but you look at those five numbers. If the ADA says he's liberal, and the ACA says he's liberal, and the AFL–CIO/COPE says that he is prolabor, and the U.S. Chamber of Commerce says he's the most antibusiness son-of-a-bitch you ever saw, and BIPAC says he doesn't have an ounce of fiscal responsibility, you got a fix on him. It doesn't matter what he tells you.

The analyses by BIPAC are particularly useful, because they also make an effort to seek out promising "free enterprise" challengers:

BIPAC analyses are good; they're hunting for the same kind of candidates as we are; therefore, they tend to be very relevant to us. . . . They're very active in this, and they've got some first-rate people doing the analysis. We don't always agree with them, but we always find their analyses relevant.

Academic studies often use ratings as predictors of corporate campaign contributions. The results are generally disappointing, and our interviews make it clear why this is so: Most corporations are *pragmatic* and access oriented. Therefore, they are concerned with a candidate's position on a specific company issue, rather than with their broad general philosophy. As one access PAC officer said:

Some people use ratings, which I hate because they are the grossest generalizations that you could ever imagine. Those people that may be on the Chamber of Commerce good government scale, or whatever they say, know nothing about our business, don't care about our business, and in fact if they are from the northeast, would vote to screw our business. It has nothing to do with reality. I haven't looked at a rating. . . . I have people throw those at me all the time. Generally, I can come back and say, "So what? Since when did they vote yes on natural gas decontrol?" Or "I know he is a screaming liberal but he helped us go get our coal permit. Helped us get that land out there to mine because he knew the situation that was involved. If he hadn't been paying attention, we wouldn't have been able to get it."

Three other factors are more problematic for ideological than for pragmatic corporations: political party, social issues, and preexisting friendships between executives and candidates.

Political party is perhaps the most surprising factor. We found that virtually no corporation pays any attention to political party. Without a single exception, access-oriented corporations insist that it is irrelevant whether a candidate is a Democrat or a Republican, that this isn't a consideration except to the extent that political party predicts who will have power in Congress. (The 1994 Republican takeover of the House and Senate did change corporate donation practices, as we will discuss in Chapter 5, but this was primarily because of pragmatic, not ideological or partisan, considerations.) Ideological corporations are more likely to be concerned with political party: Some of them consider it significant, others do not. Most ideological corporations would prefer to be strictly bipartisan, but given their orientation find that difficult:

The direction of our political views is for fiscal responsibility, and it tends to be for conservative candidates, it tends to be in favor of Republican candidates. We try very hard to be bipartisan, but given the current makeup of the parties, and the ground rules we have, we have some ground rules that make it hard to find Democrats. The guidelines are that you've got to have a competitive race for us to make a contribution to you. You've got to need the money in terms of the sources available to your opponent. In addition to that, you've got to be meritorious in terms of public policy values that are reflected by our PAC.

Most of the Democrats that are attractive to us are extremely well funded and win overwhelmingly and do not have serious competition. . . .

We work hardest trying to find Democrats that we can support and that our members want to support. The trouble is, if you've got a PAC of American manufacturing managers in the U.S. in the late 1980s, and you only give to contested races, you are unlikely to have a Democrat running against a Republican and more attractive to a business manager. There are some Democrats who meet that criteria, but golly they're safe. They've been in there a long time. They got a lead-pipe cinch. We don't give to Republicans like them either.

There's nothing that has frustrated me as much. . . . The one thing that I think we've failed at is having a sufficient partisan balance, and I don't know how to do it. I've tried like hell, but it seems to me that the partisan bias is a reflection of the realities of American politics today. And I can't do anything about that. We could change our criteria; we could say, by God, we're going to support at least one-third Democrats, whether they need it or not.

Some ideological corporations are so concerned about remaining bipartisan that they give to Democrats who don't really fit their criteria:

Well someone says, how come you only contribute to Republicans? Well, we are only contributing to pro-business candidates. It just so happens that the pro-business candidates are Republicans. Nine times out of ten. In the last election I searched out pro-business Democrats. I came up with some and I came up with some that we had missed in years past. And we made a point to contribute to them this time around if they needed the money. Sometimes lesser contributions even when they didn't necessarily need the money.

A few ideological corporations expressed a clear preference for Republicans. As one said, "We are obviously a more Republican PAC than a Democratic PAC." Speaking before the 1994 Republican congressional takeover, he said:

We have contributed heavily to Republican senatorial candidates, and that's been primarily a strategy on our part to help maintain a Republican majority in the Senate. . . . When one party controls Congress for so long you don't have the balance that I feel is good for the free enterprise system. So if you look at our contributions, we have specifically targeted Republican challengers and incumbents to help maintain or help increase the Republican majority to give balance in the Congress.

One or two companies that expressed a preference for Republicans nonetheless gave most of their money to Democrats. As one of the latter explained to us before Newt Gingrich became speaker:

You've got to be pragmatic about it as well. As I've said, we support very heavily Republicans in the Senate, but in the House the Democrats are in the leadership. They control the committees; all of your legislation that you are vitally concerned about has to go through them, so obviously you'll find many of our contributions are to Democrats in the House. . . .

[Our CEO] was invited up earlier this year to speak to a Republican leadership group. I forget what they call it, they've got a lot of these little caucuses in the House. Bob Michel [Republican leader in the House] was there, and there must have been twenty Republican candidates. Because they all know he's a Republican, strongly Republican, one of the questions they raised to him was, "Why are so many of your contributions to Democrats? Why aren't we getting more of them?" And he had to say "Well, just pragmatically, you aren't running the Congress." He said, "We do give to challengers and to others that we would like to support, but by and large many of our contributions on the House side are to those in the leadership positions and they are Democrats."

These are problems that access-oriented PACs need never face.

Social issues, such as abortion, school prayer, censorship, and the like, seem to have the same potential to cause problems for ideological corporations. In practice, however, every corporation we spoke with insisted that they do not consider social issues. Even the most ideological corporation among them said, "We don't have a position on pro-choice or pro-life" or other social issues. Many corporations take a strong stand in favor of "free enterprise," but social issues were important only by their absence. As one ideological PAC officer noted, "If you looked at people's voting records on abortion, you'd probably make half the people that contribute to the PAC mad one way or the other."

As for *friendships,* ideological corporations do have trouble with preexisting friendships between candidates and executives. For a pragmatic PAC, this is a pure benefit. Since their aim is to gain access to and support from a member, such a friendship is an ideal entrée. It hardly matters what the candidate's politics are; the corporation can only benefit from having a friend in Congress.

> I think we have to make a more personal decision based on our experience with the individuals. That's one of the things we are looking for. We tell our people that if you know somebody that's running for office that you think deserves to be supported by the [company] PAC, tell us about it. Because there is nothing better than having a personal contact, next-door neighbor, or some close association.

Many corporations have at least a few contributions that are determined in this way: A candidate had gone to school with a top executive, or was a fraternity brother, or was an ex-company employee, or was in some other way an acquaintance. For an ideological corporation, however, this contribution could pose problems if the candidate had a moderate or liberal voting record, while the company normally supported only "free enterprise" diehards:

> From my perspective, it is somewhat of an embarrassment with our PAC, but it's only one candidate. We contribute to him every year, and he doesn't have a pro-business voting record. He just happens to be a *frat brother* of the number-three person in the company. Fortunately we only have one of those. But we were able at least to cut his contribution back to $500 this year instead of $1,000. That's the one where the other executives are giving the one grief. There is a lot of kidding back and forth about, "Are we going to support that communist again?" But no one's going to say, "Why don't you just contribute to him yourself, instead of having the PAC do it?" We don't do that. We just honor that request. It's the only one we have.

CONTROVERSY: WHY AND HOW OFTEN?

At many corporations PAC committee contribution decisions are made peacefully, and controversy is almost nonexistent. Issues are settled "pretty much by consensus. We don't have many heated exchanges at all." Sometimes this is because "everybody pretty much agrees on the general orientation of the PAC," as one ideological corporation reported. In other companies, controversy is rare because the high-level executives on the PAC committee have other duties they see as more pressing:

Sometimes I get a question: "Why did you give to him?" Recently one of my vice chairs asked me why I gave to more Democrats than Republicans. But I've never had a serious complaint or an issue that wasn't easily resolved. Most of these people are so busy themselves that they couldn't care less about the PAC.

A small number of PACs, however, experience a great deal of controversy. The most common and heated disagreements are in pragmatic PACs operated by diversified corporations whose divisions have differing interests. One highly diversified corporation, when asked if there ever were any differences of opinion about whom to support, replied:

Oh, absolutely. I could think of numerous examples where one of our business sectors wants to support candidate A and the other says, "Golly, he's not really one of our very good friends. We ought to support his opponent. He's not supportive at all. Stay out of that race." So we do have a lot of disagreements. We have our PAC executive committee comprised of a representative from each of our business sectors plus the corporate staff, so those business sectors have ample opportunity and ample voice to get involved in our decision-making process.

Several corporations reported some version of this experience, where the division of opinion *inside* the corporation was extreme:

There may be candidates who have taken a high profile on an issue. . . . Some guy is all for wilderness. That's death for our exploration division, they wouldn't give him a dime. But maybe that same guy is on Ways and Means, and he's been very helpful for taxes.

Some of these corporations report that committee meetings often become heated: "It gets pretty exciting sometimes. When the pitch reaches a certain level, we have to table the issue till the next meeting." The hope is that by then tempers will have cooled down, they'll have more information, or something will help resolve the issue. A few candidates get set aside until people have cooled down:

On rare occasions we come to loggerheads. Ninety percent of the time we reach consensus; 10 percent of the time we can't. But 90 percent of that time we will come to the point of voting for the record, and the disagreeing party goes on record as being opposed but we contribute on the basis of the vote. In extraordinarily few circumstances since I've been here has the conflict been so great that it cannot be resolved. The two parties were so fiercely in disagreement that the other board members wouldn't even vote, that they've said the issue has to go out of this room and be resolved in some other way. That's happened maybe twice.

At the great majority of corporations, relatively few donations are challenged, or even questioned, but the concerns that are raised are ideologically motivated complaints about pragmatic donations. These objections are generally infrequent and muted, with little or no open conflict. Such concerns may be raised by members of the PAC committee, by ordinary managers, or by top executives. Typically they take the form of someone wanting to know, "Why are we giving to such a liberal Democrat?"

Most ideological controversies stay mild; the tone of these disputes differs from pragmatic controversies between corporate divisions with differing interests. Typically,

One person will say, "I cannot vote for that individual." And the other one might say, "Well, I can understand how you might feel, but here's some good things." And the other one will say, "I don't care. I cannot vote for that person. I do not believe that they stand for what this PAC stands for."

Another common response is, "One person will say, 'Well, okay, but I want to be recorded as voting no.'" Contributors who question PAC decisions can usually be persuaded to go along:

Occasionally somebody raises a question, but usually they can be satisfied. We don't ever give to somebody without some reason. Generally, the people who ask are satisfied.

Some complaints are more vigorously pursued:

We have members of the PAC who believe firmly and strongly that we should never give to somebody that doesn't have a voting record that is exactly consistent with theirs. And when we give those people money or make contributions to them, they get very upset. And they call. Or they make their views known at the PAC meeting if they are on the steering committee.

Dissenters aren't always satisfied with the responses they received, or the PAC officer doesn't consider it worth the effort to persuade them:

We have had a couple of people drop out of the PAC because they didn't like the fact that we were giving to, for example, a Democrat on the Energy and Commerce Committee who represents [an area near headquarters] who isn't necessarily all that good a friend of business. We were trying to establish a relationship with him because of his committee spot. The PAC member that wanted to drop out, he had some problems with a couple of other contributions, and he was very, very conservative. I told him that it would probably be best if he did drop out because I didn't think he was going to be able to learn to live with contributions that we were making.

Top officers' concerns are much like those of other managers. Most of the time, in most corporations, they have no complaints: "I've been chairman of this PAC for three years, and I have yet to have an officer call and quiz me about a contribution"; "I have never had one senior manager ever say, 'Why did you do that?'" On the other hand, such queries are by no means unknown:

INTERVIEWER: Do they ever call you up and say, "I have problems with the PAC having contributed to So and So?"

PAC DIRECTOR: Yes. And you try to explain why you did it. Usually, in fact always, they say "Okay." They never say, "Don't do it" or "Get the money back."

INTERVIEWER: Do you ever come out of a conversation feeling you are in trouble?

PAC DIRECTOR: No. They are kind of rational guys. If you have a rational explanation. He didn't get to the top of this company because he was emotionally involved, except for the business of course. So they tend to take your explanations as long as they are rational. But they get emotional once in a while. They are like citizens. They are fans. They read the newspapers and they see the guy holding a demonstration outside. But I say, "Yes, the guy's holding a demonstration. That's what he has to do to get elected. You can't take that personally. What we have to deal with is how did he respond on an issue or how did he help us ameliorate the problem that he is addressing in another way."

There was a clear sense that a substantial number of complaints could be expected if the corporation donated to a well-known liberal who represented an area near a main center of corporate employment. "Liberal" in this context could mean someone who, on the national scale, is regarded as a moderate—either a Democrat or a Republican. However, when the PAC officer explained the reasoning, people were usually satisfied:

Generally if an employee says that they're unhappy with what we have done, if we have an opportunity to talk to them before they get so bent out of shape, we can explain why the contribution was given. Generally it satisfies them. If you can maintain a level of communication with your membership, and they understand that this PAC is not involved with the social issues, that it's involved strictly with industry issues, then they will be satisfied.

Crucial to going along with the corporation's contributions is a recognition of the purpose of the PAC.

The thing that the committee has to keep in mind is this: What we do is not a manifestation of our own personal political preferences. It is a manifestation of what we collectively think is good for [the company]. I've got Bill Gallagher, who is our corporate treasurer, he's to the right of Attila the Hun, so when we have to give money to a liberal it's very hard for him. But the purpose of the PAC is *not* to pander to his particular political leanings.

Virtually all these ideological disputes involve conservatives objecting to donations to liberals. The reverse is almost, but not quite, hypothetical: One corporation could not actually remember a specific controversy, but knew liberal sentiments were a consideration:

We also have liberal Democrats who are unhappy. I don't know what would happen if somebody ever suggested we give money to Jesse Helms. I'm not sure we have ever given money to Helms. I don't think we have ever been asked.

The vast majority of the PAC officer's suggestions are accepted, but the PAC steering committee nonetheless exercises an important influence, since it must approve all donations. If a PAC officer proposes 100 donations, of which 90 are accepted routinely, 10 are vigorously debated, and only 3 of the 10 rejected, then the committee has approved 97 percent of the PAC officer's recommendations. Nonetheless, the 3 rejected and the 10 disputed are likely to be long remembered and to influence future suggestions. The discussion, and the occasional rejection, of the recommendations is a part of the process by which the government relations office comes to better understand the company's operating divisions and their concerns. At the same time, the operating units learn what is politically possible and how issues should be presented for maximum political effectiveness.

The character and frequency of these internal disputes is, however, counterintuitive. Controversy is frequent and heated when PAC committees argue about which of two incumbents should receive a pragmatic access donation. It is mild, rare, and usually polite when people voice ideological objections to giving to candidates they consider too liberal. Why?

Controversies over pragmatic donations can become so heated for at least two reasons. First, in a pragmatic controversy neither side is speaking for itself; both are defending the interests of the corporation as they understand them. Second, to the extent that each PAC committee member is primarily accountable to the head of his or her division and is serving as his or her representative, standing up aggressively for the division's interests will help, not hurt, his or her career. This kind of dispute is sanctioned by the corporation. The PAC committee members may be primarily or exclusively concerned with the interests of their particular part of the company, but members who engage in such behavior are likely to be rewarded, not penalized, by their superiors.[36] Therefore, in diversified corporations with pragmatic PACs, such disputes are frequent, and people are unafraid and prepared to hold their ground.

Ideological disputes are different. In an ideological controversy, particularly if the PAC is primarily pragmatic, the objection to the candidate can be seen as coming from someone who is putting personal values above the best interests of the corporation. Therefore, disputes are tentative and understated—even though committee members are likely to care much more deeply about these ideological disputes than they do about pragmatic arguments among divisions; that is, the most important factor shaping disputes is not individual feelings and preferences, but rather what the corporation encourages or discourages.

MORE THAN CAMPAIGN CONTRIBUTIONS

Virtually all corporations use political action committee contributions as a mechanism to form a connection with a member (or nonincumbent candidate), and increasingly they use soft money as a means of solidifying a relationship with presidential candidates and top party leaders. The next section analyzes these publicly reported donations, but first we consider some of the unreported, end-run ways of establishing connections to politicians. The specific mechanisms vary over time: When one gimmick receives wide public notice and hostility, some sort of regulation or control is introduced; meanwhile, the smart players are developing a new loophole. The congressional abuses that attracted the most attention at the beginning of the 1990s (speaking fees lining politicians' pockets, free trips to vacation spots, and personal gifts)[37] are now subject to (more-or-less effective) regulations, but new loopholes have been created or expanded. Some of these scams can still be used for state legislatures, however. For example, in 1996 and 1997 Charlie Williams, a member of the Mississippi state legislature, went to "Spain, Belgium, Australia and Costa Rica, all courtesy of the New York Society for International Affairs." His June 1997 trip to Costa

Rica included a stay at a posh resort and a jungle boat safari; all expenses, including accommodations for his guests, were paid for by the New York Society. It turns out that the nonprofit New York Society "receives almost all of its funding from Philip Morris,"[38] which had earlier paid for Williams to attend the Super Bowl. Williams hopes to be the Republican gubernatorial candidate in 1998; a likely opponent is Mike Moore, a Democrat and the state's attorney general, who negotiated a deal requiring the tobacco industry to shell out $368 billion nationally over the next twenty-five years (see Chapter 4).

The aim of the various other mechanisms, some accepted as legitimate, some extremely dubious, is to skirt the law and create a special relationship, with advantages for both the politician (who gets more money) and the donor (who creates a greater sense of indebtedness and a stronger relationship).

To begin at the most legitimate end, the company can aid the candidate in gaining access to constituents, something that most would consider appropriate.

We also invite the member of Congress to come to our facility. And they love to come. They get there in the morning before [work gets going and makes access difficult]. We usually give them a chance to make a speech, and usually arrange coffee and donuts or something. Any member that visits with us remembers us. We'll do that during election time; if the challenger wants to visit us we'll give him the same opportunity.

A member may benefit more from a visit to a major company facility than from a PAC contribution of $500 or $1,000. Companies sometimes provide a member free publicity through their PAC newsletter, with a picture of the member and a text explaining what he or she has done for the company and why the PAC considers this candidate to be worth supporting.

Companies can also help a member do favors for constituents. Constituents occasionally call or write their member of Congress for help in dealing with gas, electric, or phone companies. Someone on the member's staff calls the company's government relations unit, and that person straightens out the problem, or at least explains it. The customer is guaranteed careful attention, and it's reasonable to suppose they are more likely than the average customer to get the rules bent in their favor; a voter whose problem is solved through congressional intervention is likely to support the member at the next election, and companies can be more cooperative with "friendly" members.

Far more dubiously, politicians can—and often do—form organizations that can accept donations of unlimited size.[39] Often they can conceal the names of donors, and the money given counts as tax-exempt charitable contributions. As with soft money, corporations may contribute directly, without having to use PACs. Most such organizations are supposed to be nonpartisan and only for educational and research activities, but this is interpreted so loosely as to have little meaning.

The top Republican leaders of 1996 illustrate a range of such practices. Bob Dole's foundation for the handicapped can serve as a best-case example: a worthwhile, relatively nonpolitical goal, an issue of personal concern to Dole, and money apparently used in a meritorious fashion. Even in this best-case example, however, if a corporation donates to Dole's charitable foundation instead of, say, to the March of Dimes, the donation doesn't just help the poor and deserving—it also helps the corporation gain Dole's notice and gratitude, a gratitude that may well be repaid at some future time. Dole's running mate, Jack Kemp, was the leader (with William Bennett) of another nonprofit, called Empower America. In 1992, Theodore J. Forstmann, whose fortune is estimated at $250 to $300 million, wanted to support Kemp's tax-cutting ideas. He told Kemp to "figure out what it costs, and I'll underwrite the thing for you."[40] First-year contributions were $8.6 million; the organization enabled Kemp—and his ideas for tax cuts that give huge benefits to the rich—to stay in the limelight. Nor did promoting these ideological views involve personal sacrifice by Kemp: The organizational base enabled him to earn $1 to $2 million a year by giving speeches (at up to $35,000 apiece). Had Dole and Kemp been elected, their "nonprofit" contributors might have profited handsomely.

The other key Republican leader of 1996, Speaker of the House Newt Gingrich, had more trouble with his nonprofit.[41] Newt Gingrich solicited tax-deductible contributions for his "educational" program broadcast nationwide on television to "provide the structure to build an offense so that Republicans can break through dramatically in 1996."[42] The House later voted to fine him $300,000 for various abuses involved in this process.

Sometimes the process lacks even fig-leaf legitimacy. The National Foundation for Women Legislators was established "to provide strategic resources for women to be strong and effective state legislators." In 1996 the organization blatantly sold access rights, with a list of prices ($2,500 to join a roundtable with state legislators; $15,000 to conduct an issues workshop; $30,000 for a lunchtime speech). A number of top businesses found this a good deal: A representative of the American Automobile Manufacturers Association spoke on clean-air legislation, someone from General Motors explained the need to restrict lawsuits targeted at defective cars and the accidents they cause, and slot machine manufacturers made a pitch for gambling. In marketing this access, the organization explained that "women legislators are a critical target audience because of the credibility they engender in their statehouses." Needless to say, "balance," so much in demand at other times, was never a concern.[43]

With the end of the speaking-fee scam, it is more difficult to put significant cash directly into a politician's personal pocket, but it can still be done. The most notorious recent example: Book publisher HarperCollins offered Newt Gingrich a $4.5 million advance on the anticipated royalties for a book he wrote. Public outcry forced him to return the advance and make do with the actual royalties—a hefty $1.2 million in 1995 and $185,109 in 1996 (less than a third of the proposed advance).[44] Why did HarperCollins offer an advance so wildly in excess of the book's actual earnings? Presumably, the publisher's defense would be: It's a chancy business, and we miscalculated. But other possibilities suggest themselves: HarperCollins is owned by Rupert Murdoch, whose total profits depend far more on some of his other companies—the Fox Television Network, several major newspapers, various cable, satellite, television, and telephone operations—and he may well have been happy to shell out millions in the hope of influencing the regulation of these businesses. The $4.5 million payment could have been good business even if Gingrich's book never earned a cent in royalties.

Campaign contributions can themselves effectively enrich members. There are virtually no controls on the way campaign money is used. "For instance, Representative C.W. Bill Young, Republican of Florida, bought a light blue $30,000 Lincoln Continental with campaign funds. Carroll Hubbard Jr., Democrat of Kentucky, decorated his office with a $3,000 portrait of his father. Stephen Neal, Democrat of North Carolina, took $57,173 in campaign funds for rent and improvements on his home, which conveniently doubles as his permanent campaign headquarters."[45]

On the federal level, strict limits now apply to outright gifts to politicians. But with a little creativity they can be evaded. "Club level" tickets for the Washington area's new hockey and basketball arena cost season ticket holders $91.46 per ticket. Senate rules allow senators to accept gifts valued at less than $50. (Their House compatriots are only allowed to accept "nominal" gifts.) A naive observer might hastily conclude that senators and their staff could not accept tickets from corporate lobbyists. Wrong: Abe Pollin, the arena owner, is no dummy. He calculated that, conveniently enough, the ticket to the game was only worth $48 (even though no one can buy them for this amount), and the remaining $43.46 is actually for indoor parking, membership in the restaurant, and access to the Executive Business Center. Therefore, he said, senators *could* accept tickets to the games. But he realized this wasn't a decision he should make himself, so he took the issue to a neutral body, the Senate Ethics Committee. Are you surprised to hear that they agreed with him? It would, they decided, be hunky-dory for them to accept free tickets, since luckily enough the tickets made it under the $50 limit.[46]

One other kind of unusual gift deserves consideration: contributions by one politician to another, usually by means of "leadership PACs." Ten Republican and two Democratic leadership PACs had 1995–96 receipts of more than $400,000; and Trent Lott's New Republican Majority Fund, Newt Gingrich's Monday Morning PAC, Dick Armey's Majority Leader's PAC, and Richard Gephardt's Effective Government Committee all had receipts of over a million dollars.[47] Powerful congressional leaders collect far more money than they can use themselves, enabling them to contribute to the races of struggling party candidates. The ability to raise money thus becomes a factor in making leaders; a candidate who refused to participate or who did not appeal to big donors would find it harder to move into a leadership position. Despite his 1996 unpopularity with the public, Newt Gingrich remained the Republicans' top fundraiser; "one reason for such a reservoir of loyalty towards Newt is because of his tireless efforts on behalf of his G.O.P. colleagues," efforts that included 132 events in 18 months.[48]

PAC CONTRIBUTIONS BUILD NETWORKS

By far the most common form of gift, however, is the campaign contribution—more than 122,000 PAC contributions for the 1996 election, along with 41,000 soft money donations. These should, therefore, be the primary focus of analysis. Corporations can—and do—defend their PAC contributions, pointing out that the money comes from "voluntary" contributions by corporate employees, and that the donations are for modest sums. Soft money donations—for unlimited amounts and involving no consent from or participation by employees—are more problematic, but they can be defended as open and available for public scrutiny. Campaign contributions, corporate officials and sympathizers imply, are a disinterested part of the democratic process.

This public defense captures an important reality: Corporations don't want to engage in practices that might harm the corporate image. Therefore corporations think carefully about how to present their campaign contributions. They want to build personal networks with presidential candidates, top party leaders, and members of Congress, but they want to do so through open and aboveboard practices that can stand public scrutiny. Although the primary corporate aim is to build networks and create obligations for use at some future time when the company faces a problem, the process of presenting the money is usually also part of the next step in the process: using this sense of obligation to gain access to the president or a member of Congress.

JUST DROP IT IN THE MAIL? If campaign contributions were made solely to aid the democratic process and to promote the best candidate, with no ulterior motive, then it would not matter how the money was delivered. If politicians were never influenced by the money they received, then it would make no difference whether or not they were aware of the contribution. The very same people who say their campaign money gives them absolutely no power or influence also insist that it is extremely important that donations be given in person. As one said, "When push comes to shove I'm the one that they expect to get the job done, so I want to be the one that the member knows is the guy who has delivered."

When we asked executives how their corporation delivered the contribution, virtually all of them insisted that "you don't just write out a check and drop it in the mail." In fact, "the very last thing that we do is put a check in the mail. That, in my opinion, is the worst thing to do."

BACK HOME FUNDRAISERS. For members of Congress, Washington fundraisers cost much more than those held in the home district. Today the minimum entry price for a Washington fundraiser is around $500, and it is unlikely that even a handful of the member's constituents will be in attendance. Fundraisers in the home district are more likely to charge $15 to $100; virtually everybody there will be a constituent.

One advantage of attending a fundraiser in the member's district is that "you can get a whole table for a back-home fundraiser for what you would have to pay for one ticket at a Washington fundraiser." As a result, "We get much more bang for the buck with minimal PAC dollars if you have the money presented out in the field." A company can pay for all of the local managers to attend a picnic or barbecue, have a good time, meet other local influentials, and be introduced to the member of Congress. The event can be fun for employees; one corporation reported that it passed out tickets, and "a bunch of people went, took their kids, and really liked it." A back home fundraiser like this emphasizes to the member that many constituents are employees of the corporation, so he or she depends on the corporation not only for money but also for votes. The corporation is responsible for employees' jobs, salaries, and benefits: Anything the member does to harm the corporation is likely to hurt the employees and influence not only their votes, but also the votes of their friends and relatives.

On the other hand, such an event has many limitations. In the first place, it is only possible if the company has employees in the member's district, and most companies have operations in a limited number of districts. Unless the corporation is prepared to confine its PAC contributions to the ten or twenty districts where it has a significant number of employees, this home-district contribution pattern is insufficient. The members who serve on the committees most crucial to the corporation may well represent districts where the company has no employees. Moreover, although these fundraisers are useful in creating a sense of dependence on, and connection to, the company, they do relatively little to aid the lobbying process, since at a large affair no one individual makes much impression on the member, and the company's lobbyist is unlikely to attend a function outside Washington.

PERSONAL VISIT. Many of the PAC officers said they disliked fundraisers, and it's easy to see why: PAC officers put in a nine-to-five day and then have to go to (one, two, or even three) fundraisers before they can head home. Moreover, a large fundraiser doesn't offer much contact with the member, nor is the corporation as likely to be favorably remembered: "To tell you the truth, even when I was in Washington, I rarely went to fundraisers. Why in the hell should you give somebody a thousand dollars in the presence of a hundred other guys giving him a thousand dollars?" Corporations that had the clout tried to avoid the fundraiser and instead get one-on-one time with the member: "If it's a big fundraiser, what we may do is go earlier and deliver the check to his office and sit and talk with him."[49] Of course, this defeats some of the purposes of the fundraiser: The member wants to get everybody together at once in order to reduce the time he or she spends dealing with campaign contributions and, at the same time, to show the world how much support he or she has.

WASHINGTON FUNDRAISERS. Despite all the reservations and frequently expressed preferences for delivering the money in the home district, Washington fundraisers are the most common way of making a contribution. There are so many of them that a newsletter was started just to list them all. Increasingly, the functional equivalent of a Washington fundraiser will be held in other cities around the country—that is, a Minnesota member will hold a $500-per-person fundraiser in Houston. We will discuss congressional fundraisers first, then presidential events.

Fundraisers provide advantages for donors as well as politicians. First, they offer a chance to see and speak to the politician. The very largest corporations may have little difficulty reaching members of Congress, but most corporations, even multibillion-dollar ones, don't always find it so easy to talk to members, or even to their staffs—much less to top party leaders or to the president.

> Everybody thinks we spend all our time up on the Hill and every time you pick up the phone, Senator X's staff calls you back right away and you go up and sit down and talk. Sometimes it takes you days to have phone calls returned. If it's a crisis and you say I'd really like to talk to him, that's different. But I know people that I've called, and they will call you back at 6:00 at night because they have just got done with a committee meeting or doing something in the Senate. By then you are gone. It's tough to catch these busy, busy people. So it's an opportunity to see them.

But access at the fundraiser can lead directly to a solution of the company's problem:

> These guys are very hard to see; it's hard to get an appointment with these guys because they're so busy. But at a fundraiser you get a chance to shake a hand, to talk to somebody for a couple of minutes. I know one example perfectly, in fact, the issue we were talking about earlier. I just happened to mention to the member, I said, "Look, we've got a unit that probably knows more about this subject than anybody, and particularly this segment of the market—the small business market that you're concerned about; and we've got an enormous amount of data, and our guy's an expert in this area and would like to help." And this particular senator said, "Boy, I would be delighted to have a chance to talk with him further," and he grabbed his appointment secretary and said, "Please talk to Bill, get an appointment. I want to do this." But the fundraising event and the PAC enabled me to be there and to raise that question in a way that would have been a lot harder if I had to go through a formal appointment.

Some fundraisers, especially for important members, are huge, but probably the most common variety is the cocktail party attended by forty or fifty people. Everyone meets the candidate, the candidate makes some remarks and then fields questions. "The ones I've been to, there's never been a case where the candidate was not asked to say something, and where the candidate did not respond to questions." More focused fundraisers bring together a small group concerned with the same issues. Typically this means a breakfast organized by an industry trade association. "The most opportune kind of fundraiser that we prefer to go to is an intimate breakfast or dinner with less than twenty-five or thirty people, and you place your guy next to the person . . . In fact, I don't care if you sit at the end of the table. The fact of the matter is there is some personal interchange, dialogue, that goes on."

Second, the fundraiser is an opportunity to show support for, and connection with, a particular member, and to let other people see you talking with the right people. Even PAC officials who prefer to avoid fundraisers may attend to show support: "Sometimes if it's a friend, somebody we are particularly close to, they might not only want the money but want the bodies there, want the physical support as well as the money."

Third, it is a chance to see *other* members of Congress and their staffs, many of whom attend the fundraisers of friends and associates.

Fourth, it is a chance to see government relations staff from other corporations—a great many of whom will be attending the fundraiser—who can provide useful information about issues of concern, who is doing what, who might be able to help with a problem, and the like. Many of the same people attend these affairs, and attendees sometimes commented that they would see the same twelve people three times in the same night, but each fundraiser has a slightly different cast of characters. As one PAC director said, "Issues develop where we need to work with these other lobbyists, and it's interesting to see who shows up." Fundraisers become one of the main ways that corporate personnel, lobbyists, congressional staff, and members of Congress meet and interact with each other, forming friendships and networks that facilitate future cooperation.

Normally, congressional fundraisers are attended by one or two key government relations personnel from the company. Sometimes the person attending the fundraiser in the name of the corporation, or making the private visit, is an independent lobbyist retained by the corporation. This happens when a lobbyist has a particular area of expertise (or set of connections; the two are virtually inseparable in these circumstances), or when the corporation's government relations operation is too small to handle all the issues. If the lobbyist represents the corporation on some key issue, he or she is the person who should present the check, in the name of the corporation, to the member or staff: "It helps to focus the member's sight on where that funnel is. Where they get these contributions." Occasionally the corporation's CEO presents the check. This may be a reflection of the importance of that member, but as often it may be largely the result of an accident of scheduling: The CEO is in town for other reasons and available. One company for whom government actions are particularly important reported:

Depends on who the person is. We don't use our CEO unless the person whom we're dealing with is heavy duty. What happens is that our chairman is one of our most effective lobbyists. We get him into the scene when he can be particularly useful, and that's usually with leadership people. Or particularly our home-state delegations. He is involved in lobbying, and sometimes also hands over the check. But a senator may stop by here [at the home office], or he may be in Washington and go to a cocktail party. Usually if we don't have to, then the chairman will not hand over the check. Somebody will go along with him and . . . give the check. We don't want to be unseemly about it. Our chairman is very much involved in our political efforts, which may include dispensing PAC money—[but]that is fairly rare. His actual talking with members is becoming increasingly common.

When company survival depends on government action (or inaction), as in this instance, the CEO is likely to be directly involved. This was most common in heavily regulated industries. In other companies, the CEOs generally seemed to be less involved, with individual exceptions based in part on the CEO's personal history and interests.

PRESIDENTIAL FUNDRAISERS. Most of the same considerations apply to presidential fundraisers (or, for the party out of power, fundraisers with its top leaders, whoever they may be), with obvious adjustments for scale. Big fundraisers are huge events. In some cases donors can get in the door for as little as $1,000. That certainly doesn't provide access to the president, but it might be a ticket to (at least some of) the other powerful figures at the gathering. President Clinton has said he grows "frustrated going to meetings and goings where all you do is shake hands with somebody or you take a picture,"[50] but to many business executives, this picture itself becomes a marketing tool, establishing that they have a one-to-one relation with the president.[51] Generally speaking, only contributors of $10,000 or more get their pictures taken with the president; admission to intimate gatherings with the president or top leaders is far more expensive, typically $100,000 for a White House coffee involving a dozen people, and still more for a chance to spend the night in the White House Lincoln Bedroom. (These issues are discussed in Chapter 4, on soft money.)

USING THE MAIL. Most companies want to be sure politicians know who has contributed to their coffers. Those companies make every effort to present their gifts in person in order to create more personal contact and increase the sense of obligation. But some companies do send checks through the mail. Who are they, and why do they do so?

Mail delivery appeared to be used in three kinds of situations: First, as an exceptional move for a company that normally delivered checks in person:

Occasionally when you get down to the end of a year, they need the money. You can't do it personally. But they are asking you, so you mail it to them. But in general it's all hand delivered in some form or fashion.

Second, by companies with access oriented government relations programs that were, in our opinion (an opinion sometimes but not always shared by the company itself), weak operations. One company had been subjected to a major raid by a Boone Pickens–type operator, and had been forced to split itself in two and downsize radically. The government relations staff had been reduced from eight people to two. The PAC officer agreed that, if it were possible to deliver the check in person, "sure, that's the best way to go. Sometimes it works out that way but, like I said, with fewer people doing this stuff, sometimes it's hard to orchestrate things the way we used to be able to."

The final situation in which the mails may be used is when the PAC is not oriented to access, when its concern is ideology and it self-consciously renounces pragmatic considerations. Many ideological PACs do deliver checks in person, but others do not, and personal delivery does not seem to have the same priority for them. Thus, one of the PACs that gave the heaviest emphasis to its ideological orientation reports that it totally separates the PAC from its lobbying activity. It does not approve of fundraisers; if one is held in their headquarters city, and the PAC supports the candidate, staff members might attend, but this would be a "very rare exception." Their normal delivery procedure is mailing the check (about 70 percent of the time). If one of the company's divisions is working closely with a member, the check will be sent to the division to hand carry it—but on reflection, the chair of the PAC steering committee said, "The check goes out to the divisions, but what they do with it when they get it, I don't know." The PAC officer for another ideological PAC indicated that, when the company had a facility in the district, the check was delivered by people from that facility; in other instances she tried to make personal deliveries where convenient, but often used the mail.

CONCLUSION

Campaign contributions are best understood as gifts, not bribes. They are given to establish a personal connection, open an avenue for access, and create a generalized sense of obligation. Only rarely—when the normal system breaks down—does a contributor expect an immediate reciprocal action by a politician. Even then, the donor would normally use circuitous language to communicate this expectation. Open and explicit comments are rare, dangerous, and likely to be counter-productive. The networks and feelings of obligation created by gifts are crucial, however, when corporations want access to ask for favors from the president, members of Congress, or top party officials. Given how many donations corporations make, it is a struggle to make them all personal. But corporations make every effort:

> Counting state legislatures, last year we were involved in 532 races. I can't make that many contributions personally. So we use the networks that we have. Our corporate lobbyists. Our people on retainer. And our employees. We try to make the contributions as personal as possible.

It can reasonably be asked whether politicians even remember who has contributed to them. In corporate executives' experience, by the time someone gets to Congress,

> At that point they have proven they are good enough at the game, that they've got a pretty good idea, and if they don't know, they can find out. They may only know two days a year, and that's when their political staff briefs them on what they are doing. But at some point in there, they are aware of it.

President Clinton, in fact, got into trouble because—can you believe it—he "kept close tab on cash raised at coffees,"[52] and was informed of "the most minute details of the Democratic Party's fundraising."[53] The media treated this as surprising; corporate donors take it for granted. In fact, the politician's memory is one crucial test of the success of the corporation's government relations office:

> If we are making a contribution to somebody who doesn't know it, we're screwing up. So that's one of the tests. That's one of our internal tests. If we are just sending money out to somebody and they are not aware of it, we've got no business giving them a contribution because they are not doing any good.

It is in the access process, the subject of the next chapter, that the corporation finds out just how much "good" their contributions are doing.

◆ 3

ACCESS

LOOPHOLES AS A SYSTEM

ACCESS: THE MAGIC WORD. THESE DAYS, CAMPAIGN FINANCE DISCUSSION centers on "access." Some politicians try to deny that donors gain access. Most politicians admit that donors do get access, but insist that's all they get. When a reporter asked President Clinton what political donors "get in return" for "big-money contributions," Clinton's response was: "What they get from me, I think, is a respectful hearing if they have some concern about the issues. . . . They should get a respectful hearing."[1] This chapter and the next ask: What are the consequences when the way to get a "respectful hearing" is to contribute big bucks to the elected official? And what else is involved in this process besides a "respectful hearing"? We show that access for donors means much more than a respectful hearing, and that this practice has become so widespread that today loopholes are not exceptions but, rather, a fundamental part of the system.

Our analysis challenges four misconceptions about corporate political activity in the access process: First, that what matters to corporate donors is the thumbs-up or -down decision (votes for members of Congress, signature or veto for the president) on highly publicized laws. Second, that corporations exert influence through an explicit exchange of campaign money for congressional votes or presidential decisions. Third, that Democrats and Republicans, or liberals and conservatives, differ fundamentally on the issue of special benefits for corporations and industries. Fourth, a belief held by some of those on the left of the political spectrum that this process operates automatically, with no significant effort by corporations, but that, in any case, has minimal consequences. In this chapter we focus primarily on PACs and Congress; the next chapter examines soft money and the presidency.

◆ MYTH ONE: WHAT CORPORATIONS WANT

Many critics of big money campaign finance seem to assume that a corporate donor summons a senator and says, "Senator, I want you to vote against raising the minimum wage. Here's $5,000 to do so." This view, in its crude form, is simply wrong. The (liberal) critics who believe this recognize the existence of power only when it is most obvious and blatant; they miss the more insidious (and pervasive) ways that a field of power shapes and distorts action, and does so most effectively when no one even knows that power is being exercised. When the gift process operates smoothly, the typical politician (or donor) can say, "I am an honorable man" and mean it, can truly believe it, can have lines he or she would never cross—and nonetheless the system as a whole advantages the rich and subverts democracy.

We recognize that payoffs and outright bribery are a continuing fact of political life. Sleazy characters—*and* respected business leaders—pass wads of cash to politicians, usually to pad the individual's pocket, but at other times simply to hide the true source of the money.[2] Several people have told us stories of firsthand involvement in these processes (usually in local, not federal, races). Some of the money raised in 1996 by John Huang clearly did not come from the listed contributor (though, at least as of this writing, there is no clear evidence that donors received any actual rewards, other than White House invitations, in exchange for these contributions). The Abscam court cases of twenty years ago made it clear that more than a few members of Congress were prepared to introduce legislation in exchange for packets of used bills. In 1997, a Chicago alderman representing Hyde Park and the University of Chicago, a reformer with a squeaky-clean image, was arrested for allegedly accepting a $2,000 bribe and a $10,000 campaign contribution from fictitious individuals. Informed that his "contributors" would include the names of dead people, the alderman reportedly replied, "The more dead the better."[3] For obvious reasons, it's difficult to uncover such activities, and we don't want to dismiss their importance. Nonetheless, we will devote little attention to outright bribery for two reasons: First, we believe that, at least at the federal level, it is a small fraction of total fundraising; second, because *everyone* already agrees that such practices should be forbidden.

Not only media accounts, but most academic analyses as well, frame the debate over campaign finance as follows: "Did this or that special interest buy the politician's vote on a key issue?"[4] Posed in this way we have to agree with the corporate executives we interviewed who said: no, they didn't. But they believed it followed that corporations have no power, and maybe not even any influence, and we certainly don't agree with that. If power means the ability to *force* a politician to change his or her position on a major bill, corporations rarely have power. However, corporations and their campaign contributions have a great deal of power if power means the ability to exercise a field of influence that shapes the behavior of other social actors. In fact, corporations have effective hegemony: some alternatives never receive serious consideration, while others seem natural and inevitable; some alternatives generate enormous controversy and costs, while others receive almost no attention. Candidates are reluctant to take *any* position critical of business because, as campaign consultant Robert Shrum explained, that "will make it more difficult to raise money. Do people in a campaign say that directly? No. What they say is: 'What's the responsible position on this issue?' That's a code word for fund raising."[5]

HIGH VISIBILITY ISSUES

A corporate PAC officer could stress two key facts: First, on important, highly visible issues he or she cannot determine the way a member votes; second, even on low-visibility issues, the entire process is loose and uncertain.[6] As to the first: The more visible an issue, the less likely that a member's vote will be determined by campaign contributions. If the whole world is watching, a member in an environmentally conscious district can't vote against the Clean Air Act (discussed in Chapter 1), because it is simply too popular. A poll by Louis Harris and Associates Inc. reported that when asked, "Should Congress make the 1970 Clean Air Act stricter than it is now, keep it about the same or make it less strict?" 73 percent of respondents answered "make it stricter," 23 percent "keep it about the same," and only 2 percent "make it less strict" (with 2 percent not sure).[7] Few members could risk openly and explicitly voting against such sentiments. To oppose the bill they'd have to have a very good reason: perhaps that it would cost their district several hundred jobs, perhaps that the bill was fatally flawed, but never, never, never that they had been promised five, ten, or fifty thousand dollars for doing so.

The corporate executives we interviewed understood this, though they weren't always careful to distinguish between high- and low-visibility issues. (As we discuss below, we believe low-visibility issues are an entirely different story.) Virtually all access-oriented corporate executives went out of their way at some point in the interview to make clear that they do not, and could not, buy the vote of a member of Congress on any significant issue. Not one corporate official felt otherwise; moreover, their opinions sounded honest and genuine, rather than uttered by rote for public consumption. The executives pointed out that the maximum legal donation by a PAC is $5,000 per candidate per election. Given that, in 1996, the cost of an average winning House campaign was nearly half a million dollars, and several times that amount for the Senate, no individual company can provide the financial margin of victory in any but the closest of races. A member would be a fool to trade 5 percent of the district's votes for the maximum donation an individual PAC can make ($5,000), or even for ten times that amount. As a result, most PACs feel they have little influence. Even the one person who conceded possible influence in some rare circumstances considered it unlikely:

> You certainly aren't going to be able to buy anybody for $500 or $1,000 or $10,000—it's a joke. Occasionally something will happen where everybody in one industry will be for one specific solution to a problem and they may then also pour money to one guy. And he suddenly looks out and says—I haven't got $7,000 coming in from this group, I've got $70,000." That might get his attention—"I've got to support what they want." But that's a rarity, and it doesn't happen too often. Most likely after the election he's going to rationalize that it wasn't that important and they would have supported him anyway. I just don't think that PACs are that important.

This statement, by a senior vice president at a Fortune 500 company, is probably a roughly accurate reflection of one part of the reality: Most of the time members' votes can't be bought; occasionally a group of corporations are all supporting the same position and their combined resources are enough to influence a member's vote even on a major contested issue. But even if that happens, the member's behavior is far from certain.

What about megabuck soft money contributions for $70,000, or even for $700,000? Aren't those big enough to settle the issue and *force* the politician to do what donors want? Peculiarly enough, our answer is no. Donations of that size are given to the national parties and, in effect, to the president or to the top leadership of the party. At that level, $100,000 is the price for *access* to talk about the issue; it's not even remotely sufficient to guarantee the outcome on a high-visibility issue. If campaign finance is not reformed, it may become routine in the future for corporation X to funnel $100,000 or more in soft money to congressional candidate Y. But so far that hasn't happened and, in our opinion, it's unlikely because the publicity and adverse reaction would turn the money into a liability, not an asset.[8]

LOW VISIBILITY ISSUES: NONISSUES

However, "politicians aren't for sale" is true only if we limit out attention to highly visible, publicly contested issues. As ex-Representative Eric Fingerhut (Democrat–Ohio) noted:

> The public will often look for the big example; they want to find the grand-slam example of influence of these interests. But rarely will you find it. But you can find a million singles.[9]

Most corporations and government relations units focus only a small fraction of their time, money, and energy on the final votes on the big issues. So-called access-oriented approaches have a different purpose. Their aim is not to influence the public vote on the final bill, but rather to make sure that the bill's wording exempts their company from the most costly or damaging provisions. If tax law is going to be changed, the aim of the company's government relations unit, and its associated PAC, is to be sure that the law has loopholes built-in to protect the company. The law may say that corporate tax rates are increased, and that's what the media and the public think, but Section 739, Subsection J, Paragraph iii, contains a hard-to-decipher phrase. No ordinary mortal can figure out what it means or to whom it applies, but the consequence is that the company doesn't have to pay the taxes you'd think it would. For example, the Tax "Reform" Act contained a provision limited to a single company, identified as a "corporation incorporated on June 13, 1917, which has its principal place of business in Bartlesville, Oklahoma."[10] With that provision in the bill, Phillips Petroleum didn't mind at all if Congress wanted to "reform" the tax laws.

Two characteristics of such provisions structure the way they get produced. First, by their very nature such provisions are unlikely to mobilize widespread business support since they are targeted to one (or at most a few) corporations or industries. Other businesses may not want to oppose these provisions, but neither are they likely to make them a priority, though the broader the scope, the broader the support. Business as a whole is somewhat uneasy about very narrow provisions, though most corporations and industry trade associations feel they must fight for their own. Peak business associations such as the Business Roundtable generally prefer a "clean" bill with clear provisions favoring business in general, rather than a "Christmas tree" with thousands of special interest provisions. Most corporations play the game, and part of playing the game is not objecting to, or publicizing, what other corporations are doing. But they don't feel good about what they do, and if general interest business associations took a stand they would probably speak against, rather than in favor of, these provisions.

Second, however, these are low-visibility issues; in fact most of them are not "issues" at all in that they are never examined or contested. The corporation's field of power both makes the member willing to cooperate and gets the media and public to, in practice, accept this as a noncontroversial matter. Members don't usually have to take a stand on these matters or face public scrutiny. If the proposal does become contested, the member can probably back off and drop the issue with few consequences, and the corporation can probably go down the hall and try again with another member.

WHAT A TYPICAL BILL IS LIKE

People usually think of a congressional bill as a relatively short and simple statement specifying new tax rates or mandating cleaner air. Japanese laws are typically very brief: a single paragraph authorizing the appropriate government department to formulate policies to clean up air pollution.[11] In the United States, however, most important bills are "Christmas trees" covered with dozens of special provisions. Congress itself insists on writing many of the details of the regulations.

For example, the Tax "Reform" Act as printed in the U.S. Code *Statutes at Large*, is 880 pages long. Much of it is incomprehensible—and intentionally so—even to a tax lawyer, unless he or she knows the hidden references. That is, a provision is written to apply to one and only one company, but in order to protect the guilty (both member and corporation), the company is delineated without being publicly named. The purpose of the description is to be sure that reading the act won't be enough for anyone to learn what's going on. Large sections of these 880 pages are filled with passages like the following:

D) A project is described in this subparagraph if—

(i) such project is part of a flat rolled product modernization plan which was initially presented to the Board of Directors of the taxpayer on July 8, 1983,

(ii) such program will be carried out at 3 locations, and

(iii) such project will involve a total estimated minimum capital cost of at least $250,000,000.[12]

This sort of material goes on for pages and pages. A huge amount of detective work is necessary to figure out which companies are referred to or how much money the taxpayers are giving them. It would be much simpler to write the law to say:

(5) SPECIAL LOOPHOLES—The rest of you suckers have to pay the full taxes specified in the law, but the following corporations are exempt from most taxes:

(A) Octopus Oil

(B) Monopoly Phone Company

(C) Oligopoly Phone Company

(D) Super Steel Inc.

However, some people reading this section and finding it outrageous might know where to focus their attention. As things now stand, the long descriptions sound as if they must in some way be general explanations of circumstances in which the taxes would not be appropriate. In fact, their only real purpose is to specify one and only one corporation without naming it and making its loophole visible to public scrutiny. Even if you know the provision is an outrage, there still isn't any way to know who is getting away with theft.[13]

The task for a curious voter is made still more difficult by the fact that tax provisions are not necessarily contained in tax laws (and similarly with any other category). A persistent member, perhaps under the pressure and inducements of a needy or greedy business, can try again and again. If a measure is rejected by the tax committee, sometimes it can be slipped into a bill in an entirely different area. In 1996, the greatest victory for labor unions—and for millions of American workers—was passage of a bill raising the minimum wage, which had been stuck at the same level for over a decade. But that's not all the bill did:

◆ One provision "clarifies that foreign trade income of an FSC and export trade income of an ETC do not constitute passive income for purposes of the PFIC definition." Whatever the hell that means, it's estimated that it is worth $22 million to Hercules Inc., a $3-billion-a-year chemical manufacturer. In theory, any such giveaway must be paid for by identifying an offsetting tax saving. An early version of the bill did so; the final version classified this as a "technical correction," with no loss to the Treasury.[14]

◆ Presumably to help America's lowest-paid workers, the bill suspends the tax on diesel fuel for recreational motorboats.

◆ The bill repeals a tax that was intended to make it less attractive for companies to send jobs overseas. This will save companies $427 million over the next ten years and, of course, will also make it more profitable to move jobs from the United States to overseas.

◆ There's a deduction for convenience stores that have gas stations attached. Its largest beneficiary will be Japanese-owned Southland Corp., the $6.7-billion-a-year operator of five thousand 7-Eleven stores.[15]

◆ There's a giveaway to big bank trust departments.

◆ A subsidiary of a French company, Rhone-Poulenc, "persuaded Congress to repeal an excise tax on ozone-destroying chlorofluorocarbons (CFCs) found in one of its major products, asthma inhalers."[16] The U.S. company (Minnesota Mining & Manufacturing) that developed an asthma inhaler without CFCs will therefore lose business; and companies will learn that the best way to deal with environmental regulations is to use political muscle to win loopholes, rather than engaging in costly research and development to actually improve the environment.

◆ Two provisions, one especially designed for newspaper companies, make it easier for businesses to classify workers as "independent" contractors. The corporation, which may be their only employer, is thereby exempted from a host of labor standards and employment-related taxes. These workers end up without pensions, medical coverage, or unemployment insurance; companies get higher profits—clearly the sort of provision our country needs, and no better place for it than in a bill to raise the minimum wage.

◆ And there are dozens of other giveaways to business, many too complicated to explain (which, of course, makes the ideal loopholes—people who can't understand a loophole are unlikely to mobilize to oppose it).

The corporate welfare in this one bill totaled up to $16.2 billion (that's *billion*, not million).

We could fill an entire book with additional examples of this process— the 73 words in a spending bill that would remove a safeguard for wetlands,[17] the special break for Alaskan seafood processors above 53 degrees north latitude,[18] big brewers' pressure to restore the right of U.S. soldiers based in Korea to buy thirty cases of duty-free beer a month—eight cases a month, the proposed new limit, would have reduced the black market but also have lowered beer company sales.[19] Congress has lost all perspective on this issue. Robert L. Livingston, the Louisiana Republican who heads the House Appropriations Committee, explained that in a 1996 catchall spending bill, "We kept the extraneous legislative language to a bare minimum."[20] Just how bare was the minimum? *Three thousand* pages.

A particularly outrageous example is a provision in the so-called welfare reform law; it deleted a single word ("nonprofit"), thus permitting for-profit companies to get federal funding to take care of poor children who are removed from parents judged to be unfit to raise them. Under the welfare reform law, this "is now the last unlimited pool available for poor children," and funds for this kind of care have increased 400 percent since 1988. This type of group care is always expensive: The per child cost, on average, is 11 times the cost for AFDC ("welfare"). The change was inserted in the bill by Senator John B. Breaux (Democrat–Louisiana) at the request of Kenneth M. Mazik. Does Mazik's record indicate it's good policy to allow for-profit companies to take care of these, the poorest and most vulnerable children? Mazik has "his own plane and pilot, a home on a former du Pont estate in Wilmington, Del., and one in Eustis, Fla." Mazik's companies specialize in especially disturbed children, charging more than $140,000 per child per year, but a New York City inspection team found the children cared for by Mazik's company "in trailers that reeked of urine and feces," with one deaf child immobilized in a "wrap mat" that cut off his circulation.[22]

THE BOTTOM LINE

In our interviews, when we asked corporate executives to give us an example of what their office tries to do, about 90 percent offered us an example of a tax loophole they had won. It reached the point where we started saying, "an example of anything but taxes." The Tax Code has become the de facto U.S. industrial policy, a policy made in the most haphazard and particularistic process imaginable.[22] Though we didn't ask PAC officers to give us examples of their successes, virtually all of them did, presumably because it validated their worth and contribution to the company. We suspect this is also part of the reason they preferred examples of tax loopholes: The benefits can be precisely quantified, as in "this provision saved our company X million dollars." Many government relations departments emphasize the bottom line: "That's one question I always ask people when they call up, what's the dollar impact on the business?" Or, as another said: "We don't do things altruistically. We don't do things just because it's the right thing to do. There ought to be a bottom line approach to it."

How much do these tax loopholes cost? It's hard to know. Congress estimated the revenue loss in the 1986 tax law at $10.6 billion, but this number is taken seriously only by those who still believe in the tooth fairy. As Barlett and Steele note:

The cost of one break was originally placed by the Joint Committee at

$300 million. After passage of the legislation, the figure was adjusted upward to $7 billion.

That worked out to a 2,233 percent miscalculation, a mistake so large as to defy comprehension. It would be roughly akin to a family who bought a house expecting to pay $400 a month on its mortgage but who discovered, belatedly, the payments would actually be $9,332 a month.[23]

Or consider the cost of the special tax provision to help the Long Island Power Authority buy and shut down the Shoreham nuclear power plant. This provision was buried in what Congress referred to as a deficit-reduction measure. The Joint Committee on Taxation originally said the bailout would cost $1 million, then revised that figure just a tad to $241 million. The true cost is estimated at $3.5 to $4 billion.[24]

There is another way to assess the dollar value of these provisions, and that is to consider two instances where corporations did *not* get the bills written to their specification, went ahead and did what they wanted anyway, and then—this is the shocking and unusual part—got caught. First, Sears and bankruptcy law. Sears pressured hundreds of thousands of bankrupt customers to sign so-called reaffirmation statements that said that, despite their bankruptcy, they would nonetheless pay their credit-card debts. The law requires that any such agreements be disclosed to bankruptcy courts; Sears did not do so, and "as a result, customers ended up paying debts that had legally been erased." Why didn't Sears disclose the statements? "Sears apparently didn't file the reaffirmation agreements with the bankruptcy courts out of fear that they would be rejected." Some poor soul named Latanowich, who had signed such an agreement,

> struggled to pay his $28 a month to Sears, but in a handwritten note to Judge Kenner in November 1996, he said the payment was "keeping food off the table for my kids." He asked Kenner if his bankruptcy case could be reopened and the Sears debt wiped out. Kenner investigated and discovered that the agreement Sears negotiated with Latanowich had never been filed for her review. She said she would have rejected it out of hand, in part because it was too onerous but also because Sears overstated the amount Latanowich owed.[25]

How often had Sears done this, and how much money was involved? Sears admitted "it had also failed to file the agreements in as many as 331,500 cases nationwide," involving a trifling $265 million. Arthur Martinez, Sears CEO, provided an example of the modern corporate approach to taking responsibility, explaining that it had all been done by lower-level staff, who would be disciplined, and that "senior management had no knowledge of the practice." Presumably decisions about three hundred thousand cases and more than two hundred million dollars are made—at Sears—by file clerks and first-line supervisors.

Second, SmithKline Beecham agreed to cough up $325 million to settle claims that it had overcharged Medicare by billing the government "for millions of laboratory tests that were not medically necessary, were not ordered by a doctor or were not performed."[26] Following the Sears approach to accepting responsibility, SmithKline executives said the violations were accidental, with the company CEO explaining that "'ambiguities over regulations and guidelines' contributed to the violations."

The job of a corporation's government relations unit should have been to insert language that, if it did not permit these practices, at least made them difficult to prosecute. Note, however, that even when corporations have stolen hundreds of millions of dollars, the executives do not risk jail—in fact, newspapers quote them respectfully. Given the amount of money involved—where a single company, in dealing with a single provision, can have to shell out hundreds of millions of dollars—the government relations unit is a bargain, even if the company puts several million into soft money and other donations (and few companies spend that much). We have focused on examples where the dollar value is easily quantified, but many of the other instances—environmental protection, workplace safety, education, health, or welfare—matter far more. In these areas, people's lives, and not just dollars, are at stake.

BUSINESS HEGEMONY

One of the best indications of the power of business is that corporations are not only able to win themselves billions of dollars through loopholes, but that they are able to do so without much public exposure or blame. Hegemony is most effective when its operation is invisible. Companies not only receive what amount to large government handouts, but these are rarely discussed and exposed. The obscure language is an admission of guilt, a clear indication that these provisions cannot withstand public scrutiny. And yet Congress and (virtually all of) the media cooperate in handing over the money and keeping the public from knowing what is happening.

Two Pulitzer Prize–winning journalists, Donald L. Barlett and James B. Steele of the *Philadelphia Inquirer*, tackled the job of uncovering the loopholes in the 1986 Tax "Reform" Act, and in the process won themselves a second Pulitzer. Despite their reputations and the resources available to them for their search, it still took them fifteen months to track down a small fraction of the thousands of tax breaks buried in the law. "The congressional tax-writing committees and their staffs refused to provide any information, insisting that the identities of the beneficiaries of the preferential tax provisions had to be kept secret." Barlett and Steele wrote to the chairs of the relevant committees—not one of their letters was answered. In fact, even members of Congress aren't allowed to know what they are voting for:

> In 1986, congressional leaders withheld even a partial list of tax preferences from House members until after they voted in favor of the legislation.

> The process has become so byzantine that, at times, key lawmakers involved in writing tax bills profess their ignorance about breaks that they personally approved.[27]

Barlett and Steele were able to identify the beneficiaries for many of the tax loopholes, but hundreds more remained hidden. Even when Barlett and Steele found the beneficiary, it was often impossible to determine which member(s) of Congress deserved the "credit" for the loophole.

The same kind of secrecy, we might add, is sometimes applied to the fundraising process itself. Two New York reporters attempted to attend Governor George Pataki's April 1997 fundraiser at the Waldorf-Astoria Hotel. They were arrested for trespassing, even though they stood outside the festivities in a part of the hotel normally open to the public, simply trying to determine who went where.[28] The people with power know that their actions—whether inserting loopholes in legislation or giving and raising money for candidates—cannot stand public exposure. In a manner befitting a totalitarian state, the power brokers maintain a cloak of secrecy to protect the guilty.

On those rare occasions when the media do identify and focus on a provision, the company and member can and do defend themselves, providing a thousand reasons this provision makes good policy, why this provision isn't really a loophole at all, but rather a way of improving the bill, of preserving the spirit of the bill without creating unfortunate consequences that were never intended for this particular situation. If the provision will benefit a company in the member's district, there is adequate reason to support it. A member who helps a respectable business to increase its profits is almost never vulnerable. If the business is going bankrupt, or is held to have immoral purposes, the member is potentially vulnerable, but even then it will rarely come to public notice. If the company is not in the member's district, and if he or she has received a *lot* of money from the company, there is potential negative publicity—but rarely very much. Since most voters (correctly) assume that most members will engage in such behavior, being caught is unlikely to become a major issue.

◆ MYTH TWO: MONEY IS EXPLICITLY EXCHANGED FOR VOTES

ARE THESE LOOPHOLES AVAILABLE TO ALL?

A reader imbued with the me-first spirit of Reagan–Gingrichism ought to be asking him- or herself: "How can I get in on the action? How much would it cost me to get out of my taxes and to whom should I give the money?" Even a cautious cost-benefit analysis shows that campaign contributions to members are one of the best "investments" available. Philip Stern calculated that AT&T's $1.4 million in campaign contributions saved it $12 billion in taxes[29]—a fabulous "rate of return." Not all companies are so successful in evading taxes as AT&T, but hundreds of companies regularly receive special exemptions. An educated guess would be that $1 in campaign contributions produces at least $100 in a tax loophole (in the AT&T example, almost $1,000). Applying this same ratio to individual taxpayers, if I (Dan) decide that I'd rather not pay taxes, could I just walk in and offer Richard Neal, my member of Congress, $200 to write a provision declaring: "Anyone living on Munroe Street in Northampton, who was born on August 18, 1948, doesn't have to pay taxes"?

No one will be surprised to hear that working stiffs can't do this. Part of the reason is simply economies of scale: Members would need to process 2,000 loopholes for individual taxpayers to equal one corporate loophole.[30] But of course that isn't the primary reason: Loopholes for corporations are regarded as sleazy, but only slightly so, and members who write or support such provisions do not need to worry about public exposure or condemnation, but a member who proposed 2,000 loopholes for ordinary people would be regarded as a nut and immediately exposed. The media would have a field day; members would fight for interviews to condemn this behavior and deliver "holier than thou" sermons.

Rich people occasionally get private tax bills that save them millions of dollars. Domhoff gives the example of the Du Ponts, who were forced to divest themselves of the General Motors Corporation (because the courts ruled their simultaneous ownership of both companies was an antitrust violation and in restraint of trade), but arranged to reduce their tax liability from $45 a share to $7.25 per share, paying Washington lawyer Clark Clifford $1 million for arranging this special loophole.[31] Similarly, over an eight-year period, Ernest and Julio Gallo contributed $325,000 to members to promote an amendment to the tax code that would reduce Gallo's tax liability by $27 million.[32] While the focus is understandably on these multimillion-dollar arrangements, members also sponsor some small-scale deals: Senator Moynihan submitted a proposal that would have applied only to five biomedical researchers in Rochester.[33]

In a sense, these examples only prove the point: The laws are made for the benefit of business and the rich. They are the ones with the power and resources to pay people to work out plausible sounding rationales, to coerce the media not to expose these private deals, to have already (or to know how to make) the connections to powerful government officials, and to enjoy the large-scale operations that provide opportunities for sheltering income through unique arrangements. Moreover, somebody has to pay the taxes; if ordinary people could obtain the same sort of loopholes that are routinely dispensed to the rich, the government wouldn't have enough money to operate. As New York real estate mogul Leona Helmsley explained: "We don't pay taxes. Only the little people pay taxes."[34]

The notion of thousands of ordinary taxpayers each shelling out $100 campaign contributions to be exempted from taxes sounds silly, and of course it is. The reason it's silly, however, is not because the government would never agree to special giveaways, nor is it because members of Congress would never violate tax equity for a campaign contribution. To see why ordinary individuals can't do what corporations (and a handful of rich individuals) can, we need to examine how a successful corporate government relations operation is run. Ordinary individuals wouldn't know what changes were being considered or where to go to intervene effectively, have the ability to craft appropriate legal gobbledygook to give themselves a break without opening things up for everyone, have access to key decision makers, have the know-how to present and defend this rip-off as public policy that advances the general interest, or be able to defend the change through the long legislative process. To understand the corporate access process we examine each of these points in turn.

KEEPING TRACK AND KNOWING THE PLAYERS

In order to win special legislative provisions, an individual or company needs to know what is being proposed. Only rarely will special privileges be embodied in a totally independent bill; usually they are incorporated as minor parts of a general purpose bill. Basing our questions on the general sense in both the media and academia that government is a threat to business, hampering its operations, we tended to ask our questions in terms of how companies learned about threats. Almost invariably they would add "or opportunities"—for legislation provides many of these as well. But whether threat or opportunity, a company needs to know what is happening, what's possible, what another company has of a similar nature.

To find out what is going on, corporate government relations personnel read a host of newspapers and specialty publications, hire consultants and lobbyists, talk to members and their staffs, go to fundraisers, and constantly network in the world of Washington insiders (see Chapter 6). One of the factors simplifying the task of keeping track of legislation is that, at least in Washington, things move slowly:

It's not a tough job today because things take so long to get done in Washington, and there are so many chances to have a change made or to say to someone, "Look, you shouldn't go this way. You should go that way." A new concept that becomes law in less than five years in Washington today is pretty unusual.

The same processes are used not only to learn that an issue is likely to be considered, but also to find out which members or staff people are most involved in the issue, and the best way to approach these people. Reading is likely to be less important in this process than networking, informal contacts, and attending fundraisers.

GETTING ACCESS

The crucial first step in the corporate access process is knowing what has been, or is likely to be, considered. The second step is knowing whom to see to influence the outcome. The third step is actually obtaining access.

The campaign contribution plays its most crucial role in helping the corporation to gain access, but even here no one-to-one correspondence exists between money and outcome. Corporate government relations officials sometimes talked as if it were normal that anyone who wanted to see a member of Congress could do so—even if the person didn't live in the member's state or district. One executive saw this as a right, not a privilege: "You want to have access to the member so you or your experts can tell your story. That's what the Constitution guarantees." At other times, gaining access was presented as a significant problem, and the campaign contribution as vital to this process. Fairly typical was a company that described a particular problem, arguing that while its plant in a specific area had come under attack for environmental pollution, "the entire economic framework of that whole section of the country" depends on its plant and therefore the company was in a strong position. Some academics argue that this alone should guarantee the company success,[35] but this executive didn't agree:

> INTERVIEWER: So does the PAC really change anything? Suppose you didn't have a PAC? You'd still have 2,000 employees and a $50 million payroll—
>
> CORPORATE EXECUTIVE: I wouldn't have the access, and it may sound like bullshit, but I'm telling you very sincerely, I wouldn't know Governor X to the degree that we know the governor and his staff; we wouldn't know Bob Y, the local congressman as well as we know him; and we wouldn't know the junior senator as well.

The impact of campaign contributions is greatest at the level of access, a point nicely illustrated by Bob Dole's handling of a 1996 merger between the Union Pacific and Southern Pacific railroads. Dole publicly announced that, as a matter of principle, he was recusing himself from participation in the issue:

> "I also want to acknowledge that there are a number of individuals involved in the merger who are active supporters of my Presidential campaign," Mr. Dole said. "In order to avoid any appearance of a conflict of interest, this Senator wants to make clear his intention not to become involved in any discussion related to the proposed merger."[36]

"Active supporters" was code language for "big contributors" from out of state. Philip Anschutz, CEO of Southern Pacific, was a long-time big-money Dole backer, and Drew Lewis, CEO of Union Pacific, was cochair of Dole's campaign finance committee; Union Pacific was the twelfth-largest contributor to the campaign. Although Dole made a public point of recusing himself from the issue, he did not do so until *after* he had helped guide the deal through key steps. According to a spokesman for Lewis, "Mr. Dole spoke twice about the subject to Mr. Lewis last year as legislation crucial to the merger was moving through Congress," and Dole voted to kill an amendment that would have delayed or derailed the merger. During this same period Dole refused (twice) to meet with Kansas constituents who opposed the merger as likely to raise costs for farmers. Bob Glynn, the executive vice president of the Chamber of Commerce in the small town of Hoisington, Kansas, a loyal Republican who had always supported Dole, said: "It makes me feel I wasn't being represented by my Senator, that he had to recuse himself because of a big business deal. . . . I have the feeling we were sold out."

This is a case where campaign contributions by themselves were probably a significant reason big business had access that was denied to the small town Chamber of Commerce, though even here the long-term relationship (built, admittedly, around giving money) may have been equally important. Once again, the campaign contributions paid off handsomely: Anschutz and people affiliated with his companies had contributed $170,000 and made a $318 million profit on the merger.

SHAPING A SOLUTION

Not everyone can get in to talk to every member, but when a lobbyist does get an appointment, she or he must be prepared. This means going in with a carefully thought out proposal and supporting evidence or exhibits. The company lobbyist can't prepare all this by him or herself; many other company officials must be actively involved.

> When legislation appears on the horizon, we send a copy of the bill to one of our government relations people, and he has the ability to go around to our different business sector units and talk to people. If it's a tax bill, talk to our tax department. If it's a product liability bill, talk to the legal department and flesh out how that bill would affect our company. Based on that, we might have a couple of meetings with some of the people from our Washington office that covers that legislation and people from the business sector it would affect. They'll sit down and say, here's what the bill says, we think it's great or we think it's terrible. We can maybe amend it to say this instead of that, we can live with that, and that's how we come up with our positions on the issues.

The PAC steering committee is potentially valuable here, providing contact people in each area of company operations. However it is done, government relations cannot be isolated from operations personnel, but needs help both in identifying problems and in formulating responses; this process contributes to the forced political education and involvement of a broad array of company managers.

The more carefully a company's proposal is crafted, and the more fully their arguments are supported, the more likely the member is to accept their proposal. Congressional staffs have expanded, but are still minimal. If a small company went in, correctly identified a technical problem with the proposed wording of a bill, but was unable to suggest a modification that would fix this problem without abandoning the entire bill, it is unlikely that the member's staff would have someone with the technical expertise needed to cope with the matter. The more effort required by the member, the less likely he or she is to work on the problem. The ability to provide technical expertise becomes a further structural factor favoring big business over most alternative groups, whether small business, the homeless, or environmental activists.

Thus Jane B. Williams, a health policy adviser for the 1996 Senate panel overseeing legislation that would speed up Food and Drug Administration approval of food additives, explained that, in order to be sure she knew what to do, she regularly sought advice from Peter Barton Hutt, a Covington and Burling lawyer for the Pharmaceutical Research and Manufacturers of America: "I talk to him all the time. He's extremely helpful. I've always felt like I could talk to him not as a person who was representing a particular industry, but as an expert in the field."[37] At the prices Covington and Burling charges, we assume that Hutt *is* an expert, and that he is able to provide solutions that a small business could not by itself develop—even if it had made enough campaign contributions to gain access to the relevant congressional staff.

As corporate lobbyists view it, when they meet with a member or key staffer, they have to have full and complete information, present it honestly, explain why their alternative proposal is reasonable, and make a case for it as better policy. "It's all education—that's what lobbying really is. In fact, if you do it right, it's to supply the best information you can about your side, but the information you supply cannot be so biased that it's no good to them." Lobbyists seem to be able to convince themselves that the changes they request are not just reasonable, but right, honorable, and meritorious. In this they are no different from many of the rest of us, who generally manage to see our self-interest as benefiting the general good; the difference, of course, is that lobbyists argue for additional benefits for those who are already the most powerful and privileged in our society. For the most part, they did not seem to be struggling with their consciences or having trouble living with themselves. It is necessary to give the member the full picture, even facts that might hurt the company's case:

> You lose your reputation for honesty and integrity, and that's it. You are finished. So as much as you might say, "Well, I'll tilt this or scratch that," or "I'll take that column out of the chart," that doesn't pay in the long run. It really doesn't.

Once information has been presented fully and accurately, lobbyists then make the case for their proposed alternative, which is never presented as naked self-interest: "Screw the environment, we'll make an extra $50 million if we poison the river." Rather it needs to be put in practical and high-minded terms, as in this *hypothetical* example: "No one cares more about the environment than we at the Loot-and-Pillage Corporation. We have been moving to upgrade our facilities as rapidly as is economically practical. However, our plant in Flaming River was built before this concern with the environment, and there is no rational way to fix it so it will meet these unreasonable standards. If this law were passed, we would have to close that plant. The issue here is not just the effect on our bottom line, but jobs for our loyal employees in Flaming River.[38] The modification we propose would allow that plant to continue producing; the plant would improve its environmental record and 'as soon as economically practicable' it would meet the more rigorous standard. We have a study here showing that this would have a negligible effect on the environment and would save 1,247 jobs.[39] If you are prepared to make this change, we'll be able to live with this bill. I realize that we don't always see eye-to-eye on all issues, but you've always been reasonable, our PAC has supported you in the past and hopes to do so in the future. We've worked together on other issues, and the change we are proposing here is totally reasonable."[40]

In some instances, the member simply accepts the proposed change for any of a variety of reasons: It does seem reasonable, the plant is in his or her district and it is conceivable that the company would close the plant (though such actions are threatened ten times as often as they actually take place), the member has a long-time friendship with the corporate lobbyist, always feels that "what's good for business is good for America," or just wants the campaign contribution(s) and doesn't care that much about the environment. In many other instances, however, the member has a set of tough questions to put to the lobbyist and is not prepared to accept the company proposal—or not until it is substantially modified. If the member asks, the lobbyist must give an honest and knowledgeable assessment of the likely political impact:

CORPORATE EXECUTIVE: They [The members] say: "What do you think the steel guys will really think if I support this? Can I get away with that, is this too tough an issue for me?" I try to give them an honest answer. If I can't give them an honest answer, then I better. . . .

INTERVIEWER: Is that a good opportunity for you, is it useful when they call?

CORPORATE EXECUTIVE: No, it isn't, because you've got to be honest with them. The whole thing is that they are going to call you back . . . so you've always got to be 100 percent honest with them: "You can take that issue but it's going to kill you back in the district, that's not popular with the steelworkers." Or: "I can't say that's a good issue for you because the pensioners don't like it." I'd like to say: "Support us," but you can't do that because you've got to think about tomorrow.

The friendly, live-and-let-live nature of relations between PACs and members of Congress means that if members can't accept the company's initial proposal, they often ask the corporate lobbyist to help them fashion solutions:

They say, "Here's what I think, here's what you think, can you rework this out so I can give you a little piece of the pie and still not screw the other 93 percent of my district who want it the other way?" And we say, "Yes, if you can just do this. It doesn't change the bill, but at least it allows us to do this." It's the fun of the game.

Even if the company is reasonably sure the legislation is not going to pass this session, "You still want to get in there and shape it so as to set its character for the next session, because the odds are it is going to be coming back again."

What if the member is unwilling to help and feels that the company's request is not reasonable, either because of the member's perception of good policy or because of the political realities? As an experienced politician, the member is unlikely to say, "There is no way I'll ever support that." The response is more likely to be, "I would have serious difficulties with that, I'm not prepared to support it at this time, and I doubt I could support it unless you can make the changes we discussed." The company then has two choices: If the member is not vital to this issue (for example, does not chair the key committee or subcommittee), the company can just move down the hall and try other members. If the member is vital to the issue, or if the concerns the member expressed seem likely to be widespread, the company can go back and modify its proposal, which probably means another round of meetings with the corporate managers, experts, and lawyers who were involved earlier. The lobbyist needs to explain the member's concerns, and then the assembled company group needs to consider alternative solutions and see whether any of them will be satisfactory to both the company and the member. The corporation can also, of course, work to alter political realities—through soft money contributions, new expert studies, a media public relations campaign, or by hiring a firm to mount a "grassroots" letter-writing campaign. Many of the best minds in America are paid very well to help corporations justify their actions; there are few "better" jobs (for those who can avoid thinking about the consequences of their actions).

DEFENDING THE CHANGE AND GETTING IT THROUGH

In many cases all that is needed is one respected member on the appropriate committee. He or she simply accepts the company's proposal and incorporates it in the bill word for word. If other subcommittee members ask about the change, a brief reply reviewing the rationale is sufficient, and once the subcommittee and committee have accepted this, others in Congress are unlikely to reexamine the issue. But the more costly and far-reaching the change, and the more it deals with an area of known controversy, the more likely it is to be challenged and examined. In these circumstances it is the company or industry's responsibility to help defend the provision. This defense takes at least two forms: lining up other members who will support the provision or at least not publicly challenge it, thus reducing the level of controversy; and orchestrating appropriate public relations if needed. The nature of the system is such that most of these changes do not receive much publicity. If they do, the company and the member have failed, since the aim is to present the change as minor, technically driven, not subject to partisan disagreement. On many issues "you don't want to get too far out in front and get tagged that you are the worst offender, the one this especially applies to." The better the case a company or industry makes and the more they do to build support for their proposal, the easier it is for a member to vote for them or defend them publicly.

Most of the time a corporation's known power, resources, and legitimacy are enough for it to get its way. Other actors, reacting to its field of power, don't oppose it. But corporations need to be willing and able to exert leverage if an opponent takes them on, and push comes to shove. Proctor & Gamble, for example, was targeted because its Folgers brand contained coffee from El Salvador. Neighbor to Neighbor, a small human rights organization, produced an ad featuring Ed Asner, former president of the Screen Actors Guild and the actor who played Lou Grant on the Mary Tyler Moore and Lou Grant shows. The ads focused on El Salvador's notorious abuses of human rights, noting that the regime had sheltered those who murdered priests and nuns. Ed Asner then called for a consumer boycott of Folgers because it contained coffee from El Salvador. Neighbor to Neighbor bought time on a local television station at the going rate, just as any other advertiser might do. They managed to come up with a total of $4,150 to run the ad eight times in the Boston area.[41]

Proctor & Gamble's response was hardly "I disagree with every word you say but will defend to the death your right to say it." Instead, Proctor & Gamble fought to silence Neighbor to Neighbor, denying it the rights that would be conceded to a competing soap or coffee company. Proctor & Gamble announced it would pull all its advertising from any television station that agreed to run the Neighbor to Neighbor ad. Since Proctor & Gamble's advertising budget was $1,506,892,000, with over $683 million of this for television,[42] and Neighbor to Neighbor had to scrape hard to come up with $4,150, television stations had no trouble making the choice. To hell with free speech, they decided, and pulled the Neighbor to Neighbor ads. Corporate pressure rarely needs to be so blatant, however, because business's field of power is so well known and recognized by others in our society that reporters and others avoid direct confrontations. Nonetheless, members of Congress try to minimize situations that could lead to public condemnation. One of the key reasons corporations give to members representing company facilities is that those members are much less likely to receive negative publicity for doing favors for the company, because they can always argue the action was undertaken to save people's jobs, not simply to garner a campaign contribution.

CAMPAIGN CONTRIBUTIONS ONLY A PART OF THE PROCESS

Campaign contributions by themselves are never enough to create or maintain a viable government relations operation, but they are a useful, perhaps even a necessary, part of the total strategy. One corporate official captured what seems to be the general attitude toward the role of its campaign contributions:

> Yes, I believe the PAC is important. But nevertheless, might we have won the issue without the PAC? I think so. It made it easier with people with whom we did not have a close relationship. We went to the AA [administrative assistant, top congressional aide] and said: "Here is a letter which Senator X is going to be the lead signer on"—because he knew our company very well. "And so we'd like to ask you, John Doe, who is vaguely aware of our existence, to sign this letter. And, oh, by the way, it goes without having to say, we contributed $2,000 to the senator's last campaign." It sure didn't hurt. Now would he have signed the letter anyway? I suspect he probably would have.

Even PAC officials agree that some of what they seek is dubious, but for the most part they feel they are simply seeking to improve policy:

> I'm not going to say that I haven't in the past lobbied for things that are just straightforwardly to advantage my corporation, because I have. Although, more realistically, people who we employ have; I don't do a whole lot of lobbying myself. But far and away the vast majority of things that we do are literally to protect ourselves from public policy that is poorly crafted and nonresponsive to the needs and realities and circumstances of our company.

Most PAC officers insist that money alone is not enough.

> I think two hours of constituent participation at a charitable event with a member of Congress, getting a bunch of employees to go to the

Bowl-a-thon, the Cancer Society, is worth, I don't know how much, but a bunch of PAC money from somebody that they don't really know and whom they deal with in a strictly "business" relationship. I think the truth of the matter is, except for some major companies, any company that has more than a handful of members of Congress with whom it enjoys a genuinely close relationship, genuine mutual respect, is fortunate indeed. In the final analysis, that's really all it takes. Because I'd rather have one guy who sincerely cares than I would twenty who are superficial. . . . The one that is your friend, you are going to be his primary concern. The PAC certainly is an important part of that, but only a part.

For small-scale issues or a one-time vote on a minor wording change, a strictly monetary relationship with a member might be sufficient, but if the corporation is suddenly in some kind of major trouble, the offer of a campaign contribution won't be much help. At that point no member will find it rational to assist them simply in hopes of a future donation. There has to be something more. Bringing in a check

might make the AA [administrative assistant; top congressional aide] happy because he has to raise $10,000 that week, and you walk in the door with a $3,000 check[43] and you are a hero today at least, but I think the meaningful relationships are those that develop over time and that have many dimensions to the relationship.

Corporate government relations specialists, members of Congress, and their staffs get to know each other and become friends. Most of these people, on both the corporate and the congressional side, are extremely likeable. The proportion of warm, friendly, outgoing, genuinely nice people is about as high as you will find anywhere. It's their job to be like that, but it's clear that it is much more than that, that the job attracts people with that kind of personality. The people who aren't like that probably don't succeed at the job and tend to leave it, but whatever the reason these are people you can't help liking. We have a lot more in common with academics than with corporate lobbyists, but the corporate lobbyists were often easier to talk with, and despite the differences in our viewpoints they were friendlier and pleasanter to be with.[44] While this point is difficult to convey, it is crucial to understand how outgoing and nice lobbyists are, and that this was not just a pose put on for professional purposes.

In addition to being the kind of person whom everyone always likes, who smooths over social situations and helps put people at ease, corporate government relations personnel inhabit the same social world as members and their staffs. To a considerable degree this is true even for personnel located at corporate headquarters far from Washington, but it is overwhelmingly so in Washington. Wherever corporate headquarters are, government relations personnel have to spend significant amounts of time in Washington. Moreover, they will interact with virtually all members of their home state's congressional delegation, and with many of the other members who regularly hold fundraisers around the country. In the nation's capital, however, all this is raised to new heights. Many corporate lobbyists formerly worked as congressional aides or political appointees in one or another government agency. People shift positions fairly frequently; the key person to contact may be someone you worked with not long before, or a fraternity brother, or a member of your club, or someone who serves with you on the board of a local charity. The men regularly play golf together. One of our interviews was interrupted by a phone call to make arrangements for a golf foursome with the chair of the House Ways and Means Committee, the committee in charge of all tax legislation; our interviewee and the other person on the phone discussed the need for a fourth with the right level of golf skills and the right personality who would make an enjoyable golf partner. Our man explained it was important that everyone have a good time, but that didn't mean you couldn't also talk a little business.

Women are unlikely to be included in golf dates. They are, however, a substantial fraction of corporate government-relations personnel, perhaps one-quarter of the total,[45] and often meet elsewhere, probably on the tennis courts, but perhaps at the hairdresser:

> I was getting my hair done a couple of weeks ago, and I had a very early appointment. . . . I was amazed by the women in the beauty shop . . . a number of well-known, well-connected, high-placed, high-powered women—and a lot of talk was going on.

Unplanned contacts come easily and regularly for people who live in the same neighborhoods, belong to the same clubs, share friends and contacts, and inhabit the same social world. Some companies pay for lobbyists' memberships in country clubs and the like, seeing these as sensible business expenses. One corporate lobbyist told about having car problems when driving her babysitter home: A man she didn't know stopped and helped her; he turned out to be a member of the House Ways and Means Committee, and she has continued to have dealings with him since. In fact, as one PAC officer noted, "It's hard to quantify what is social and what is business."

> I can go to lunch with people and take two minutes of their time talking about my issue, and then we can spend the rest of the time catching up on what's new. Some of those people are my best friends on the

Hill. I see them personally, socially, and they're very good to me; they always help me with my issues. I don't think you have to spend two hours of somebody's time groaning and beating an issue into their heads.

WHY CORPORATIONS CAN DO WHAT OTHERS CAN'T

Legally, campaign contributors may not explicitly exchange cash for influence. Unlike the explicit exchange of an outright purchase in the market, campaign contributions are gifts based on a fundamental trust that the gift will be reciprocated if and when that becomes appropriate. But these gift exchanges are always uncertain and problematic; people may not understand the rules or may not be able to negotiate the appropriate implicit understandings. The more people have in common, the more they share networks, and the more they know and accept the rules of the game, the greater their confidence that things will work out. An explicit request for a quid pro quo would be not only illegal (and therefore risky to both parties), but gauche and inappropriate. An analogy can be made to a date: If a man takes a woman to an expensive restaurant and then to a major event, sparing no expense or courtesy to show that he cares about her and regards her as special, the probability increases that she will agree to, want to, have sex with him. However, were a man to propose an explicit exchange (I'll buy you a steak if you'll spend the night with me), the odds are high that the woman would be offended and the date a disaster. Similarly, members of Congress distinguish between being *asked* to do a favor, which they see as appropriate, and being *required* to do one in exchange for a donation, which is unacceptable.

For [Tony] Coelho, [Democrat–California, and chair of the Democratic Congressional Campaign Committee], putting the official machinery of the House of Representatives to work on behalf of a $5,000 donor was no more out of line than giving him fancy luggage tags. He said he became offended only when the donor suggested an explicit entitlement to official favors. "There is a fine line," Coelho explained. "I don't mind [donors] bringing up that they have a problem [with the government]. But don't ever try to create the impression with me, or ever say it—if you say it, it's all over—that your money has bought you something. It hasn't. There's a real delicate line there, and it's hard for people to understand how we do it."[46]

Similarly, at his press conference in March 1997, President Clinton insisted, "I don't believe you can find any evidence of the fact that I had changed government policy solely because of a contribution."[47] Some people would emphasize "can find any evidence" and ask whether this meant Clinton had done so but thinks no one will ever be able to prove it. We are inclined to think Clinton's emphasis falls on the second half of the sentence—that the change never came about *solely* because of a contribution, though Clinton would (at least off the record) acknowledge that in many instances the contribution had facilitated access and made it possible for the contributor to make a case for a change.

Participants need to realize that sometimes friends can help you out, sometimes they can't. Sometimes relations balance out evenly; more often you have given more to some people than you've received, but received more than you've given from others. What matters is not simply the specific gift, but a relationship of trust: a reputation for taking care of your friends, for being someone whom others can count on, and knowing that if you scratch my back, I'll scratch yours. A month after the *Valdez* spilled millions of gallons of oil into the waters of Alaska it is unlikely that many politicians would have regarded it as sharp political strategy to speak up for Exxon. No corporation knows when it might face a similar disaster—a company plane bursting into flames while carrying illegal cargo, a chemical plant emitting fumes that kill thousands, a feed additive found to cause cancer in cattle and humans, or a car or a plane responsible for dramatic accidents. But it is precisely in such situations that a corporation may most need a politician willing to help out—not by dramatic announcements but by stalling a resolution, or amending it to remove some of the penalties, or arguing that some other forum should consider the issue first.

This culture gives enormous advantages to long-term big players. Even if a corporation hasn't contributed to the member it most needs to see, other politicians and other corporate officials can provide introductions and testimonials. The member knows that the corporation is a major player, has been around for a long time, and has the resources to deliver. The corporation will be able to give a contribution every election for as long as the member is in Congress, and that without straining corporate resources. Moreover, the corporation will be able to draw on reserve power if need be. It is this sort of reputation that both individuals and corporations work for years to achieve. With such a reputation, very little needs to be made explicit. A wink and a nod communicate everything—even the wink and nod may be superfluous. Without such a reputation, a person looking for a favor is a much greater risk. A risk in several ways: that they will put the issue as an explicit exchange, thereby compromising the politician (and potentially forcing a rejection of the request); that, with no reputation to safeguard, they will be more likely to double-cross you; or that if asked for extra help, they won't have the networks necessary to deliver.

Therefore individuals, small businesses, or nonprofit organizations are in a different structural position from major corporations, *even if they are willing and able to contribute the same amount of PAC money.* A corporation is also able to draw on, and promise access to, a host of resources not connected to campaign money. It can not only deliver a campaign contribution, but also provide the expert information the member needs, contribute to a nonprofit organization, or line up campaign contributions from other corporations. If the company has a facility in the member's district, it can provide entrée to its employees, it will have leverage with both its customers and suppliers, and its managers will have personal networks in common with other key figures in the community.

Moreover, most of the time most major corporations have a high degree of legitimacy. Even if the politician is helping them to pollute the environment or evade taxes, the special benefit is still likely to be widely regarded as at least defensible and perhaps honorable. A news story, if there were to be one, would be a "balanced" presentation of "both sides." In part this is simply because of the special place business occupies in our society, but it is also important that the businesses that make large donations are large operations. A tax break need not stand out; rather it will be seen as a complicated provision applying to special circumstances faced by this corporation and intended only to create fair conditions in this unusual situation.

The 1996 campaign finance scandals, for example, focused primarily on the Asian connection to Clinton donations. Because the donations came from marginal players, even though the companies and individuals had money to contribute, they found it difficult to do so in appropriate ways. Moreover, because they were marginal, and because they were Asian by origin, their contributions received more intense scrutiny. Illegal contributions by Dole's Cuban supporters were not newsworthy, nor were donations by a German businessman who claimed his donations stemmed from an innocent ignorance of the law forbidding foreign donations.[48] (See Chapter 7.) Money by itself is not enough; the money gains its potency by being part of a general field of power; big contributors who are not backed by an appropriate degree of power are regarded as in some sense illegitimate.

The example of the Social Security "notch" for those born between 1917 and 1921 illustrates the differing treatment accorded to nonbusiness groups. In 1972, Congress adopted a formula to ensure automatic increases in benefits for Social Security retirees in order to protect them from inflation.

For technical reasons, however, the formula was flawed, and it led to greater increases in benefits than had been intended. In 1977 Congress again revised the formula, preserving the raised benefits for those who were already receiving them but lowering benefits for future retirees, and providing a five-year transition period to phase in the new benefits. The new benefit levels for those born from 1917 to 1921 were intended to be 5 percent lower than the old benefits.

The new regulations, however, produced substantially more reduction in benefits than most people had expected. The "notch" in benefits for those retiring under the new law produced some anomalous results. Critics of the notch point to the example of Edith Detviler and her sister Audrey Webb. The two sisters went to work on the same day in 1957 at the same southern California bindery, where they did the same job for the same pay. "They retired 25 years later on the same day, October 8, 1982. They earned almost the same amount over their careers and paid virtually the same in Social Security taxes."[49] However, one sister was born fifteen months later than the other—in 1917 instead of 1916—so her monthly retirement benefit was $184 less than her sister's ($695 instead of $879, a 20.9 percent difference). More generally, for two workers with average lifetime earnings retiring at age sixty-five, the one born in 1916 received $716 a month and the one born in 1917 received $592.[50]

Older Americans are not without political clout, and those born in the notch certainly noticed the discrepancy. When "Dear Abby" ran a column on the issue, she received a million responses—the largest number for any column she had ever run. The issues director for a congressional campaign reports, "It's no exaggeration to say that during the campaign I received more calls about the notch issue than on any other subject."[51] Nonetheless, the powers that be insisted that there was no issue. Frank Batistelli of the Social Security Administration explained that "we don't see it as a legitimate problem."[52] A *New York Times* editorial called on "responsible representatives of the elderly . . . to denounce the Notch Baby fix for what it really is: a budget-busting giveaway fired by greed, not fairness."[53] A report by the Academy of Social Insurance concluded that the problem was that prenotch retirees were receiving too much, and that therefore no change was appropriate.[54]

Without getting involved in all the arguments, it can be said: (1) "Notch babies" were not aware ahead of time of the impact of the 1977 revision; (2) they made no serious effort to introduce a formula that would have led to more gradual cuts; (3) millions of people would have been prepared to support such an effort; (4) a correction would have been far more justifiable and meritorious than most of the loopholes corporations win for themselves; and it's obscene that the *New York Times* habitually overlooks handouts to corporations but denounces as "greedy" two sisters who did exactly the same work and wonder why their retirement payments are so different. The failure to be properly organized, the lack of an effective access operation at a crucial time, the fact that older Americans do not have the same legitimacy and clout as business—all this meant that "notch babies" received lower benefits than their older brothers and sisters. It is hard to believe that any corporation that could point to such a disparity—say, in the tax rates for companies incorporated at dates a year apart—would be unable to mount a successful campaign to get the most favorable rate then prevailing.

◆ MYTH THREE: POLITICAL PARTY MATTERS

One popular conception labels the Democrats the party of the common people, and the Republicans the party of big business.[55] Alternatively, one could believe that true conservatives would not want government to do anything that would interfere with the free market and the need for a level playing field. We found, to the contrary, that essentially all members of Congress participate in the access process. The country doesn't have two major parties, it has just one: the money party.[56] Members of Congress, governors, presidents, and virtually all of the "serious" challengers are past winners in the money primary; in order to win that primary they had to make implicit (or explicit) commitments to the money party.

When we began our interviews with corporate executives, we already knew that many Democrats, and many well-known liberals, were happy to do special interest favors for corporations. Nonetheless, we assumed corporations would have many enemies in Congress, people who were out to get them and whom they in turn wanted to defeat. We regularly asked about this in interviews, and were surprised to learn that corporations didn't really feel they had enemies in Congress. Yes, there were plenty of members who opposed them on a given issue, but no, there weren't any they considered unreasonable. Essentially *all* members of Congress, they believe, are at least potentially willing to help them out, to give them access, to let them make their case. One PAC official told us, "you have guys that will hold rallies right outside this building here, hold news conferences and picket lines periodically, every year," attacking the company and its policies. However, "when they go to the Congress . . . they tend to ameliorate their anti–big business or pro-consumer stance." Even the people who once

led demonstrations against the company over time become more reasonable, more open to information from, and dialogue with, the company. "I
don't want to say that they are the best friends we have in government, but
you can go to them."

This doesn't mean that every corporation is happy with every member,
only that there were almost none regularly mentioned as hostile to business. For example, one corporation refused to contribute to the late Mickey
Leland because they felt he was too "communistic." But another had a
different attitude:

> Mickey Leland [Democrat–Texas] is a good example. Mickey works
> with us all the time. You know what he is going to do. On a social issue
> he is going to be a liberal. You know: Let's get arrested on apartheid.
> Let's try to force businesses to paint those old shacks that his constitu-
> ents live in. Let's set up extra help for the food stamp programs. All
> that sort of stuff. But when you get down to an energy issue, he is right
> there with us. And that comes down to, we don't have anything against
> doing those things he is talking about, but that's not the purpose of
> this company's PAC. The purpose of this company's PAC is to pay at-
> tention to this business.

Similarly, Jim Florio was a liberal Democratic member of the House
and, as governor of New Jersey, instituted soak-the-rich tax-and-spend
policies. Yet one company official explicitly stated that "we support Florio
strongly in Washington. And the reason is because he helps us on all sorts
of stuff."

We are *not* saying that there are no differences between Republicans
and Democrats. On certain large-scale ideological issues, there *are* differences;
votes on most major bills show a sharp partisan split.[57] At the same time,
however, virtually all members of Congress, both Republicans and Democrats, will participate in the access process of creating loopholes for individual corporations and industries. Most of these provisions will never be
known to the public, and most of the members responsible will hide their
responsibility—from everyone but the company that benefits. Thus Richard Gephardt (Missouri), Democratic leader in the House of Representatives, presents himself as something of a populist, and in some sense he
is—but that didn't stop him from proposing that the airline industry be
exempted from a fuels tax. (TWA is based in Gephardt's district.) Charles
Rangel, Democrat of Harlem who is in line to be chair of the House Ways
and Means Committee if and when the Democrats become the majority
party, notes that "just because I don't go to the country clubs doesn't mean
I don't understand business."[58] "Understand business" in this context means

"support loopholes." Are the Republicans sometimes a little more blatant about it, with private corporate lobbyists explicitly writing the legislation and speaking as representatives of the congressional committee?[59] Probably. But these differences should not be exaggerated: Most of the loopholes, for Democrats as well as Republicans, are written by the corporation and inserted in the bill unchanged by the member of Congress. For some publicly debated issues there are two parties, but there is only one party when it comes to the question, "Are you willing to take money from business and in exchange help create loopholes that will undermine the stated purpose of the law?" That party is, of course, the money party, and it includes nearly every Democrat and Republican.

Not only are virtually all members accessible to business, but it is also amazingly cheap to gain such access. In general, on a day-to-day basis, access to ordinary members of Congress costs $500 or $1,000, though to be really sure a corporation should contribute that much in each election for a period of years. Or this is what the records of campaign contributions appear to indicate: In 1996, the average corporate PAC contribution to members of the House was $1,313; to members of the Senate, $1,942. Seven out of ten (71.3 percent) donations to members of the House and six out of ten (59.1 percent) donations to senators were $1,500 or less. These costs are exceptionally modest considering that corporations gain access to make their case for special privileges that can save them hundreds of millions of dollars. Easy access is available even to members who are regarded as *not* sympathetic to business. Maria Hsia, one of the Democratic party's most successful fundraisers (best known for teaming up with John Huang to arrange the 1996 visit to the Buddhist temple that got Vice President Al Gore into trouble), began her campaign contributions in a small way. She operated a business that assisted Asians in their efforts to gain U.S. visas. With a couple of other people, she made contributions of a few thousand dollars apiece to one senator and three representatives, and then asked them to write letters to the immigration agency demanding an end to unfair treatment for her clients. A senior immigration service official responded at length, analyzing the status of each of the twenty-five cases and assuring the members that all cases were being handled properly. "'That was when the light went on for her,' said a person who knew Ms. Hsia then. 'She said so. She was amazed that with so little money you could do that.'"[60]

The nonadversarial character of the relationship between corporations and politicians depends on at least two factors. First, business is accorded great legitimacy and acceptance; there is a widespread notion that what's good for business is good for America, a notion held in some fashion even by many of the critics of business. Except in rare instances where a highly visible disaster threatens lives or the environment, business is regarded as a pillar of the community—even when it is arguing that it should be able to pollute the atmosphere, threaten its workers' health and safety, and avoid its fair share of taxes. Business is treated as almost a part of the state, an extension of congressional staffs:

> We get a lot of calls from committee staffs who respect the company and its standards of operations. They will ask us questions on "how would this provision work?" or "how would that work?" and they know that, when they do that we give them an honest answer.

Second, while the opponents of business became much more visible and effective in the late 1960s and have retained much of their political capacity,[61] public interest movements rarely have the resources to contest the *details* of congressional (or regulatory agency) actions. Environmental movements can and do put their issues on the agenda, arguing for a "clean" bill without special exceptions, and they manage to focus attention on a handful of the most visible corporate attempts to cripple the law. They are the main opposition corporate polluters need to worry about, but they have not been in a position to engage in hand-to-hand combat over each and every one of these provisions. Exposure by such movements is the main thing a member needs to fear, but there are tens of thousands of corporate special deals struck each year, and public interest movements are lucky if they can attract major attention to ten of these and minor attention to another hundred. Still less able to contest corporate tax loopholes is the labor movement, or any other organized representative of the bottom half of the income distribution. Corporations are in a no lose situation: There is no pressure from any group to impose extra burdens on corporations that attempt to win loopholes. If such groups existed, and if more members were frequently sympathetic to their claims, corporate lobbyists might modify their policy of honesty and full disclosure. This policy could be interpreted as an indication that members and corporations generally see themselves as basically on the same side, even if they differ on specifics; this interpretation is further supported by the sheer number of occasions when members allow corporations to write the specific wording they want incorporated in a bill. To date, these practices have been fully developed only at the federal level. However, a number of corporations talked about branching out to the state and local levels: "Out there is a whole new field. Nobody is doing this. Taking a Washington approach to issues and coming out and trying to attack it all across. It scares the shit out of people when you do it to them. It's effective."

If corporations can get the "minor" wording changes they want, then they may not care how a member votes on the roll call on the final bill. As a senior vice president explained:

> We are not big on voting records . . . because frequently the final vote on a particular bill isn't really important. . . . Probably what's more important is what's thrashed out internally in some of the important committees in Congress. And it doesn't much matter how people vote afterwards. It's what they argued for or tried to get done or stopped from happening, getting done, in those interpersonal discussions that take place.

Another corporation was willing to be understanding if a member voted in favor of Clean Air: "In some cases, maybe because of local environmental people, the senator was not able to vote for [the company] on the floor, but there are a lot of ways that members can help with an issue without actually voting on the floor." Companies would like to see members vote for the company even when the heat is on, but

> Ultimately, we understand they are not going to vote against their own interests. If it comes down to the bottom line and the issue has gotten such public heat that it becomes their holding the job another year or [our company], we would like to see them take the profile in courage,[62] as they say. But we understand. We hope the issues don't get to that point. You try to defuse them ahead of time, or find alternatives.

The fact that corporate lobbyists can potentially gain access to any member, that it is cheap to do so, and that when they get in the door they talk honestly, does not mean that success is automatic. If it were, corporations wouldn't bother to make campaign contributions.

◆ MYTH FOUR: BUSINESS WINS WITHOUT EFFORT

A different sort of misconception about the access or special interest process is held by some people on the left of the political spectrum: that this process operates automatically, that business is guaranteed to win with no significant effort by corporations, and in any event that the consequences are minimal. Some people believe that Congress is unimportant, that all key decisions are made by the president and executive branch—though, as we argue in the next chapter, with the explosion of soft money, the president is fully involved in a similar dynamic. The access process described in this chapter is what G. William Domhoff calls the special interest process, and it is the simplest and least significant of his four processes of ruling-class domination. Structural Marxists, such as Nicos Poulantzas or Fred Block, argue that business does not need to have a consciousness of its interests or mobilize to achieve its aims, that the nature of the system requires politicians and the state to do what business wants in order to maintain a healthy economy.[63]

To some degree we agree with this reservation. The access process is not the sole basis for corporate power. The primary foundation of business power is the ability to make day-to-day business decisions unless and until the government intervenes. This, together with control over vast resources, makes it possible for a measly $1,000 ($100,000) to win the corporation not only access to a member of Congress (the president), but also the member's (president's) support for a multimillion-dollar corporate benefit. However, access through a carefully placed campaign contribution is one component of corporate power, and by no means a trivial one. A range of commentators agree that Congress has become increasingly important,[64] and any analysis of business's political problems must focus on congressional actions. In the 1960s, the presidency may have been far more important than Congress, but that is no longer so, except for foreign policy. David Vogel's analysis of business's *Fluctuating Fortunes* led him to conclude that for the decline of corporate political power in the late 1960s as well as for its revival in the late 1970s, "the key to this shift was Congress."[65] The most important business group formed in the 1970s, the Business Roundtable, differed from previous peak associations in that its primary mission was *not* to develop policy behind the scenes, but rather to lobby Congress openly. Nor would it be fair to interpret Domhoff's work as arguing against the importance of the processes we have been discussing. While the access process is most centrally concerned with Domhoff's special interest process, it also has a major impact on two of his other processes, candidate selection and policy formation. The large sums of money that flow to members of Congress willing to do favors for corporations make it difficult for any challenger to unseat them. As we argue below, the access process complicates policy formation in ways that both aid and frustrate business domination.

The next chapter, on soft money, deals more with executive branch decisions, but much of the analysis here also applies to the executive branch. For better or worse—and most people would say it is for worse—the president, certainly President Clinton, is increasingly involved in the minutiae of decision making.[66] With the decline of the Soviet Union and the absence of credible challenges to American power, the presidency is less about foreign policy, less about broad visions, and more about wheeling and dealing. President Clinton's campaign, and his governance, have been about a host of minor, even trivial initiatives: "Vision" for Clinton (and for Dole) consists of finding the best compromise.

Corporations find it cheap to gain access, but the process also demonstrates the limits to business power and the effort corporations must make to hold on to their privileged position. The access process is a limited response to legislation that business wishes had never been proposed. Corporations seek special provisions to protect themselves only because they can't totally defeat the legislation. We asked one PAC director whether his aim was, in general, to defeat legislation or to modify it. He explained:

> I think it depends on the bill, and also it depends on the company. I think, as a general statement, the business community normally goes in and says they [members of Congress] should vote against the bill. And ultimately when you get done saying that, you sit down and say, "We really would like you to consider a, b, and c." My personal attitude is that certain things are going to happen. You obviously try to make the end product as palatable as possible.

This is a pragmatic approach by someone who hardly feels in control of the process. Much of his effort has gone into fighting environmental regulations. On the one hand, he has helped win many modifications; on the other, the legislation always passes by a wide margin.

The limits to corporate power need to be recognized both theoretically and politically. Failure to do so can lead only to cynicism and despair, a sense that nothing can be done, that people can't make a difference. No question about it, the odds are stacked in favor of business and the rest of us have to engage in massive struggles to win small victories. But victories are possible. We have won them in the past, and we will win them in the future. Not token victories only, but real changes that bring substantial improvement. Unions have brought millions of workers higher living standards, along with limited power at the workplace; on average, unionized workers are paid 30 percent more than nonunionized workers in the same industry, and that success is a direct result of struggle. The environmental movement is responsible for some improvements and for some instances where we have been able to hold the line in the struggle to preserve the earth. The fact that environmental degradation will destroy the earth and all of us with it is hardly proof that corporations would have done anything about it if left to themselves. As Marx said about the nineteenth-century movement to limit the length of the working day:

> [Capital] allows its actual movement to be determined as much and as little by the sight of the coming degradation and final depopulation of the human race, as by the probable fall of the earth into the sun. In

every stock-jobbing swindle everyone knows that some time or other the crash must come, but everyone hopes that it may fall on the head of his neighbour. . . . *Après moi le déluge!* is the watchword of every capitalist and of every capitalist nation. Capital therefore takes no account of the health and the length of life of the worker, unless society forces it to do so.[67]

Even the special exceptions that corporations win for themselves require persistent effort. If members of Congress were always eager to do what corporations wanted, corporations would not need to contribute to safe incumbents or make certain to establish personal connections by attending fundraisers. Corporate government relations departments wouldn't have to mount major campaigns to get their special exceptions. While people can't be sure exactly how much difference the campaign contributions make, most have a clear sense that they provide a critical edge. In one interview, a top company executive complained about a host of problems with PACs and government relations, so we asked him, "What would be the consequences if you didn't do any of that?" He answered, "I'm not sure, but I'm not willing to find out."

Good government relations executives are the ones that make the right decisions, giving gifts to politicians and establishing relationships with them *before* their corporation needs a favor. These decisions involve large measures of uncertainty, not so much in terms of who will be defeated or move to a more powerful committee, but rather in terms of what government actions the corporation may need, or want to stop. A profitable company today may be in bankruptcy five years from now; today's steel or electric company may be tomorrow's oil or television company. The corporation therefore wants to build trust and relations with the widest possible network of politicians, and to do so well before it has any favor to request. It is cheap and easy to make a contribution, and it doesn't require much effort to attend a fundraiser or make a friendly personal contact. Compared to a big corporation's income and resources, $1,000—or $100,000—is a truly insignificant contribution. No individual contribution is a big deal; if in doubt, better to have contributed the money. On the other side, however, the politician's actions may save the company hundreds of millions of dollars; may in fact be critical to preserving the company's very existence. Such actions probably (though not necessarily) require the member to cash in some of their political chips, to call in favors from other members, to say, "Give me this one and I'll help you out when you've got a problem." There is always a (slim) chance that this special interest activity will be exposed and cost the politician dearly, perhaps fatally, in the next election.

If a past history of $1,000 contributions can substantially increase the possibility that the politician will be willing to help in a crisis, then it constitutes a cheap insurance policy for the corporation.

But in doing so corporations sometimes find themselves coerced into making contributions they resent. Part of this is just the endemic pressure by candidates discussed in the previous chapter. Another part, however, is PACs that would prefer to be ideological,[68] to support conservatives without regard to access. They sometimes find that they have to play the game—have to contribute to liberals who are anathema to them—in hopes of future access. Again, is this glass half-empty or half-full? On the one hand, virtually every member of Congress is willing to do favors for corporations; there are virtually no members who are hostile to business, able to act effectively on this hostility, and unwilling to take business money. On the other hand, the corporation is being "forced" to contribute to liberals, as we hear in this 1988 interview:

PAC DIRECTOR: I give some money to some people I don't agree with merely because they are working on a bill or something, and then I'm playing access so it's not entirely ideology. There's sometimes I have to give the money: I think we've given [Representative Henry] Waxman [Democrat–California] some money, and I cringe because he's not representative of our philosophy. . . . I got a note from another guy on the PAC committee who's more conservative than I am, and he said, "Why are you giving to that turkey?" But I'm more pragmatic. I realize I've got to live with some of these people.

Now if they weren't on that committee, I'd never give them any money. Now Teddy Kennedy and Howard Metzenbaum are—one's chairman of Labor and Human Resources and the other's way up there. And yes, I need access sometimes with those people. But I just can't—they're just so far that way. Now Waxman's just so far that way—but Waxman, you're never going to get him out.[69] He's very important to us, and we may give him a modest amount of money. Now you say, is there any rationale? Well, not really, it's sort of working with the system.

INTERVIEWER: Let's take that as a contrast. You give the donation to Waxman, you don't give one to Kennedy.

PAC DIRECTOR: That's right.

INTERVIEWER: You need to talk with both of them sometimes, or the committees are dealing with things—

PAC DIRECTOR: That's right.

INTERVIEWER: What difference does it make?

PAC DIRECTOR: [Laughing] Because Kennedy is usually a $1,000 minimum, and I can get to Waxman for $250 probably—so my principles—we know what we are, we just don't know what we cost.

This PAC director wasn't happy prostituting himself and his company by contributing to a member he regarded as "just so far that way," but he felt it was necessary. Since he could get access to Waxman for a $250 contribution he was willing to do so, but he drew the line at the $1,000 that would be needed to gain access to Kennedy.[70] In a similar instance, one corporation reported it had contributed to a moderate senator based in the same state as company headquarters, even though "there isn't a member on my PAC committee that voted for him."

But we don't want to push this argument so far that we appear to be agreeing with pluralists. Business doesn't win automatically, but pluralists sometimes seem to argue that the existence of a struggle proves it's an even contest. To us, it appears a very one-sided struggle, with business clearly having disproportionate power. Take clean air (discussed in Chapter 1) as an example. Should we be impressed that, after twenty years, the bill was revised? Or appalled at how weak the bill is despite strong popular support for an effective bill? Does the Clean Air Act show us that corporations are too weak to stop environmental legislation? Or does it suggest that even when the corporate position has virtually no popular support, corporations are still able to sabotage the legislation and guarantee it will be weak and ineffective?

LANGUAGE AND EUPHEMISM

Language reveals a great deal, not only by what is said, but also by what is not said. When something is regarded as unpleasant, embarrassing, or degrading, people develop euphemisms. The euphemism attempts to deny whatever it is about the word that's considered unpleasant or unfortunate. Euphemisms can help us locate those activities and areas that cause strain or discomfort in a culture. Our culture, like many others, has difficulty confronting death. Thus, we say that people "passed away," not that they "died"; we avoid referring to someone as an "undertaker," and replace it with "mortician."

A euphemism helps us deal with a problem area by removing from thought "that part of the connotation of a word that creates the discomfort."[71] Thus the euphemisms for "toilet" take us away from the idea of excrement and substitute the idea that we are there to bathe, wash, or rest. The language used by the people we interviewed indicates that the corporation only wants "access," that it is not there to lobby or influence, it isn't asking for favors, and it most certainly isn't asking for a quid pro quo for a past campaign contribution. As the term "access" gains notoriety, PAC officials search for new and still more distant euphemisms. As one PAC director we interviewed explained, "I call it courtesy. You might call it just good manners. The opportunity to deal with staff, to meet with them to persuade them."[72]

The euphemisms used by PACs imply that the purpose of their donations to and their interactions with members of Congress is not to buy, bribe, or corrupt—not even to influence or lobby—but rather simply to gain "access."[73] If a person goes to the "washroom," they may actually wash. But they will probably be unhappy if that is all they get to do. Similarly, corporate PACs do want "access" to the member. But if all they get is access, they will be disappointed. At a minimum, the corporation hopes to lobby and influence the member, and it is certainly willing to use money as one of those influences. However, a corporate PAC official would never say aloud, "I've got an appointment to bribe Senator X this afternoon." Nor would a member say, "That loophole will cost you ten thousand bucks." Both corporate and congressional officials would have a great deal to lose if they regularly used such language to describe their interactions.

The language of corporate officers is, of course, intended for public consumption—but not *only* for public consumption. Every group creates and nurtures illusions about itself; euphemisms are as necessary to the speaker as they are to the audience. Many, though by no means all, of the corporate executives we spoke with are uncomfortable about the access process. They don't like what they do, feel it is slightly sleazy, are embarrassed and defensive about it. Generally speaking, they resent having to buy access and influence. The corporate government relations officials don't feel embarrassed about the policy changes they ask for and don't feel these are indefensible special interest legislation. Their concern is that politicians ought to be making better policy and should not be giving their companies a hard time. PAC directors are uneasy that the corporation is supporting liberals who don't belong in public office. The people we interviewed are troubled not by their exercise of power—which they see as not real power at all, but simply helping politicians to craft better public policy—but by the *limits* to that power, by the fact that they are drawn into cooperating with "liberals" rather than throwing the bums out. A few of the most pragmatic PAC directors didn't seem to mind this, because they recognize that these "liberals" are actually happy to cooperate and do favors for business. But many people we interviewed seemed uncomfortable contributing to people they consider antibusiness liberals. They wish they didn't have to do it, but feel it is necessary to get the results they need from Washington. Corporate PAC directors are often defensive about these donations; most corporations respond by reserving some of their money specifically to support "pro-business," "free market" candidates who are either running for open seats or challenging entrenched incumbents.[74]

POLICY IMPLICATIONS

How much difference does it make in the end? That is a key issue in any discussion of the access process. What does it add up to? Do loopholes for business, even if there are a great many of them, actually have much influence on the distribution of power in society as a whole? Do they change the basic thrust of the legislation? Our answer: yes. Cumulatively, these minor changes, introduced through the access process, have a substantial impact, one that both aids and frustrates business control of U.S. society. (A politician's skill in this access–fundraising process also influences election outcomes—an issue we consider in Chapter 5, on ideology.)

The access (or special interest) process furthers business control of society in at least two inter-related ways. First, the cumulative impact of these minor changes is to subvert the stated intent of the policy. When "minor change" is added to "minor change," the ultimate bill does little to reform taxes or ensure clean air. Thus the Internal Revenue Service is surprised to find corporations paying less in taxes than they had anticipated from the Tax "Reform" Act. Thus the Clean Air Act is passed, but the air doesn't get much cleaner.

Second, the access process serves and promotes business power because it is uniquely suited to frustrating the popular will. The process introduces endless delays and complications and moves the issues out of the spotlight and into the backrooms, where only "experts" and power brokers are allowed. These actors introduce provisions designed to prevent the public from knowing what is happening. The process is successful in that it keeps people's anger uninformed and diffuse. A major investigation is necessary simply to find out what the government is doing. The consequence is that people without lots of time and resources grow discouraged and go away.

The access process thus becomes a major weapon for frustrating and sidetracking social movements. People become cynical and discouraged, convinced that meaningful change is impossible, that the more things change the more they stay the same, that all politics is dirty, that "you can't fight

City Hall." This disillusionment can serve business's purpose, since an ineffective government leaves business in control of most decisions.

Today, voter anger, distrust, and resentment are all high. People feel they have lost control of their government, that the government serves the interests of the few, that politicians can't be trusted. They are, of course, correct. But the access process helps incumbents direct attention away from larger issues of principle. Frequently key choices are made in the hidden abode of committee and subcommittee hearings or in one-on-one meetings in a member's office. This activity is not generally subject to media scrutiny, and by the time the bill finally comes to a public roll-call vote, virtually everyone lines up on the same side.

The line-item veto—which took effect on January 1, 1997—is intended to address exactly this problem. The law authorizes the president to veto tax breaks that affect one hundred or fewer taxpayers, as well as some spending items. The 1997 tax cut contained 79 provisions that met the technical requirements of the act and were thus potentially subject to a line-item veto; President Clinton used the veto "judiciously," applying it to only two of these items and permitting 77 of the 79 provisions to remain in the act. One veto concerned the ability of financial service companies to defer taxes on overseas operations. The other concerned Harold C. Simmons—a billionaire who heavily backs Republican candidates—who would have been able to defer $104 million in taxes through a special provision for the sale of a beet-processing plant. Among the provisions that Clinton allowed to stay in the bill was one that enabled tobacco companies to count $50 billion in taxes as part of whatever settlement, if any, comes out of Congress (see Chapter 4). Clinton has been equally fainthearted in his spending vetoes. For one traditionally pork-laden bill, he announced that he was stopping "unwarranted corporate subsidies," but found only $19 million worth in a $20 billion bill, or less than one one-thousandth of the total.[75] Moreover, it's important to realize that the line-item veto applies to only a small fraction of the provisions that ordinary people would identify as loopholes. Lobbyists are already running seminars on how to design future loopholes so that they do *not* meet the provisions of the act and, hence, are not subject to the line-item veto.[76] The line-item veto is a small step in the right direction. But no one could mistake it for an end to the old system.

Ending that system would require both the media and politicians to turn their attention to exposing and stopping the use of loopholes as a system of governance. Members could refuse to vote for a bill unless it publicly identified the member(s) who had proposed each loophole, the corporation(s) it would benefit, and the estimated dollar value of the loop-holes. If the proposed provision is good public policy, bring it out in the open and defend it. If no one is willing to admit responsibility for the provision, eliminate the loophole from the bill. Totalitarian states need to keep the public ignorant about what the government is doing. What, then, does it mean that the U.S. government is doing so as well?

The access process also creates problems for business and indicates the limits to its power. Thousands of special deals that subvert the general thrust of legislation make it difficult to develop and implement *any* coher-ent policy, including one that addresses the needs of business as a whole. When a rising world power has a unified and powerful ruling class, such arrangements are probably minimized. If no other group is able effectively to challenge that class for power, there is less need to pretend to enact a bill to clean up the air. The power of the dominant group and the weakness of its opposition make it possible to be more explicit and open about both intentions and consequences. Thus, if an attempt is made to clean the air, both the rhetoric and the law can clearly indicate the limits to this and not pretend to do more than is actually intended. When a ruling class is most powerful, unified, and effective, individual companies that attempt to pur-sue their own interests probably will be disciplined by other businesses in a host of ways,[77] which help ensure that policy promotes the interests of business as a whole, not just those of specific companies. If the U.S. busi-ness establishment did not have to take account of alternative social move-ments and centers of power, and if businesses were able to unify more effectively around the principles that best support their collective long-run interests, much of the access process would be eliminated. While the pro-cess may help to frustrate and sidetrack popular movements, it also under-cuts the effectiveness of (business-dominated) public policy. To pass key legislation, deals must be cut with individual businesses, and this makes it more difficult to develop policies in the best interest of business as a whole.

Consider health care policy—probably the most important issue of Clinton's first term. The United States health care system is deeply flawed. Not only is the United States the richest country in the world, but health expenditures make up a greater percentage of the gross domestic product (GDP) in the United States than they do in any other country. The absolute amount we spend is therefore substantially higher than it is in other coun-tries—50 percent more than the second highest country in the world, Swit-zerland. The United States spends 13.6 percent of its GDP on total health expenditures, or $3,086 per person; Japan spends 6.9 percent of its GDP, or $1,376; Canada spends 10.3 percent, or $1,949; and the United Kingdom spends 7.1 percent, or $1,151.[78] But despite those higher expenditures, higher both absolutely and relatively, United States residents have *worse* health. The infant mortality rate is 4.43 (per 1,000) in Japan, 6.39 in Canada, 7.38 in England (and lower in Scotland), and 8.94 in the United States (which ranks 24th in the world). The United States also lags in life expectancy— for men it ranks 25th, below Greece, Costa Rica, and Cuba, and for women it ranks 16th.[79]

Addressing this problem would be very much in the interest not only of working people, but also of American business. If U.S. health care expenditures took only the same percentage of GDP as in Canada, an additional $199 billion would be available; if they were at the same level as in Japan, over $400 billion would be saved. Since business pays a substantial fraction of the cost of health insurance, reducing these amounts could increase corporate profits and/or make U.S. products more competitive worldwide. There are also dangers for business, which doesn't want socialized medicine (as in Britain), and apparently isn't even willing to accept a Canadian-style single-payer plan. But a system that worked effectively *for business* would be able to meet this challenge by mobilizing a powerful block of corporations willing and able to impose a major revision that cut the costs of health care without endangering business's ideological position. Clinton's health care proposal, however, was from the beginning huge, complicated, loophole ridden, and access–compromise driven. The bill was defeated by a conservative ideological mobilization; Clinton was never able to develop a constituency for his proposal because it was so filled with compromises and concessions to business that the public could not understand the bill and saw little benefit in it.

The consequence is that our health care policy, to the extent that there is one, continues to be shaped by the access process. In place of a larger vision, we have lobbying and special deals for every financially powerful group. Effective government policy is shaped by "dizzyingly technical" changes "built on what many would consider minutiae" that transfer billions of dollars out of Medicare and into private health plans.[80] The first comprehensive audit of Medicare concluded that "the government overpaid hospitals, doctors and other health care providers last year [1996] by $23 billion."[81] Our previous discussion of how a single company, SmithKline Beecham, overbilled the government by $325 million, helps explain why. Clearly, many specific companies benefit from provisions inserted in health care legislation through the access process. Businesses can't stop themselves from engaging in the process, and because they want their own special deals, they aren't willing to oppose similar deals made for other companies. Although each company benefits from its provisions, the overall effect is in many ways harmful to business as a whole, helping to create a distorted and inefficient system. Business then complains about "government inefficiency," as if this had no relation to the millions of loopholes that business itself fought to create.

The situation has become increasingly serious, because this lack of vision and the politics of deal making have spread from Congress to the presidency. Not coincidentally, changes in campaign finance practice have been central to this change: The rise of "soft money" has made the president the fundraiser-in-chief.

◆ 4

SOFT MONEY AND THE
PAY-PER-VIEW PRESIDENCY

SOFT MONEY HAS DRAMATICALLY CHANGED CAMPAIGN FINANCE. A DECADE ago, contributions were $10,000 or less; today, megabuck donations are routine. The access process, long dominant in Congress, now rules the presidency; scandals center around soft money. Unless and until the law changes, future contributions will grow ever larger and soft money become increasingly dominant.

But what in the world *is* "soft money"? The complete answer is complicated and ambiguous, providing employment for innumerable lawyers. Here is the short answer: any political contribution that is *not* subject to federal law; in practice, big bucks given at fundraisers hosted by the president or top party leaders. The only limitation on soft money is that it cannot (legally) be used explicitly to advocate the election of a specific candidate. Creative consultants and lax regulators are making this restriction less and less significant, but, all other things being equal, politicians still prefer "hard money" given within the law. Of course, all other things are seldom equal.

In understanding soft money—the focus of most of the 1996 election "scandal"—the best first approximation is that soft money is the top-level equivalent of PAC contributions to individual members of Congress. "Top level" means, above all, the president, but it also takes in the congressional leaders of both parties and the presidential candidate of the opposing party. Some elements of the soft money process closely resemble a higher level version of the access process discussed in the last chapter, but soft money can also involve a looser and more general shaping of the positions of a party or a president, including the background discussions that create the unstated (and often unrecognized) parameters structuring all policy proposals.

RULES AND FRAMEWORK

Federal campaign finance rules require full disclosure of contributions over $200, and limit campaign contributions by individuals ($2,000) and political action committees ($10,000) to candidates for federal office.[1] Donations to political parties are regulated if they are to be used to assist specific candidates. The 1970s laws, however, did not specifically mention donations to political parties that are used for "party building" or "get-out-the-vote drives." In 1979, this ambiguity in the law was presented to the Federal Election Commission. The FEC could have ruled that such donations were subject to the same limitations and reporting requirements as other contributions, but it did not do so.[2] Instead, as in most cases, the FEC left the practice unregulated. At first, there were few such donations, but over time their numbers grew exponentially. In 1997, eighteen years and many millions of dollars after the FEC nonregulation, President Clinton came out (verbally) in favor of reform, writing a letter to the FEC "to request that you take action under your existing statutory authority to ban '*soft money*' and end the system under which both political parties compete to raise unlimited sums from individuals, labor unions, and corporations."[3] Some people might compare this advice to Jack the Ripper advocating respect for women. Even after his verbal commitment to a ban on soft money, Clinton continued to work hard to raise more, and he failed to appoint FEC commissioners who would enact the soft money ban he claimed to favor.[4]

The absence of *any* regulation means that an individual or organization can donate a million dollars (or ten million, or a hundred million). At least as important, corporations no longer have to operate only through their political action committees—which can raise money only by soliciting "voluntary" contributions from managers and stockholders—but can simply treat politics as a business expense, a budget item like advertising, research and development, or public relations.

From 1979 through 1990, soft money donations did not have to be reported. Both parties kept their donors' names secret, though beginning with the 1988 election, each voluntarily released some information, typically on (some of) the largest contributors. For the 1992 election (that is, from January 1, 1991 on), the FEC mandated reporting for soft money contributions, though it required less information and less uniform reporting, than for other donations. In the sense that these donations are now subject to reporting, they are no longer entirely unregulated. The FEC has also imposed rules on the funding of joint activities that benefit both nonfederal and federal races, such as voter drive activities, requiring that 60 (in 1995) or 65 (in 1996) percent of the costs come from hard money accounts.[5]

Soft money has increased rapidly. The best available estimate of early soft money expenditures are $19.1 million in 1980 and $21.6 million in 1984 (with the Republicans accounting for just over $15 million in each of those years).[6] In 1992, 7,000 thousand donors made 13,000 donations totaling $84 million; in 1996, 28,000 donors made 41,000 contributions totaling three times the 1992 sum.

But each step forward has been matched by at least one step back. Reporting requirements for federal soft money donations have led to increases in other kinds of—even less regulated—campaign spending. A host of new forms of evasion are developing; we can discuss only a few of these.

The most important at this point are so-called independent-expenditure issue advertisements. The biggest spenders on issue ads are the political parties, but if ads are run by independent groups and not coordinated with the political parties, then they are not even considered "soft money," and, depending on how they are done, may not be subject to any reporting or disclosure requirements. If expenditures are made independently of the candidate and the campaign, they are subject to no limitation; if ads do not explicitly advocate the election (or defeat) of a candidate, the people or organizations who paid for the ad need not be identified.

In the 1996 election, total spending on "issue ads," including spending by the political parties themselves, totaled $150 million, one-third of the spending on political advertising. The AFL–CIO's independent expenditures received far more attention than those of any other group: It spent $35 million to influence the election, with $20 million of this going to independent-expenditure television ads. These ads were extremely effective; they drove Republicans and business nuts, and framed much of the debate in the election, in part because the AFL–CIO focused on the issues most important to the public, not on those most important to labor officials. The ads did not tell people how to vote. They simply announced, "Your member of Congress voted to gut Social Security and Medicare, to pollute the environment, and to cut spending on education," and then left voters to make up their own minds.[7] Steve Rosenthal, political director of the AFL–CIO, has said that, even if there were no laws regulating advertising, he would prefer to run ads setting out the facts, and then let voters decide for themselves who should get their vote.

In 1996—for the first time in many years—labor was a major player, framing the political debate and focusing on issues of importance to workers. Because business had been having things so much its own way, some of the commentary and debate questioned labor's right to run such ads. Although labor's ads received the most attention, many other groups were buying space and time for their causes. Business routinely runs enormous quantities of advocacy advertising, though many of the business ads are sedate and genteel, like the Mobil ads on the *New York Times* Op-Ed page. Each year, a typical U.S. resident is exposed to hundreds of business ads that implicitly or explicitly try to persuade people to see the world in a particular way (Corporation X is concerned about the environment, helps little kids, and carefully monitors conditions for its workers in Third World dictatorships).

Business, conservative, and Republican groups intervened aggressively in the election, but—given who dominates public discourse—their ads attracted far less criticism than labor's. As one example among many, consider Grover Norquist and Americans for Tax Reform. Norquist, a good friend of Newt Gingrich, is the coordinator of the "Leave Us Alone" coalition, which meets every Wednesday morning, bringing together representatives of the Christian Coalition, the National Rifle Association, a range of other conservative groups, and members of Congress or their staffs. Late in the 1996 election, Republican congressional candidates were in trouble. The party had more money than it knew what to do with, and in many congressional districts the party had already made the maximum legally permissible contribution. The Republican National Committee then *gave* $4.6 million to Norquist's Americans for Tax Reform, which used the money to flood 150 congressional districts "with a direct-mail campaign assuring voters that the Republicans had no intention of cutting Medicare and that voters were being subjected to 'political scare tactics' to think otherwise."[8] None of the mailings revealed that they were paid for by money from the Republican party; the mailings carried the name of Americans for Tax Reform and were presented as though they came from an independent group. These expenditures would be illegal if they were coordinated with the Republican party (which after all paid for them), and there is every reason to suspect they were (though—as yet—no proof). Norquist insists that there was no coordination and that there was nothing illegal about the mailings:

"'It doesn't say "Vote Republican" and it doesn't name candidates. It doesn't say who to vote for, it just says "Here are the facts." It fits comfortably within the law.'"[9] Given the way campaign finance laws are being interpreted these days (by both politicians and courts), Norquist's interpretation is likely to hold up; if it does, it will open yet another major means of avoiding the regulations. There are, of course, dozens of other groups that ran issue ads of one kind and another, including the Christian Coalition, the National Rifle Association, the Sierra Club, and business groups that mobilized explicitly to counter labor activity.

Another major step backward is the expansion of donations to state—as opposed to national—political parties. These are not subject to federal reporting statutes, state disclosure requirements vary widely, and most states have not computerized their data. In 1996, in order to hide donations, the Democrats apparently systematically channeled them to state parties.

Contributors' checks routinely were sent to DNC headquarters before being passed on to the state parties, but documents show that DNC officials kept meticulous records of the donations so that donors and fundraisers received credit.

Because the money was not deposited in the accounts of the national party, the identities of the donors did not appear on the DNC's federal disclosure reports. Instead, the donations were reported on the state level, where they are far more difficult to track.[10]

For example, in order to avoid angering Michigan's Republican governor, the Sault Ste. Marie Chippewas, a Native American tribe in Michigan's Upper Peninsula, gave $100,000 directly to the DNC, but gave an additional $270,000 to five state Democratic parties. Pamela Liapakis, former head of the American Trial Lawyers Association, gave $5,000 to the DNC, "but was listed on the internal documents as giving another $150,000 to state parties." On the federal level, Mirage Resorts, Inc. gave the Republicans $250,000 and the Democrats only $35,000, but it gave an additional $215,000 to Democrats at the state level. Therefore, anything that we or others report about soft money represents the minimum case; there were certainly additional donations, and we simply can't tell how significant these might be.

The Democrats have introduced another way around campaign finance rules; essentially, it provides the opportunity to expand soft money (that is, unlimited contributions) into individual congressional (especially Senate) races. What happens when an individual contributor has "maxed out" on a Senate (or House) race, having given $2,000, the maximum amount legally permissible? The senator or representative who wants (naturally) to get more out of the donor, then suggests that the contributor give soft money to the party, putting no notation on the check ("For some reason, it is very important that you not put Senator Levin's name on the check itself," a party fundraiser wrote to Robert Nathan[11]), but writing a cover note asking that the money be credited to the senator. The Democrats then maintained a "tally account" showing how much money had been credited to each candidate and used a variety of dubious mechanisms to spend that money on those races. The 1996 Democratic Senate candidate in Illinois, Representative Richard J. Durbin, "said in August the 'only way' he receives DSCC [Democratic Senatorial Campaign Committee] money 'is if I raise the money and it is tallied to me.'" Even a reformer like Paul Wellstone, who accepts a maximum of $100 per person for his campaign, wrote a contributor that "anything you can tally would be a tremendous help." The Republicans, who have not made such direct and explicit use of the tally system, have objected to the Democratic practice and filed a complaint about it; the Democrats paid a $75,000 fine to settle the complaint and then proceeded to refine the system slightly so it would meet legal objections. Democrats argue that "the amount candidates have raised in their 'tally' accounts does not in any way guarantee that much will be spent on their behalf, and, therefore, the practice passes legal muster." If this practice goes unchecked, the likelihood is that soft money, today confined primarily to national-level interventions, will soon dominate the funding of individual congressional races as well.[12]

THE DATA

A great deal is said about soft money, but few have examined the actual data, except perhaps to look at lists of the largest donors. Any discussion of soft money needs to be grounded in an understanding of some information that is typically omitted, concealed, or distorted.

The FEC has done wonders in making its data more available for public inspection. In 1993, in order to analyze soft money data about the 1992 election, we had to file a Freedom of Information Act request and pay for the information. Now the data are available and free to anyone through the FEC from their World Wide Web server (www.fec.gov); the Center for Responsive Politics website (at www.crp.org) also has useful information. In this chapter we present data for the 1996 election, but we have also analyzed the data for 1992 and 1994—all the data that are available—and, where appropriate, compare 1996 to previous elections.

Easy access to the FEC data is a major step forward, but numerous problems remain: Donors are identified only by a 35-letter name, names are not uniformly reported (one donation may be from Atlantic Richfield Company and the next from ARCO), and donors are not classified by category, so we have had to make our best judgment as to whether a donor is a corporation, labor union, association, individual, or political committee. When computing the total amount given by a donor that made multiple contributions, it is easy to miss the fact that two donations actually came from the same entity (especially since ARCO, for example, may give some contributions from a Los Angeles address and others from a Washington address). We may also, of course, have miscategorized a donor—assuming, for example, that some newly formed "Walt Disney" was an individual, when actually it was a corporation, or adding together two "John K. Smith" donations that actually came from two different people. Because of assorted difficulties in working with the data, no two lists are identical. Most commonly cited are the figures released by the Center for Responsive Politics (CRP). We created our own version of the data in order to do analyses not possible from any existing data source.[13]

Two issues sometimes complicate our presentation of the data. First, we must distinguish between contributions and contributors. Some contributors made many separate contributions; specifically, 28,000 contributors made 41,000 contributions. Unless otherwise specified, we present data on contributors and focus on the total of their contributions over a two-year period. Second, a substantial amount of money was transferred from one party committee to another. We eliminated this money from consideration to avoid counting it twice.

THE LITTLE GUY

Public statements nearly always stress the thousands of small contributors who are responsible for the party's or candidate's funds. At the opening of the 1997 Senate hearings investigating campaign finance abuses, especially those by the Clinton campaign, John Glenn noted that the committee and the media had identified problems only with a handful of contributors out of what he said were 2.7 million contributors. Similarly, during the 1992 election, Rahm Emanuel, the Clinton campaign's finance director, "said that the Democrats received their most contributions through the mail on the Monday after the Republican convention, when $852,000 arrived, mostly in sums of $5, $10 and $15."[14]

Small donors, "ordinary people" who use this money to "have their say" and "participate in the democratic process," serve an important ideological and legitimation function, but they are not especially important in actually raising the money needed to get through the money primary. It is unclear who is included in Glenn's 2.7 million figure; Donald Fowler, the former chair of the Democratic National Committee, said that the party had 1 million small donors who contributed $26 million during 1995 and 1996—but 42 percent of this money was needed to pay for the cost of the solicitation, so the net to the party was only $15 million.[15] (These small donations were presumably "hard money" that did not go beyond the bounds of the law; the party could therefore use them to promote specific candidates, and they are not included in the soft money figures presented below.) The cost of raising money is an important factor; getting money from small contributors is expensive, so the net gain is often much less than the total raised. Not infrequently, a first-time solicitation letter costs *more* than the amount it brings in. The figures we are about to present therefore *understate* the importance of big contributors, because the cost of a cup of coffee doesn't make much of a dent in a $100,000 contribution.

How important are small contributors? Not very. Let's say that a contribution of $1,000 is "small"—and most of us would regard it as huge. As shown in Figure 4.1 and Table 1, these "small" contributors made 71 percent of all the 1996 soft money donations; however, this accounted for less than 4 percent of all soft money contributions. An additional 5,009 contributors gave between $1,001 and $10,000. All the $10,000 and under contributors together—89 percent of the total—gave just over 12 percent of the total amount of soft money. At the other end of the spectrum, the contributors who gave $100,000 or more accounted for very close to half of the money; that is, financially these 487 contributors were four times as important as the 24,000 giving less than $10,000. If you were a politician,

---

TABLE I

LARGE AND SMALL SOFT MONEY CONTRIBUTORS:
NUMBER OF CONTRIBUTORS VS. AMOUNTS RAISED, 1995–96

CONTRIBUTION	TOTAL RAISED DEM. REP. (IN $ MILLIONS)		PERCENTAGE OF MONEY	NUMBER OF CONTRIB.	PERCENTAGE OF CONTRIB.
0–1,000	1.3	7.0	3.6	19,670	71.3
1,001–10,000	10.2	10.4	8.8	5,009	18.2
10,000–50,000	24.5	23.3	20.6	1,907	6.9
50,001–100,000	19.6	20.2	17.1	523	1.9
100,000 and up	54.2	61.9	49.9	487	1.8
TOTAL	$109.8	$122.8	100.0	27,596	100.1

FIGURE 4.1

LARGE AND SMALL SOFT MONEY CONTRIBUTORS: 1996

TOTAL CAMPAIGN CONTRIBUTIONS AND PERCENT OF
CONTRIBUTIONS BY CONTRIBUTOR CATEGORIES

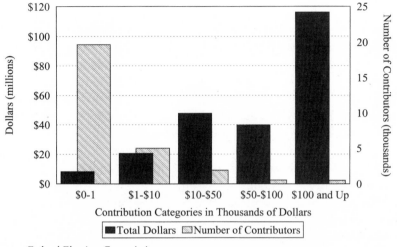

SOURCE: Federal Election Commission

party leader, or fundraiser, these 487 contributors might seem as important as all the (27,000+) other soft money contributors combined—not to mention the voters. Offending all of the "small" contributors ($10,000 or less) would cost about as much money as offending the 39 largest corporate contributors. If you were a politician struggling to get through the money primary, whose views would most concern you?[16]

BUSINESS VS. LABOR

Discussions about political influence in general, and campaign finance in particular, often counterpose business and labor as if they were two equally powerful groups; even sample lists of large donors may convey this impression.[17] Reporters (or editors, or newspaper owners) appear to believe that "balance" means including labor alongside business in stories on the influence of soft money. Or, in a variation, the opponents of business are said to include not only labor, but also environmentalists and women's groups, and the combination of these forces is presented as a match for business. Typical are the remarks of Robert A. Farmer, the treasurer of the 1992 Clinton–Gore campaign (and the top fundraiser for Michael Dukakis as well). "Mr. Farmer said the party had found new sources of contributions this year from women, homosexual groups and health-care companies, along with a substantial increase in support from corporations."[18] This picture of a balance between business and its opponents is not accurate for PAC money, and it is ludicrous as a characterization of soft money: Business dominance is overwhelming.

When dealing with "ordinary" campaign contributions by PACs and individuals, it is easy to conclude that the regulations are so porous that they create no effective limits. Accounts by reformers sometimes read as if the campaign finance regulations hardly matter—the wealthy are not at all constrained. We now have two parallel systems: PACs, which are more or less regulated, and soft money, which is almost completely unregulated. As an indicator of whether regulation makes any difference, we can compare these two systems. In the PAC world, corporations outspend labor by 1.6 to 1; adding in business-oriented associations, the ratio is 2.9 to 1. If donations were unregulated, would business be any more dominant?

The answer is an unequivocal yes. In terms of soft money, in 1996 corporations outspent labor unions by $140 million to $9.2 million, better than a 15 to 1 ratio. Tables 2 and 3 list the 20 largest contributors for corporations and unions. Philip Morris, which sells both cigarettes and beer, leads the corporate list at $3.3 million, followed by a liquor (Seagram, $1.5 million) and a tobacco (R.J. Reynolds, $1.3 million) company. The remainder of the list includes more beer (Anheuser-Busch) and tobacco (Brown & Williamson), along with phone, oil, drugs, and other companies. The labor contributions come from large unions, above all those that represent public-sector workers (state, county, and municipal employees; teachers; postal workers). The total raised by the 20 largest corporations—$18.5 million—is almost three times that raised by the 20 largest unions—$6.5 million. But as the final row in each table indicates, this tells only part of the story, because the top 20 unions accounted for more than two-thirds (70.3 percent) of all the union soft money raised, while the top 20 corporations accounted for only one-seventh (14.0 percent) of the corporate money raised. To a fundraiser, it's clear which area has growth potential: There's not much more to be had from unions, but corporations could give far more.

And that is only step one in determining the full extent of business dominance. At least two more groups need to be counted in: associations and individuals. Associations gave fractionally more than labor unions ($9.7 million to $9.2 million). What is their business-labor balance? As Table 4 indicates, none of the top 20 associations—and collectively they account for more than half of all association money—are labor related, and virtually all are business groups, controlled and funded by member corpora-

TABLE 2
TOP 20 CORPORATE SOFT MONEY CONTRIBUTORS, 1995–96

CONTRIBUTOR	TOTAL CONTRIB.	REP. CONTRIB.	DEM. CONTRIB.
Philip Morris	$ 3,345,036	$ 2,849,518	$ 495,518
Joseph E. Seagram & Sons	1,515,000	650,000	865,000
R.J. Reynolds Tobacco Company	1,277,231	1,047,725	229,506
Atlantic Richfield Co. (ARCO)	1,235,843	749,471	486,372
Nations Bank Corporation	1,202,511	99,406	1,103,105
Federal Express Corporation	998,525	430,900	567,625
AT&T	981,524	534,340	447,184
MCI Communications Corporation	959,514	357,218	602,296
Anheuser-Busch Companies	779,529	363,450	416,079
Eli Lilly & Company	746,835	506,985	239,850
Walt Disney Company	743,450	291,200	452,250
Revlon Group	717,250	140,000	577,250
Chevron Corporation	702,306	526,256	176,050
Brown & Williamson Tobacco	672,500	665,000	7,500
NYNEX	659,447	429,100	230,347
Textron, Inc.	648,000	373,300	274,700
Time-Warner	641,000	350,000	291,000
Archer Daniels Midland Company	640,000	405,000	235,000
Coca-Cola	616,345	438,225	178,120
PaineWebber	590,200	434,500	155,700
TOTAL	$ 19,672,046	$ 11,641,594	$ 8,030,452
TOTAL OF ALL CORPORATIONS	$140,179,876	$81,230,964	$58,948,912
PERCENTAGE OF ALL CORPORATE GIVING CONTRIBUTED BY TOP 20	14.0	14.3	13.6

tions. For 16 of these associations—groups like the Tobacco Institute, American Trucking Association, Society of the Plastics Industry, National Soft Drink Association, National Association of Realtors, American Hospital Association, and so on—that is immediately apparent. What about the four other associations? Three are Indian tribes, each of which operates a gambling casino, and it's the casino business that led to the contribution. The remaining association is the Trial Lawyers, whose members would be just as happy to sue a union as a corporation if there were any money in it. Trial lawyers do often oppose business, because that's where they can win big bucks, but they certainly can't be considered a labor group. Not only is there no labor group in the top 20 associations, but to find a "labor" group you have to get down to the American Occupational Therapy Association ($33,750) or the American Physical Therapy Association ($20,425). What about the other opponents of business—environmentalists, women's groups,

TABLE 3
TOP 20 LABOR SOFT MONEY CONTRIBUTORS, 1995–96

CONTRIBUTOR	TOTAL CONTRIB.	REP. CONTRIB.	DEM. CONTRIB.
American Federation of Statee, County & Municipal Employees	$ 779,912	$ —	$ 779,912
Communication Workers of America	1,140,675	—	1,140,675
United Food & Commercial Workers International	582,550	—	582,550
Laborers	562,400	7,500	554,900
American Federation of Teachers	387,068	—	387,068
National Education Association	380,035	46,135	333,900
International Brotherhood of Electrical Workers	302,750	—	302,750
Committee on Political Education, AFL–CIO	270,000	—	270,000
International Association of Fire Fighters	242,506	23,950	218,556
Machinists	221,300	—	221,300
National Association of Letter Carriers	203,200	—	203,200
American Postal Workers Union	196,750	—	196,750
Service Employees International Union	191,000	—	191,000
Hotel Employees & Restaurant Employees	189,301	50,000	139,301
Local 1199 Martin Luther King, Jr.	185,000	—	185,000
Teamsters	180,800	—	180,800
International Brotherhood of Painters and Allied Trades	178,400	—	178,400
United Auto Workers	155,000	—	155,000
United Steelworkers of America	143,250	—	143,250
Sheet Metal Workers	135,400	—	135,400
TOTAL	6,627,297	127,585	6,499,712
TOTAL, OF ALL LABOR UNIONS	9,231,392	241,560	8,989,832
PERCENTAGE OF ALL LABOR GIVING CONTRIBUTED BY TOP 20	71.8	52.8	72.3

TABLE 4

TOP 20 ASSOCIATION SOFT MONEY CONTRIBUTORS, 1995–96

CONTRIBUTOR	TOTAL CONTRIB.	REP. CONTRIB.	DEM. CONTRIB.
Association of Trial Lawyers	$ 650,400	$ 196,100	$ 454,300
Tobacco Institute	517,847	422,400	95,447
Mashantucket Pequot Tribal	409,625	90,000	205,625
National Association of Realtors	389,775	225,175	164,600
American Hospital Association	323,912	204,337	119,575
American Council of Life Insurance	315,225	245,175	70,050
Smokeless Tobacco Council	268,100	250,600	17,500
Chemical Manufacturers Association	262,950	207,800	55,150
Chicago Mercantile Exchange	206,990	142,790	64,200
American Trucking Association	202,317	147,817	54,500
Society of the Plastics Industry	201,800	120,450	81,350
American Dental PAC	196,350	137,850	58,500
National Association of Home Builders	178,650	120,850	57,800
National Committee to Preserve Social Security & Medicare	158,425	64,625	93,800
American Medical Association	156,018	91,200	64,818
Sault Ste. Marie Tribe Chippewa	150,000	20,000	130,000
National Association of Chain Drug Stores	141,150	97,500	43,650
National Soft Drink Association	137,500	137,500	—
American Portland Cement Alliance	115,450	58,200	57,250
Grocery Manufacturers of America	111,925	107,425	4,500
TOTAL	$5,094,409	$3,087,794	$1,892,615
TOTAL, OF ALL ASSOCIATIONS	$9,669,128	$5,541,300	$3,931,228
PERCENTAGE OF ALL ASSOCIATION MONEY CONTRIBUTED BY TOP 20	52.7	54.2	48.1

advocates for the poor? Individuals may have contributed because they were motivated by these issues, but in the world of unregulated soft money contributors, associations representing these positions are hardly a blip on the screen. The Sierra Club may oppose business—though other such groups, such as the Nature Conservancy, emphatically do not—and it may even choose to run its own issue ads, but it does not have spare money to turn over to a political party. Table 5 lists the only associations we could find that could conceivably be seen as business opponents, and none are even remotely large enough to qualify for the top 20 list. In short, the association balance is far more than 15 to 1 for business over labor.

TABLE 5
"BUSINESS OPPONENT" ASSOCIATIONS SOFT MONEY CONTRIBUTORS

ASSOCIATION	CONTRIBUTION
National Committee to Preserve Social Security & Medicare	$158,425
International Association of Bridge Structural & Ornamental Iron Workers	50,000
American Occupational Therapy Association	33,750
American Physical Therapy Association	20,425
American Association of Nurse Anesthesiologists	14,450
Family Research Council	11,480
National Council of Senior Citizens	10,630
Interntional Traditional Chinese Herbal Medicine & Acupuncture	10,000
The ASCAP Legislative Fund for the Arts	10,000
Children's Defense Fund	5,302
California Correctional Peace Officers Association	5,000
Greater Bethel Church	5,000
Price Charities	5,000
Woods Foundation	2,000
Pemberton Charitable Foundation	1,500
Albanian American Moslem Society	1,000
Alliance for Mature Americans	1,000
Chinese American Parents Assication	1,000
Korean American National PAC	1,000
National Association for Social Security Claimants Representatives	1,000
National Organization for Women	1,000
Focus on the Family	882
National Vietnam Veterans	750
National Race for the Cure	581
Institute of Research & Education on Human Rights	522

NOTE: This table omits Indian tribes (which donate soft money in conjunction with gambling, that is, business, operations) and associations of doctors, dentists, podiatrists, osteopaths, etc.

What about individual contributions? Isn't this where the ordinary citizen, worker or owner, has a chance to be heard? Any answer to this question must be qualified because of the limitations in the data, but what can be determined is exceptionally interesting. The most serious data problem is that most individual contributors provide no information in the space for "occupation." The Republican party unsuccessfully challenged the reporting requirements in court, arguing the GOP should be able to keep information about its soft money donors hidden, but the party claims that its "omission rate has since dropped to 4 percent."[19] We're not sure how the Republicans calculate this figure; our assumption is that this is the rate for all donors of all kinds. That overall figure, however, conceals the fact that corporate, labor, and association donors are routinely (though not invariably) identified, while individual donors rarely are. Federal Election Commission soft money records list occupations for only 25.2 percent of the individuals who donated to the Republicans—marginally better than the Democrats (22.3 percent), but nothing to brag about.[20]

Individuals who made multiple contributions may provide no information when making the first contribution, "lawyer" for the second, and the name of the law firm for the third. If they identify their employer with no additional information about what they do for the employer—the most common practice—variations of the same name may be used. Thus, some contributions are identified as Lazard Freres, and others as Lazard Freres and Company. Presumably these all come from the same source, and the odds are overwhelming that all these contributors are investment bankers. Without further information, however, these data do not make it possible to rule out the possibility (however far-fetched) that one of them is a stock clerk, secretary, or receptionist:

	TOTAL	REPUBLICANS	DEMOCRATS
Perlmutter, Louis Mr.	$30,000	$30,000	
Pollack, Lester	7,500	7,500	
Rattner, Steven	92,000	92,000	
Rohatyn, Felix G.	362,500		$362,500

So, we checked Standard & Poor's *Security Dealers of North America* and discovered—surprise, surprise—that all four are Managing Directors. We do not, however, have the resources to research every individual contributor.

The limitations of the data hampered our efforts, but we searched all the records for those individual soft money contributors who did list occupations, looking for donations from people who hold working-class jobs or jobs that are frequently unionized. Legally, names and occupations do not have to be reported for those who give $199 or less. Here's the sum total of what we could find for $200-and-up contributors (among 9,349 individual contributors, 2,315 of whom listed occupations): one each for "NBA," pilot, teacher, carpenter, and janitor, plus a husband and wife who both identified themselves as "truck driver." We were excited by the National Basketball Association (NBA) listing, wondering what basketball player was taking an interest in politics, but the answer turns out to be no player: It's NBA Commissioner David Stern. The teacher contributed $110,000 to the Republican party. He may be a teacher, but his class position is not that of most teachers. Many airline pilots are unionized and as such are labor, but with average incomes of more than $100,000 a year, they aren't typical union members; this pilot gave $525 to the Republican party. The other four contributed exclusively to the Republican party, and all in relatively modest amounts (carpenter, $550; janitor, $1,270; and the husband and wife truck drivers, $1,450 each). Obviously there may be others living working-class lives: some, for example, of the 37 homemakers, 47 housewives, or 664 "retired." A number of others hold nonelite positions: a social worker, a community activist, a freelance photographer, a musician, a student, and several people who identify themselves as being at one or another university.

If labor is missing, business is present in force—especially as owners and top executives. (See Table 6.) The most common "occupation" listing is the name of a company (Lazard Freres, Dillon Read & Company, Merrill Lynch, Cargill, Philip Morris, etc.). Often these individuals are easily identified as executives of these corporations. In order to be systematic about it, let's consider only the largest individual donors. *Mother Jones* (with the help of the Center for Responsive Politics) compiled lists of the largest contributors and was able to track down information about all but a handful, thus providing a basis for assessing the proportion of individual contributors who are business connected. Of the top 50, 48 are business owners or executives, one might be (a lawyer), and one (Gail Zappa, widow of rock musician Frank) is clearly not a business person (she is the person who lists herself as a community activist), though neither can she be identified as labor. Of the top 200, 169 clearly come from business, the status of 27 is uncertain (most of these are lawyers), and 4 can potentially be classified as nonbusiness, though only one of these might conceivably be called labor— and even that is a stretch, since he is a CEO. Those four are Gail Zappa, Don Henley (a rock musician), Bernard and Audre Rapoport ("he is CEO of labor-backed American Income Life Insurance"), and Peter Buttenweiser ("an education consultant"). Looking only at the top 50 contributors, how

TABLE 6
Top 20 Individual Soft Money Contributors

CONTRIBUTOR	TOTAL CONTRIB.	REP. CONTRIB.	DEM. CONTRIB.
Schwartz, Bernard L,	$ 566,500	$ 15,000	$ 551,500
Hayes, Mariam Cannon	500,000	500,000	—
Hiatt, Arnold	500,000	—	500,000
Fisher, Larry	400,000	400,000	—
Friess, Foster	389,900	389,900	—
Ziff, Dirk	380,000	—	380,000
Rohatyn, Felix G.	362,500	—	362,500
Gandhi, Yogesh K.	325,000	—	325,000
Abraham, S. Daniel	311,500	—	311,500
Koch, David Hamilton	300,000	300,000	—
Lauder, Ronald S.	300,000	300,000	—
Cumming, Ian M.	285,000	—	285,000
Shorenstein, Walter H.	285,000	—	285,000
Trump, Donald J.	279,500	252,000	27,500
Cafaro, John J.	268,200	218,200	50,000
Fox, Sam	250,750	250,750	—
Druckenmiller, Stanley	250,000	250,000	—
Kellett, Stiles A.	250,000	250,000	—
Murdoch, A. M.	250,000	250,000	—
Pattiz, Norman Joel	250,000	—	250,000
TOTAL	$ 6,703,850	$ 3,375,850	$ 3,328,000
TOTAL, OF ALL INDIVIDUALS	$71,632,998	$34,857,266	$37,009,895
PERCENTAGE OF ALL INDIVIDUAL GIVING CONTRIBUTED BY TOP 20	9.4	10.4	9.0

much money was contributed by the 48 with a business base? $14.7 million. Of the top 100 contributors, how much was contributed by the 87 based in business? $22.3 million. If we compare business and labor contributions for individual contributors, looking only at the money given by business people among the top 100, and comparing this to *all* contributions by workers (none of whom are among the 5,000 largest individual contributors), we are "balancing" $22,300,000 by business against $5,245 by labor, a ratio of 4,250 to 1. (Note that even this "balance" involves not counting contributions by big-money lawyers; the odds are that many of the lawyers are in fact corporate attorneys. If we were to go below the top 100, the ratio would be even more skewed.)

The individual contributors are the most heavily skewed in favor of business, since many owners but few workers make individual contributions. Workers give primarily through their unions. Adding up all sources of soft money—corporations, unions, associations, and individuals—the business-to-labor ratio is at least 18.7 to 1, and, if we had information on all individual contributors, almost certainly more than 20 to 1.[21]

BUSINESS'S UNTAPPED POTENTIAL

But this balance, skewed as it is, gives only a hint of what the future may hold. Business has enormous resources, many times those of any other group in society. The total revenues for all labor unions are estimated at $5 billion, a huge sum compared to that available to any other *oppositional* group; but General Motors, General Electric, Exxon, and Philip Morris all have *profits* higher than that figure, and the revenues for the 500 largest corporations add up to roughly 1,000 times the revenues for all of labor.[22] There are 267 individual corporations that by themselves have revenues greater than the $5 billion received by all labor unions combined. Soft money rules—that is, the absence of such rules—now permit corporations to make direct contributions to politics (something that had been forbidden since the 1907 Tillman Act), thus enabling business to marshal its full revenues if needed. Corporations now may simply treat politics as a business expense, similar to advertising, research and development, or public relations. A beer company, for example, could decide to run one less ad on the Super Bowl broadcast, and instead put the $800,000 into a soft money contribution to a political party.[23]

Consider what this might mean. The largest amount contributed by any corporate PAC in any election from the beginning of PACs through the 1996 election was $2,651,493 by UPS in 1994. The 1996 *advertising* budget for General Motors was $1,681,621,700; Proctor & Gamble spent $1,493,109,500. The top 50 corporate advertisers spent $25.5 billion in 1996. Suppose these 50 corporations were to decide to shift 10 percent of their advertising budgets into politics, calculating that running a few less ads wouldn't hurt that much and that politics could provide as good a payoff per dollar spent. These 50 corporations would then be spending $2.55 billion—more than all candidates spent in the 1996 election (including all the corporate, labor, association, and individual donations, including all PACs and soft money). And they would have done so at no cost to shareholders, assuming that the political contributions paid off at the same rate as advertising expenditures. If *all* corporations (not just 50, as in the hypothetical example above) treat politics as a cost of doing business, building this into the pricing of their products, there is no effective (financial) limit to the amount of money they can spend.

Commentators often focus on the enormous sums spent on politics in the United States. From the perspective of ordinary people, "enormous" is absolutely correct. Few of us can imagine raising the $500,000 minimum needed for a single winning congressional race, never mind the amount that would be needed to change the composition of the Congress or win the presidency. From a corporate business perspective, however, the total amounts spent on politics—by all candidates, all parties, for all races—are trivial. Corporations could easily spend more, so why don't they?

We can't say with certainty, but we can point to three factors. First, business is already pretty damn dominant—where is the pressing need to put in more money? Second, people are disgusted by the influence of big money. If corporations doubled or tripled their spending—never mind if they went all out and increased it a thousandfold—a backlash might develop, and business could easily end up worse off, possibly much worse off, than it is now. Third, corporations have many other effective ways to exert influence. One indication of this is the decision by three corporations—General Motors, Monsanto, and AlliedSignal—to cease their soft money contributions (at least for now). Their decisions were apparently based far more on practical than on philosophical or moral concerns. In June 1997, Monsanto's vice president for government affairs, Linda Fisher, explained: "With the uproar over soft money, and given the fact that we hadn't found it very helpful, we decided not to do it anymore." Similarly, Bernadette Budde, a highly respected representative of the Business–Industry PAC, told the *Washington Post* that corporations were evaluating whether soft money was "as effective as channeling cash into 'issues advertising' on radio or television or giving directly to candidates through their political action committees."[24]

THE PARTY OF THE PEOPLE?

So far, we have discussed soft money as a relatively undifferentiated whole, as if no account need be taken of differences between the Republicans and Democrats. To what extent do the two major parties differ, and to what extent is there a single Money Party?

The parties do differ in some noteworthy ways, but we are far more struck by the similarities. Each party raised roughly the same amount of money; the Republicans have a slight lead ($123 million to $110 million), but that isn't very substantial. (Of course, the Democrats controlled the presidency, had a clear lead throughout the election, and still ended up with less money; it seems quite possible that the Republicans would have had a huge soft money lead had they controlled the presidency and looked like sure winners.)

Two differences stand out. First, the Republicans have eight times as many small ($1,000 or less) contributors as the Democrats (17,674 to 1,991). For many purposes this is important, but it makes surprisingly little difference in the amounts raised: $7.0 million for the Republicans, compared to $1.2 million for the Democrats, if we consider only those contributors who gave their money strictly to one party. (Split givers are another story, discussed below.) The Republicans have a total of 16,425 more contributors than the Democrats (again, after excluding split givers), with almost all of this accounted for by the $1,000-and-under group and the rest in the $1,001 to $10,000 range.[25] The two parties have almost exactly the same number of donors for those who gave more than $10,000, and raised almost exactly the same amounts of money, with the Democrats having an edge in the top group, those who gave $100,000 or more.

The other striking difference between the parties is that Democrats get a substantial amount of money from labor, while Republicans receive virtually no labor money. Unions gave Democrats $8.99 million, and Republicans only $.24 million. To the extent that campaign contributors influence policy, Republicans can completely ignore labor, while Democrats rely on labor as a minor but significant source of funding. The Democrats' funding edge from labor (an $8.75 million partisan advantage) exceeds the Republican advantage from small contributors ($5.8 million).

Overall, however, the similarities are far more noteworthy than the differences. Each party raised roughly $35 million from (mostly business-based) individual contributors, $4 or $5 million from associations (most of them business related), and most of their money from corporations—$59 million for Democrats, $82 million for Republicans. (See Table 7.) Each

TABLE 7
SOURCES OF SOFT MONEY BY POLITICAL PARTY

(IN $ MILLIONS)

TYPE OF CONTRIBUTOR	REPUBLICANS	DEMOCRATS	TOTAL
Corporations	$ 81.2	$ 58.9	$140.1
Associations	5.6	4.0	9.6
Individuals	34.6	37.0	71.6
Labor	0.2	9.0	9.2
Unclassified	1.2	0.7	1.9
TOTAL	$122.8	$109.6	$232.4

party relied primarily on large contributors, with a majority of the money in each case coming from contributors who gave more than $50,000. Both parties, the Democrats as well as the Republicans, depend on business and on megacontributors. Even within the Democratic party, labor is a very junior partner; losing *all* labor money would hurt the Democrats roughly as much as losing *one-sixth* of the corporate money (and corporations provide only a part of the total business money, which also comes from trade associations and individual owners–executives). Do the Democrats depend on business? Does a fish need water? To the extent that fundraising drives policy, Democrats obviously won't risk helping labor if it angers (or even just annoys) business.

What about the split givers, those donors who contributed to *both* political parties? We could define a split giver as any donor that gave any money at all to the "other" party (whichever party was "other" for it), or, alternatively, only as donors that split their money exactly evenly. But both those definitions are one-sided. We here define split givers as donors that gave at least 10 percent of their money to each side (that is, split their money at least 90–10, but including those who split their money 80–20 or 60–40). A PAC that contributes to both Democratic and Republican congressional candidates can reasonably argue that there is no inconsistency, that the candidates within each party differ tremendously, and that contributing to William Weld is very different from contributing to Jesse Helms. This claim is less plausible when applied to soft money, which is donated to national party organizations. Isn't it contradictory to give money to both, with one sum offsetting the other? If the purpose of a contribution is to promote the success of a candidate or a party that you agree with, then split giving is a dubious strategy. That is exactly the conclusion reached by most individual donors; more than 98 percent of the money contributed by individuals was given by contributors with a clear preference for one or the other of the two parties. Labor unions also had political convictions and stuck to them, with more than 92 percent of their money given by unions with a distinct partisan (nearly always Democratic) preference.

But if political contributions are designed to gain access in order to be able to influence government policy, then there is no reason to stick to one political party. It might make sense to hedge your bets, to be sure that whichever side wins, you have entrée. This was exactly the conclusion reached by many corporations and business associations: 46 percent of the money contributed by corporations, and 68 percent of the money given by business associations, came from split givers. Together these two groups accounted for more than 97 percent of the money contributed by split givers.

Split givers were also large givers: Among nonsplit givers, 73 percent of the contributions were for $1,000 or less; among split givers, less than 1 percent of the contributions were for $1,000 or less.

WHAT DONORS GET FOR THEIR MONEY

Soft money donors, even more than corporate PAC contributors, seek a range of outcomes. Some are ideologically committed to a party or position. They want nothing in return, and only seek victory for their causes. Gail Zappa, widow of rock musician Frank Zappa, lists herself as a "community activist." She contributed $234,500 to the Democrats; Boyden Gray, former Bush White House counsel, gave $154,100 to the Republicans. Some huge contributors hope to become ambassadors to foreign countries (such as Felix Rohatyn, giving $362,500 in 1995–96, who was appointed ambassador to France six months into Clinton's second term).

Others are delighted by the opportunity to be close to power, to receive recognition and enjoy a special relationship with the president. Clinton and his campaign tapped into this in a masterful way by inviting many top contributors to spend the night at the White House and sleep in the Lincoln Bedroom. The Democratic finance chair proposed the sleepovers, saying it would be "an excellent way to energize our key people for the coming year." Clinton eagerly accepted, saying he was "ready to start overnights right away."[26] These overnight stays were meant primarily to motivate those who were already committed. It's unlikely that any Republican became a big Democratic contributor in the hope of getting a night in the White House, but rich persons inclined to support Democrats may well have become much more active and involved and recounted their experiences to other members of their class. Bill Clinton can be incredibly charming; we have no doubt that he was usually the perfect host, friendly and genuinely interested in talking to visitors. Most of the soft money, however, came from contributors whose primary interest was in using donations to influence government policies and produce outcomes favorable to themselves and their companies.[27] Some of these concerns were very specific; others far more general.

An etiquette governs corporate requests for congressional loopholes (see Chapter 3). Proposals are put as suggestions or requests, the size of past (or future) campaign contributions may be referred to but is not explicitly or directly mentioned, and thus the illusion can be preserved that action is being taken for high-minded reasons. Most soft money discussions, including our own, focus primarily on the president. But plenty of money is raised by top congressional leaders, and the access process operates in a fashion similar to the PAC process, except at a higher level. A PAC (or individual) giving $1,000 at a regular fundraiser is likely to receive a couple of minutes with the candidate and perhaps an hour or two with a roomful of other powerful politicians and staff. Large soft money contributors to congressional funds generally receive far more extensive contact. Two examples illustrate this, one for each party. As the Senate hearings on campaign finance got under way in July 1997, Democratic senators denounced the evils of fundraising. Then they slipped away for a weekend on Nantucket Island with contributors who ponied up a minimum of $20,000. Senator Robert Toricelli of New Jersey told the hearings, "Our system of campaign finance is an invitation to any interest with a desire to compromise the policy of the United States and to use money as a lever of power."[28] At the end of the week, Toricelli boarded a corporate aircraft and flew to Nantucket for a weekend where "Democrats wanted everything kept secret—especially when it came to the real business of fundraising." What the *Globe* described as "an armada of corporate jets" landed at the Nantucket airport, many of them discharging senators accompanied by major (corporate) donors. A plane flight of this kind—a couple of hours in a luxurious plane, just the senator and the corporate executive—provides exceptional "access." In our own interviews, one corporate executive told us, "You may or may not be able to imagine the pressure that is placed on people flying in corporate airplanes." One of those senators, Richard Bryan of Nevada, said that "'Of course' the donors 'get access.'" The *Boston Globe*'s reporting was an unusual exposé, but even it protected the *donors* (though not the senators). Only a single donor was identified by name, Herb Holtz, a Boston attorney who explained that "to wonder whether there is access at high-dollar fundraisers is to wonder whether the sun is coming up."[29] Another anonymous donor noted that "the gathering was 'no different than senators meeting with middle-class people who give $200 because to some of these people, $20,000 is like $200.'" A $20,000 contribution may have been pocket change to the donors, but—given the money primary—the senators care about the cash far more than they do about the level of commitment and interest. A weekend of this sort—with sailing on a yacht, breakfast at Senator Kerry's mansion, and a host of other activities—provides all sorts of opportunities to establish personal relationships and connections—relationships and connections not available to small contributors.

Republican soft money access was even more blatant: Flyers advertising a May 1997 Republican event were left on tables at a press event. The flyers explained that contributors who pledged to give or raise $250,000 apiece would receive in return breakfast and photographs with Majority Leader Senator Trent Lott and Speaker Newt Gingrich (who promised to share their "opinions on our party's issues and strategies for the 105th Congress"), a seat at the head dinner table, and lunch with Republican House and Senate leaders.[30]

President Clinton is probably the greatest fundraiser operating today, and his famous coffees were an important part of his campaign. Nearly a hundred of these were held, with the typical session involving fewer than a dozen people. Democratic officials insist that most of these affairs followed what we would call a polite gift logic, with no crude quid pro quo. Only one person—Dan Quayle's former national security adviser—has claimed that a direct appeal for funds was made at one of the coffees, and his account was contradicted by others who attended that same event.[31] Outside the White House, the money-for-access equation was sometimes explicit: "A fundraiser told executives at the Nynex Corporation that they would receive an invitation to a White House coffee if the corporation joined the 'managing trustees' program by pledging to contribute a total of $100,000 to the Democrats."[32] Reportedly, most discussions at coffees focused primarily on background and general policy, rather than on the direct insertion of loopholes. This kind of background discussion, a chance to influence the president or top party leaders, is in significant ways different from the PAC–loophole process, though the aim is still to tilt policy toward business and the wealthy. At his press conference, Clinton defended these gatherings: "I look for ways to have genuine conversations with people. I learn things when I listen to people."[33] Some of these events, like the one held on May 13, 1996 with (CEO-level) bankers and federal regulators, had a clear agenda. Those attending included Terry Murray, president and CEO of Fleet Bank; John McCoy, chairman of Banc One; Paul Hazen, chairman and CEO of Wells Fargo Bank; and Thomas G. Labrecque, chairman and CEO of Chase Manhattan Bank, as well as Treasury Secretary Robert E. Rubin, Comptroller of the Currency Eugene A. Ludwig, Democratic National Committee Chairman Don Fowler, and party Finance Chairman Marvin S. Rosen. Other coffees ranged more widely. According to John P. Manning, president and CEO of Boston Capital Partners, who has been to the White House "often" in the last couple of years: "There was give and take on a number of business and economic issues. . . . It was everything from health care reform to why [Federal Reserve Chairman Alan] Greenspan was pushing up interest rates. The president talked the businessmen's language and asked a lot of questions. He really seemed to want businessmen's perspective on what he was doing on the economy, tax, health care."[34]

The Cheyenne–Arapaho tribes of Oklahoma also had two representatives at a $100,000 White House luncheon. Theirs is both the same story
and—in a contradiction based on their different circumstances—the opposite story. As such it provides another window on the process. The same
story: Charles Surveyor, a representative of the tribe, attended the luncheon and spoke about his tribe's wish to reclaim its ancestral land. "For 20
minutes, the President listened intently," the *New York Times* reported;
then Clinton looked Surveyor "square in the eye and said, 'We'll see what
we can do to help you.'" With that encouragement, the tribe—which had
not yet sent its check—followed through and delivered the money. This
incident closely followed the logic and customs of the campaign finance
gift system, as Lanny Davis, the White House special counsel, stressed:
There was (technically) no financial requirement to attend the luncheon
(after all, they didn't deliver the money until afterward, and no legal requirement bound them to do so), and even Mr. Surveyor's account makes
it clear that there was no explicit promise.

> "I would say, as a general matter, that it would not be surprising for
> the President to listen to a concern expressed by a visitor," Mr. Davis
> said. "In such a situation, the President would often express sympathy
> or at the very least promise to look into the matter raised."[35]

In these ways the Cheyenne–Arapaho account is the same story as a
thousand other big-ticket, personal-meeting-with-the-president, soft money
fundraisers. But as we have stressed, the money by itself is only a part of the
story, and in this instance the larger context made the incident in many
ways the opposite of the typical soft money donation. First, the Indian
tribe has what appears to be a compelling legal and moral case. Their land
was taken from them in 1883 by President Chester A. Arthur's executive
order, which specified, however, that the land was to be returned to the
tribe as soon as it was no longer used for military purposes. The fort built
there, Fort Reno, was closed in 1948, but the land was never returned to the
tribe. The land "includes unmarked graves, ritual dance grounds and an
estimated $500 million in oil and gas reserves."[36] The presence of oil re-
serves is both an incentive for the tribe and, presumably, the source of
opposition from other groups who hope to grab the land for themselves.
Second, the tribe is not a rich corporation and doesn't have the kinds of
power that back up the typical corporate megacontribution. The tribe has
11,000 members, more than 60 percent of whom are unemployed, and
those with jobs earn an average annual income of $6,074. In what appears
to be a perverse consequence of the tribe's poverty and lack of power, in
order to gain admission to the luncheon they were actually charged twice

as much as some of the rich corporate donors—the Burlington Northern and Santa Fe Railway companies paid only $50,000 each for their lunches, though Beneficial Corporation did cough up $100,000. Raising the money was a real hardship for the tribe, but based on Clinton's pledge, they cashed in their certificates of deposit and, when that still wasn't enough, found additional money. (The money—which the Democrats, due to an "oversight," never reported—was returned after it became a source of controversy.) Similarly, the tribe had earlier tried to see Oklahoma's Republican Senator Don Nickles, but was denied a meeting. The tribe drew the obvious lesson: Access depends on campaign contributions, not on a constituency relationship or the merits of the case. Third, tribal members don't understand how the Washington game is played, and as a consequence are continually outraged by the duplicity they encounter. Due to their weak and vulnerable position, they are also continually shaken down by assorted other powerful figures. For example, Nathan Landow, a Democratic fundraiser and wealthy developer, offered to help the tribe if they would guarantee him 10 percent of the oil and gas revenues. Tribal leaders said that "Mr. Landow told the tribe that without the deal, they would never get their land back."[37] This entire incident, so like an old-fashioned melodrama—tribal leaders fighting hard for what in justice is already theirs, with payoffs to corrupt figures who doublecross and threaten them—has no happy ending.

IS IT ONLY CLINTON?

Because soft money has exploded in recent years, and because Clinton has been such a masterful fundraiser who so thoroughly enjoyed the process, much of the media discussion has made it seem that Clinton and Gore were themselves the problem, that difficulties arose solely because of their failure to observe a set of rules that others implicitly recognized and honored. Clinton and Gore may be the worst offenders,[38] but they are hardly the first or the only offenders. Consider George Bush. The Republican Eagles group, whose membership requires a $15,000 contribution, visited Bush at the White House at least ten times. "Team 100" members ($175,000 over four years) were also wined and dined at the White House, entertainment that included a Bush-hosted dinner just eight days before he left office.[39] Michael Kojima gave $400,000 personally and another $300,000 through his company, International Marketing Bureau, to the "family values" candidate, George Bush. The only problem: Kojima owed more than $100,000 in child support to one of his four ex-wives, more than $100,000 to another ex-wife, his teenage sons called him a con man, and he was in debt to former business partners who were suing him to recover the money—money Kojima claimed he didn't have. The "office" of the International Marketing Bureau turned out to be a drawer in the desk of one of his ex-wives. The Los Angeles County district attorney's office filed suit demanding that the Republicans turn over the money owed for child support, and Kojima's business creditors demanded the money they were owed. The Republicans, however, refused to return the money: Evidently, deadbeat dads are far more acceptable than foreigners, and the Republicans were willing to keep money owed to children.

Or consider the companies and individuals who helped pay for Dan Quayle's putting green. The vice president's mansion was reportedly in need of basic repairs; Congress paid for those. But the Quayles felt there was also a pressing need for a private putting green and swimming pool. Rather than have the government pay the bill, they solicited tax-deductible gifts from their friends. We believe that it would have been much cheaper for the taxpayers to have built Quayle a putting green—in fact, an entire golf course—rather than have him receive it as a gift from his "friends," including:

◆ William Cafritz, a director of the failed National Bank of Washington. His brother Conrad defaulted on $17 million in unsecured loans from the bank.

◆ Lucy Crow Billingsley, a defendant in a suit by federal regulators focused on the failure of First RepublicBank Corp. The bailout of the bank is expected to cost $3 billion.

◆ Paul Arneson, a lawyer-lobbyist hired by Kellogg's to seek a change in the rules about the sugar content of cereals distributed under the Women, Infants, and Children (WIC) program. Kellogg had been excluded from the program because its cereals were too sweet; most of the business went to General Mills.

◆ Heinz Prechter, owner of American Sunroof Corporation. Prechter was one of the executives who accompanied Bush on his trip to Japan. Bush pressured Japan to buy more American products; Prechter used the occasion to wrap up a lucrative deal to supply sunroofs for Honda's American-made cars.

◆ Raymond Kravis, an oil consultant named in a number of suits by stockholders of Texas International who claimed they had been misled about the company's reserves. Raymond is the father of Henry, one-third of the famous Kohlberg–Kravis–Roberts buyout specialists who have negotiated tens of billions of dollars of deals. Henry reports that he and his father "talk about business all the time and have fun doing it."

None of these contributions counted as soft money, nor did they need to be reported to the FEC. Although Quayle's office did make available a list of contributors, we're willing to bet you didn't see this featured in your local newspaper. Was there anything illegal about these contributions? No. When Dan Quayle practiced on his private putting green, did he feel just a little gratitude to the friends and donors who made this possible? Is there a possibility that this influenced government policy?

A SMOKING GUN?

Congressional investigators of campaign finance scandals focused on the China connection, trying to show that foreigners—and still worse, certain foreigners who did business with the Chinese government—had found ways to contribute substantial amounts of soft money to the U.S. elections. This was seen as the potential scandal.

Though no one in Congress seemed interested in doing so, it might be worthwhile to begin at the other end, and to consider the donors of soft money, and what—if anything—they might have hoped to accomplish through their donations. The largest soft money contributor was Philip Morris, which gave $3,345,036—with close to 85 percent of it going to Republicans, but still almost a half-million going to Democrats. Seagram held second place,[40] and in third place was the R.J. Reynolds Tobacco Company, with $1,277,231. Other substantial contributions were made by Brown & Williamson Tobacco, $672,500 (the 20th-largest giver); the Tobacco Institute, at $517,847 the 40th-largest contributor; the U.S. Tobacco Company, $513,343 and the 41st-largest contributor; and the Smokeless Tobacco Council, $268,100.

These contributions were made at a time when the tobacco industry was under unprecedented assault. Many institutions and localities have restricted the right to smoke in public (or even private) places, new taxes have been imposed, antismoking campaigns have been launched with public money, congressional committees have held hearings, the Food and Drug Administration has considered regulating cigarettes as drugs, states have sued to recover the costs of the Medicaid money they spend on smoking-related illnesses, inside whistle-blowers (suffering from cancer) have exposed company documents, individual and class-action lawsuits threaten to win enormous judgments, and a host of other initiatives demonstrate a serious potential to drastically reduce tobacco consumption—or even to outlaw it entirely. The legal, cultural, and political climate is now more hostile to tobacco companies than at any time in the past. The combined initiatives currently underway could conceivably bankrupt cigarette manufacturers.

If you make your money by selling a product that is the single largest cause of preventable death, a product that annually ruins the lives and the health of hundreds of thousands of people, how do you respond to these assaults? The answer, of course, is: every way you can. Some years ago Philip Morris and R.J. Reynolds diversified; Philip Morris now includes Miller Beer and Kraft Foods, and RJR includes Nabisco. Philip Morris funds the arts, especially such high arts as ballet and modern dance that are patronized primarily by members of the elite, and tobacco companies are prime sponsors of various sporting events. Tobacco company lawyers are legendary: The industry has won virtually every legal case so far. Its huge stable of lobbyists on retainer includes Haley Barbour, former chair of the Republican National Committee, Howard Baker, former Republican majority leader, and George Mitchell, former Democratic majority leader in the Senate, as well as Ann Richards, former governor of Texas. Industry advertising budgets provide the leverage to effectively control the nonadvertising content of a range of publications (see Chapter 6). And, of course, cigarette companies orchestrate a fabulous advertising and PR operation.

One example may illustrate the myriad ways the industry exercises its influence. Philip Morris secretly hired a public relations firm, and the firm then used money provided by Philip Morris and other tobacco companies to create "Contributions Watch," which presented itself as an independent and nonpartisan group. Contributions Watch conducted a study of the state-level campaign contributions of trial lawyers, who represent one of the biggest threats to the tobacco industry. As a nonprofit, tax-exempt group, Contributions Watch did not have to disclose the source of its funding. Its study was reported at length in the *Wall Street Journal* and the *Weekly Standard.*[41]

The political front is a vital part of the industry's package of defense mechanisms, and soft money is one key element of a political strategy. Industry executives make individual contributions to key politicians, and tobacco companies give large quantities of PAC money, including $850,000 by Philip Morris, $652,000 by R.J. Reynolds, $554,000 by U.S. Tobacco, and $380,000 by Brown & Williamson. These donations help cigarette manufacturers to introduce themselves to legislators, establish relationships, make friends in Congress, and create a sense of obligation in the minds of many politicians. Given how visible the issue has become, few legislators will change their public stance in response to a few thousand (or tens of thousands of) dollars. Nor will a presidential candidate or major political party change sides for a million (or a few million) dollars. But even for this kind of high-visibility issue, the devil is often in the details, and here the access process, at either the congressional or presidential levels, can determine how much bite a policy actually has.

On June 20, 1997, the tobacco companies reached an agreement with the attorneys general of numerous states, an agreement that both involves huge costs to the tobacco companies *and* has the potential to guarantee the financial, legal, and political viability of the cigarette industry into the far distant future. The projected cost of the settlement was $368.5 billion dollars. The "settlement" settled nothing: It was simply one more step, admittedly a huge step, in a continuing battle.

The tobacco industry (and the attorneys general) had wanted the agreement approved swiftly, preferably by the end of the summer. President Clinton did not even respond until mid-September, and by that time it was already clear that the settlement was dead, that Congress would not act until 1998, and, when it did so, would want an active role in shaping any deal. Clinton's proposals, intentionally left sketchy to allow him room for future maneuver, involved changes that would have doubled the cost of the settlement.[42] We can imagine the scene in a tobacco company executive suite the day after Clinton's announcement: The head of the government relations unit is called in, with the CEO yelling, "You moron! We have to shell out an extra $300 billion! Why didn't you give Clinton and the Democrats an extra $30 million—that would only be one-hundredth of 1 percent of the extra money we're being asked to shell out."[43] The cost of the original proposed settlement—never mind any later increases—was about 50,000 times as much as the industry had contributed in soft money during 1995–96. What looked like a major soft money expenditure seems tiny by comparison.

As we write, the final shape of the settlement—if any—is undecided. But the issue perfectly illustrates the enormous sums that are potentially at stake in the political process. Some of the details already being discussed demonstrate the ways the access process broadly defined can make the difference: One arrangement might sound good to the public, be presented as involving enormous costs, but actually be easy for the industry to live with; another arrangement might sound quite similar, but double the costs to the industry and increase tenfold the risk that the industry would be unable to survive at all. We here review some of these details, but it is important to remember that the most successful operation of the access process occurs when the public does not know what is happening. The odds are that the final arrangement, whatever it is, will include obscure details that will be understood by only a handful of tobacco company lawyers, who look forward to chuckling over the hidden clauses and their implications after settlement. Recognizing that even on such a high-visibility issue many details remain obscure, let us consider a few of the major issues subject to political negotiation and compromise, issues where friends in high office, and feelings of obligation could mean billions—even hundreds of billions—to the tobacco industry.

TAX DEDUCTIBILITY. The projected cost of the original settlement was $368.5 billion. Both the politicians who negotiated the deal and the tobacco companies had an incentive to inflate this figure ("look at how much we stuck them for"; "look at how much we already have to pay"). The deal provided, however, that these costs would be tax deductible, which meant that taxpayers, not tobacco companies, would pay a third or more of the total cost. Clinton proposed abolishing that provision; at stake is more than $100 billion. The industry may have outsmarted itself: It managed to slip into the 1997 balanced budget deal a provision that $50 billion in tobacco taxes would count as part of the industry's contribution to any settlement, a provision so carefully hidden that it went unmentioned in news reports on the budget deal. When that secret arrangement was exposed, Congress voted by an overwhelming margin to reverse it: 95 to 3 in the Senate and by a voice vote in the House.

DISCLOSURE. In announcing the deal, Mississippi Attorney General Mike Moore said it would force disclosure of internal company documents and "make sure that every single person, not only in America but this entire world, knows the truth about what the tobacco industry has done."[44] In fact, however, the settlement permitted the industry to conceal all documents covered by attorney–client privilege. Critics could contest those claims by appealing to a three-judge panel, but the courts have been reluctant to interfere with the attorney-client privilege, and the tobacco industry lawyers have undoubtedly made sure, for many years, that all key documents are covered by privilege. Minnesota Attorney General Hubert H. Humphrey III, a critic of the settlement, says "This deal allows the lies and cover-ups to live on."

LAWSUIT LIMITS. Up to the time of the settlement, the tobacco industry had a virtually perfect record in fighting lawsuits, but tort litigation against the companies was beginning to make headway, and successful suits could quickly bankrupt the industry, just as they did with asbestos. The settlement imposes a $5 billion annual cap on claims and a $1 million limit on individual awards. The latter provision reduces lawyers' incentives to take the cases and dig up new incriminating material. Five billion a year is a lot of money, but the estimated cost of smoking-related illnesses is $88 billion a year, even without factoring in punitive damages.[45]

FEDERAL REGULATION. One of the greatest threats to the tobacco industry is the possibility that the federal government might treat tobacco as a drug and subject it to the same regulations that cover other drugs. Business usually advocates cost–benefit analyses, but, in this case, if a neutral arbitrator were making a first-time appraisal of cigarettes' benefits (smokers enjoy the product, become addicted to it, it stimulates them) and costs (lung cancer, heart disease, and a host of other illnesses), clearly cigarettes would never escape regulation. Any actual decision by the federal government would not be made on neutral technical grounds, but in relation to the political realities and balance of forces. The terms and possibilities of any potential federal regulation are absolutely vital to the future of the tobacco industry; former Surgeon General C. Everett Koop and former Food and Drug Administration chief David Kessler objected to the terms of the settlement, arguing that it would effectively limit or prohibit federal regulation. Clinton declared he would not accept any reduction in the Food and Drug Administration's authority to regulate nicotine as a drug.

YOUTH SMOKING. Under the agreement, smoking by people eighteen or younger must fall by 30 percent within five years, 50 percent in seven years, and 60 percent within ten years. If it does not do so, tobacco companies as a group are required to pay a fine of $80 million for each percentage point outside those targets, up to a maximum of $2 billion annually. These penalties may sound stiff, but companies can get 75 percent of their fines rebated if they have made good-faith efforts to reduce smoking, and the fines would be tax deductible. Clinton proposed that if youth smoking did not decline, the price of a pack of cigarettes should rise by as much as $1.50 a pack.

The tobacco industry is using every weapon available to it—including soft money, lobbying, and PAC contributions—in a rearguard holding action, using the access process to fight through the details of every controversy. Most business political activity today, whether offensive or defensive, adopts this access approach of winning small victories away from the public eye. But some businesses, and at a few points many businesses, advocate a different strategy: an ideological push for the positions that business believes in,[46] rather than a series of compromises. The next chapter considers this ideological orientation.

◆ 5

IDEOLOGY AND POLITICAL SHIFTS

S O FAR WE HAVE DESCRIBED WHAT MIGHT BE CALLED CORPORATE-politics-as-usual": campaign contributions to incumbents—any incumbents—in order to gain access, with that access used to try to win special benefits for the donor's company or industry. But in each election a few corporations do not follow this strategy, pursuing instead an ideological approach by contributing to "pro-business" candidates whose election is in doubt. First, we describe this minority tendency: the alternative perspective of these corporations and the differing challenges of their day-to-day operations. Next, we examine the 1980 election, where we show business behaving in strikingly unusual ways, best indicated by their aggressively conservative campaign contributions. In 1980 Republican electoral successes were strongly associated with a change in corporate political activity. We then look at the 1994 election, the only other election of the past twenty-five years that brought a sweeping Republican triumph. In 1994, in contrast to 1980, business campaign contributions were overwhelmingly pragmatic and therefore cannot explain the Republican electoral victory. But election outcomes, we argue, are not so important as policy changes, and for policy change extraelectoral mobilization matters more than the election results themselves. Specifically, for this period, the actions of business were decisive. The chapter concludes with a section that, at this early point in time, is necessarily speculative. Because business behavior was unusual in 1980, but not in 1994, because campaign contributions provide strong evidence

of extraelectoral business mobilization in 1980 but not in 1994, we therefore predict that the policy changes of 1980–1982 will ultimately be judged
much more decisive than those of 1994–1996. We recognize our thesis is
contrary to much of both popular and academic thinking, and that it is, in
fact, too early to make a final judgment.

◆ CHARACTERISTICS OF AN IDEOLOGICAL ORIENTATION

Criticism of an access approach comes not only from liberals and public
interest groups, but also from conservatives sympathetic to business and
from business leaders themselves. Their complaint is not that business uses
campaign contributions to win lower taxes or freedom from government
regulation, but that business isn't bold enough: that it should fight for
more sweeping benefits and should not be so willing to compromise with
(and support) congressional moderates and liberals. When Ronald Reagan
was preparing to run for president, he addressed the Public Affairs Council, the organization for corporate public affairs officers, asking, "Why does
half of the business PAC money go to candidates who may not be friends of
business? The best thing that you can hope for by following an anti-busi-
ness, incumbent contribution policy is that the alligator will eat you last."[1]
William Simon, former secretary of the treasury and member of the boards of
Dart Industries, Xerox, INA, and Citibank,[2] put the point in stronger terms:

> Businessmen, too, have intensified the despotic regulatory trends by
> their secretive attempts to fight them—not by means of courageous
> open battle, but by the pathetically short-range and cowardly attempts
> to bribe those with political power over their destinies. . . . Business,
> on the whole, has been gripped by cowardly silence in the face of this
> consistent violation of its liberty and interests. It is its final, and possi-
> bly its worst, betrayal of the free enterprise system.[3]

Corporations that reject what Simon calls "appeasement on a breath-
taking scale"[4] adopt an alternative approach, a self-consciously ideological
orientation supporting "pro-business, free enterprise" candidates, especially
if they are *not* incumbents. Ideological corporations try to target their money
to close races where a few extra dollars might change the outcome.

RELATION TO LOBBYING

In the pure case, the ideological corporation separates its campaign contributions from lobbying activity. Its basic orientation and mission is to contribute money in ways that will encourage Congress to be as supportive as

possible of business interests in general. This means that it gives donations only during election years to pro-business candidates who are in competitive races and face opponents less sympathetic to business. Corporations that are primarily pragmatic may also follow this basic approach for two, five, or ten of their yearly donations, applying an entirely different set of criteria for these decisions from the set they use for the bulk of their donations.

Our focus in this chapter is on ideological *corporate* PACs. Alongside them is a set of independent, free-standing, conservative (and ultraconservative) PACs not affiliated with any other organization. Groups such as the Committee for the Survival of a Free Congress raise their money primarily through direct-mail solicitations. Because these mailings are expensive, the costs of fundraising absorb a substantial portion of all the money they take in. Executives may contribute to these groups in addition to their corporation's PAC. These PACs were important in the 1980 election and continue to exist, though their importance has declined in recent years.

Ideological corporations generally began interviews with statements of their goals and philosophy:

The goal of our PAC is simple, and it sounds trite, and you've probably heard it a hundred times over, but the goal of our PAC is to elect pro-business candidates to Congress and keep them there once they are elected. And that's simply it.

Or, as another put it:

We are a Midwest conservative company and yet we believe in free trade, we believe in productivity, we believe in reasonable regulation, we believe that business is good for people, business helps people, and we want the people we elect to reflect that philosophy. We don't think that business is money-gouging monsters.

Some primarily ideological corporations also articulated company-specific goals more similar to those of access-oriented corporations:

The purpose of our PAC of course is to support specifically the company interest and the interest of our industry in general and beyond that what we consider to be the free enterprise system.

The basic goals of ideological corporations dictate that they not be involved in promoting the company's immediate interests. A very few corporations make it a policy not to have any lobbying operation:

We don't have a Washington lobbyist staff, we don't have lobbyists in state capitals. All we have is myself. I run a governmental affairs program as well as our PAC. Our governmental affairs program is more of a grassroots network. We have over a hundred plants across the country. We rely on those employee relations managers, personnel manag-

ers, and the plant managers to be our contacts, to be our lobbyists. So
the goal of our PAC is not necessarily to aid our lobbyist and to make
the job that much easier. It is more of a philosophical role. It's a very
ideological role to elect pro-business candidates.

More commonly, a company had lobbyists, but kept them at arm's length
from the PAC. One chair of a PAC committee explained the rules he followed when he went to Washington for meetings of the National Association of Business Political Action Committees (NABPAC):

Some of the people that were in this meeting with me were going over
to their lobbyists to have dinner and then to get a list of who they were
supposed to give money to. And that just does not happen. We don't
do this. That kind of session would never take place. I might go see
Bill X who is our lobbyist there who is a friend of mine. But it would
not be on that subject. He would not broach the topic.

Another company's executive reported:

I do know of cases where a legislator has done a couple of things to
help us, voted on a couple of issues in our favor. People have asked to
give them money, and the committee has turned them down for the
simple reason that overall they don't match what we are looking for.

However, not all ideological corporations are able to maintain their
ideological purity. As noted in the last chapter, ideological corporations are
sometimes driven to access behavior, giving $250 to Representative Henry
Waxman (Democrat–California) and others of his kind, even though it
makes the PAC officer "cringe" to do so, or supporting Democrats despite
the owner's commitment to Republicans. Another PAC officer who articulated the corporation's goals in terms of support for the free enterprise
system nonetheless acknowledged:

I don't like to think of the PAC as being a slush fund for the Washington office, but by the same token I recognize that we are sending these
people in to discuss issues and our positions with members of the Congress. . . . We like to be independent here, and yet we recognize that a
PAC should be somewhat supportive of the Washington office. I don't
think it makes sense to have a PAC if you aren't somewhat supportive of
your lobbying effort.

On the other hand, some ideological corporations argued that the separa-
tion from lobbying might actually make things easier for their lobbyist:

It takes the pressure off of them in Washington. For example, our
office there just sent me a stack of invitations to fundraisers that must
have been two feet high. What the Washington office does is call the
senator and say, "I'm sorry; this belongs to the PAC. We've sent it down

to Texas and what they do is their business. We have no control over it." Then they don't have to shell out $500 to everybody in the city. I think it is to their advantage not to be tied closely to us.

This argument was, of course, self-serving for the chair of the PAC steering committee. It absolved him of responsibility for thinking about these issues or considering what costs the company might be paying for its ideological purity.

CANDIDATES AND RACES

Since the corporation's aim is to have an impact on the ideological character of the Congress, money needs to be targeted to races where it can make a difference. In most years, most incumbents are reelected, so contributing to incumbents is unlikely to influence the composition of Congress, except in close elections. Moreover, most incumbents have little difficulty raising money, so an additional contribution is unlikely to have a noticeable impact on their situations. Therefore, a strongly ideological corporation is reluctant to contribute even to a conservative pro-business incumbent. One official summarized this position:

> The guidelines are that you've got to have a competitive race for us to make a contribution to you. You've got to need the money in terms of the sources available to your opponent. In addition to that, you've got to be meritorious in terms of public policy values that are reflected by our PAC.

Pro-business views are not enough; the money must make a difference. Races with predictable outcomes don't merit support, nor do races between opponents with similarly pro-business views.

This strategy means that ideological PACs must be reconciled to frequent losses:

> We like to win more than we lose, but we're not in it to pick all winners. That's a pretty easy thing to do. But to give where someone's going to win with 85 percent of the vote—that's not really what we're doing with the money from our managers. In fact, that's not what we do at all.

Sometimes an ideological corporation gives to a challenger who is virtually certain to lose, in the hope that the candidate can be competitive in a future election.

> You can say it's a mistake when one [of the candidates we supported] only comes in with 35 percent of the vote, but we just have to acknowledge that ahead of time. That we know that that guy is not going to do

real well. And maybe not this time, but maybe next year or two years or four years down the road. Somebody has to give him the support along the way.

Despite a willingness to support some candidates who are virtually sure to lose, most of the time the aim is to contribute to competitive races.

A guy who has no chance I usually won't support, although I have a friend running in California whose chances are minuscule and I would give him $500. Some of that money I call crapshoot money, but that's less than 5 percent of our total contributions.

This means that the corporation makes every effort to determine how viable the candidate is, which requires collecting information from all possible sources, trying to get polling data, but also finding out whether the candidate has been able to attract enough money: "I get the FEC [Federal Election Commission] reports as up-to-date as I can to see how much money they have. That will give me an idea if they really have a chance, whether they are mounting a credible challenge." Others agree:

The other aspect of this is we try to get as good a fix as we can on money, and that's always tough. Maybe it's not necessary that the candidate with the most money wins, but it's tough to throw dollars where you don't have a chance. Although we've done some venture capital, and we don't mind doing venture capital, we're not going to do that all the time. We try to get a fix on money. We try to get some polling data.

This also means that ideological PACs generally give most or all of their money during the election year. Access PACs are giving the money to gain access and establish relationships, which can be done at any time, so there is no need for them to concentrate on the period preceding an election. Ideological corporations, on the other hand, don't want to contribute unless there is a close contest between candidates with opposing views, and that usually can't be determined more than six or eight months ahead of time.

We don't make contributions in nonelection years. We just don't. We have discretionary money that our members have given us for the purpose of attempting to influence an election. It's a good idea to have an election if you're trying to influence it. So this idea that has now become popular, beginning to raise money five years before your election; or the moment you're elected, if you're in the House, have a fundraiser to celebrate your victory, is fine; it's a great way to take care of your children's education if you're in public life, but we don't make any contributions except in election years.[5]

This also means that such corporations refuse to help candidates retire their debts: "We don't make any contributions after the election is over; it's extraordinarily difficult to have an effect on the election by giving money after the election is over."

A FORMULA FOR SELF-DESTRUCTION

Ideological corporations are likely to emphasize the need for business to support and contribute to the integrity of the political system:

We've got a lot of respect for the American political system and think that American business has a tremendous stake in the American political system, and think that American business ought to try very, very, hard to contribute to its integrity.

In this view, businesses undermine the integrity of the system if they contribute to candidates "hostile" to business in hopes of gaining a narrow short-run advantage for themselves. Speaking of access contributions, William Simon argues, "If American business consciously wished to devise a formula for self-destruction, it could not do better than this."[6] Moreover, many executives of ideological PACs identify members of Congress as enemies even if they are prepared to do favors for business. In our interviews they not infrequently labeled such members "communistic," a term they use as description, not in jest. Their implicit reasoning seems to be similar to that of neoconservative Irving Kristol: "What rules the world is ideas, because ideas define the way reality is perceived."[7] Therefore, it is not enough for members to be willing to craft dozens of loopholes so that business can prevail in reality. Doing so cedes its control over public discussion in order to win short-run advantages. Practical control through compromise and wording change is not enough—business must define the broad terms of public debate, must insist on candidates who will speak up for business and the free enterprise system.[8]

Most of the time the people we interviewed avoided open criticism of other corporations, but a few did express negative opinions. One pragmatic PAC officer thought it "nonsense" to have an ideological PAC: "If you want to have an ideological PAC, then go join AMA or the National Rifle Association or whatever the hell their cause is." In his view, ideological PACs are "a manifestation of the leadership. In those situations the boss sets the tone." A few other pragmatic executives made similar comments. Ideological corporate executives generally noted the access approach and simply said, "That's their philosophy and which we've already said we don't agree with that. That's their business." Occasionally one would explain that, at one meeting or another, "I felt very comfortable talking about the way we do it versus the way they do it. They looked at me like we were a little crazy but we think they are strange too." Ideological corporation officials reported that occasionally the pragmatics' response was an antagonistic, "Oh, so you think you're so pure."

One of the most ideological executives we interviewed, a member of the board of directors of his Fortune 500 corporation, openly expressed his anger at the behavior of most corporations and his inability to understand why they acted as they did.

I think valid candidates ought to be able to wage a decent political campaign in the U.S. I believe that to be true, and I don't like a system that works in such a way that they can't. I think it is a good, good intelligent thing for American business to try to make some contribution toward that kind of a political system; because if there's anybody that's a stakeholder in the system, it's American business.

And if they keep fucking around with it long enough, and trying to suborn it by throwing money at it, they're going to have hell to pay. Because there doesn't happen to be another political system on the face of the earth that is so hospitable and so good to people who like to try to make money in business, industry, and commercial enterprises.

Now that's the basis of why we're not an access PAC, and that's the basis of why we're so Goddamned dumb. And we've got all these smart sons of bitches that know exactly what to do with their money: Find out who wins by 75 percent plus, give them a lot of money, particularly if they're chairman of a committee of importance to you.

I can't figure out what their motive is. I just look at it and look at it and I just can't figure it out. Neither can anybody else; it's just because they like chairmen better than they like everybody else. Chairmen who don't need the money and who couldn't lose if they were caught in *flagrante delicto* with the governor's wife in the public square of the capital. And they're shoving money in there. What is their motive?

◆ CONSERVATIVE SHIFT

THE IDEOLOGICAL MOBILIZATION OF THE 1970S

In most elections the vast majority of corporations pursue an access (or pragmatic) strategy. But in the 1980 election a large number were ideological, risk-taking, conservatives. To understand the changing corporate mood we need to go back at least to the early 1960s. During the 1960s, a series of social movements challenged many aspects of the established order. Blacks undertook the first major movement, first in the South and then in the North. Urban riots, Malcolm X, and the Black Panther party demonstrated that this opposition could become militant and threatening. Strong student and antiwar movements put thousands of people in the streets and took over buildings. Young men resisted the draft or deserted the military. In the late 1960s and early 1970s, the women's and environmentalist movements grew rapidly. Although most of these challenges to authority did not focus primarily on corporations, corporations increasingly felt their impact, both in worker rebellions and in demands for increased social responsibility. The host of "public interest" organizations initiated or influenced by Ralph Nader constituted what was, in some ways, the mildest and most mainstream social movement. But it was also the movement that most specifically, in arguing for more regulation of business, targeted corporate practices.

Richard Nixon, a conservative Republican, won a narrow victory in 1968 and a landslide in 1972. But policy does not depend on politicians' personal preferences, or even on electoral outcomes, so much as it does on the mobilization of power outside the electoral arena. In the 1980s, that was primarily business power. At the end of the 1960s, the forces with the power to shape the national agenda were a set of social movements. As a result, Nixon's administration enacted a host of key liberal measures on the domestic front.[9]

From 1969 through 1972, virtually the entire American business community experienced a series of political setbacks without parallel in the postwar period. In the space of only four years, Congress enacted a significant tax-reform bill, four major environmental laws, an occupational safety and health act, and a series of additional consumer-protection statutes. The government also created a number of important new regulatory agencies, including the Environmental Protection Administration (EPA), the Occupational Safety and Health Administration (OSHA), and the Consumer Product Safety Commission (CPSC), investing them with broad powers over a wide range of business decisions. In contrast to the 1960s, many of the regulatory laws enacted during the early 1970s were broader in scope and more ambitious in their objectives.[10]

As a result, corporations felt under attack and vulnerable. It appeared that even a conservative Republican president such as Nixon would inevitably be pushed to support more and more regulation of business and in-

terference with the market. Top business executives meeting in 1973 articulated their feeling of vulnerability: "We are fighting for our lives," "We are
fighting a delaying action." As one said, "If we don't take action now, we
will see our own demise. We will evolve into another social democracy."[11]

These domestic setbacks were matched by problems in the international
arena. The United States defeat in Vietnam, the rise of OPEC, and, a few
years later, the overthrow of the Shah made U.S. multinational corporations question the security of their overseas investments. Declining U.S.
economic competitiveness, the rise of Japanese and European competitors,
and the burgeoning U.S. trade deficit, made it impossible to solve domestic problems by offering costly concessions to U.S. workers and activist
movements. In the 1974 congressional elections, the Democrats made huge
gains, adding 5 seats in the Senate and 48 in the House to what had already
been secure majorities. This aftermath of Watergate only increased the sense
that the tide was running against business, that mobilization was needed to
prevent the United States from becoming a social democracy.

It would be easy to argue that business concerns reflected more para-
noia than reality. Most of the new regulatory agencies were weak, lacked
money for enforcement, and were inclined to accommodate corporate interests. For example, in 1971, when there were 47,000 commercially available chemical compounds, the Occupational Safety and Health
Administration had set legal limits on concentration levels for only about
500 of them, leaving the remaining 99 percent unregulated. Most workplaces were never inspected, and if violations were found the average fine
was only about $25. Things changed little over the years: A 1985 study by
the Congressional Office of Technology Assessment reported that the average fine for a "serious violation" was only $172, despite the fact that such
violations were defined as those that created a "substantial probability of
death or serious physical harm".[12] But while these regulations were often
weak and enforcement minimal, they established a precedent, both creating a material–institutional base for government regulation, and defining
the "public interest" as different from, and opposed to, corporate interests.
Business understandably felt threatened, and had it not responded, these
initial steps might have led to more far-reaching changes.

In the mid to late 1970s, business began its own countermobilization,
operating simultaneously on many fronts. Money was shifted out of liberal
and moderate think tanks and policy organizations (the Brookings Institution, Council on Foreign Relations, and Committee for Economic Development) to newly founded or reinvigorated conservative equivalents (the
American Enterprise Institute, Hoover Institution, and Heritage Founda-

tion). In 1965 and 1970, the three moderate organizations had more than triple the funding of the three conservative ones; by 1975, this advantage was much diminished, and by 1980, the conservative organizations spent substantially more than the moderate ones.[13]

Advocacy advertising expanded enormously. Traditional advertising tries to sell a product: Presta-Glop cleans teeth whiter than Ultra-Goo. Advocacy advertising has no explicit connection with a corporation's products but, rather, it promotes a message, often explicitly political, sometimes simply "image." In 1979 David Vogel estimated corporations were spending one-third of their advertising budgets on such campaigns.[14] The business press began the admittedly difficult task of redefining reality: "It will be a hard pill for many Americans to swallow—the idea of doing with less so that big business can have more. . . . Nothing that this nation, or any other nation, has done in modern economic history compares in difficulty with the selling job that must now be done to make people accept the new reality."[15]

Business also began to exert its muscle in more straightforwardly political arenas. One crucial step was the rise to prominence of the Business Roundtable. Founded in the early 1970s, the Roundtable differed from earlier business policy organizations in two crucial respects. First, it was open only to chief executive officers of corporations—most earlier organizations had allowed in a few hand-picked academics, not to mention corporate vice presidents. Second, previous organizations focused primarily on the process of developing "appropriate" policy, which generally involved long-range study commissions and a primary focus on the executive branch. The Roundtable, by contrast, devoted most of its energy to direct lobbying activities, often focusing on Congress, the site of many of business's political losses.

The Roundtable's influence and business's increasingly aggressive conservativism were dramatically demonstrated in the Labor Law Reform battles of 1978. Labor was a key source of both money and organizational clout for many Democratic candidates and the northern Democratic party. The Democrats controlled the presidency and had near-record majorities in both houses of Congress. The Labor Law Reform Bill was labor's number-one priority, although its measures were exceptionally mild. A few employers had been flouting the labor laws and appealing all adverse decisions by the National Labor Relations Board (NLRB). This won them years of delay. Then, if necessary, the corporations accepted the very mild penalties they received when convicted. The Labor Law Reform Bill prohibited such delaying tactics by providing that the decision of the NLRB would apply during the appeals process, until and unless a company won an appeal. It also stiffened the penalties for violations in order to reduce the economic incentives to break the law and pay the penalties. Unions saw the bill as an attempt to isolate a few companies that had been systematically violating the law. Therefore, they expected most major corporations to support the bill. Given the mild nature of the bill and Democratic dominance of government, it appeared the bill would pass relatively easily.

Instead, business mounted a major campaign against the legislation, spending more than $5 million to fight this one bill. In essence, business used all the normal tactics of pragmatic, access-oriented campaigns, but this time for the ideological purpose of defeating, rather than simply modifying, an important bill. Corporations pulled out all the stops: They cashed in their access chips so that government relations personnel could meet with members of Congress and explain their opposition. Managers from legislators' home districts were brought in to make the company's case. Small business owners were summoned as foot soldiers.

> Those representatives of big business who were lobbying Senator Lawton Chiles, Democrat of Florida, heard him complain that most of the pressure he had received had come from large corporations. Almost immediately, the large corporations switched tactics, abandoning the attempt to directly lobby Chiles, and instead used their corporate jets to fly small-business owners from Florida to Washington to take over the job of convincing Chiles.[16]

The business campaign was coordinated by the Business Roundtable. Big business has enormous resources, not just in money to spend, but in its ability to mobilize others. In 1979, when Chrysler was trying to win a federal loan guarantee, it produced a list of the employment it generated in each congressional district. The list for just one Indiana Republican's district included 436 companies with sales totaling over $29 million.[17] Since the Business Roundtable included a couple of hundred such companies, it was able to put enormous pressure on members. Labor law reform may have been the most important issue, but, in 1978, business had launched similar campaigns around consumer protection and taxes, winning significant victories in both.

THE PAC ROLE IN THE MOBILIZATION

Nineteen seventy-eight was also the year when business changed its campaign contribution behavior. The change resulted from a coordinated effort, not simply from a set of isolated decisions. During the 1978 election, two key letters circulated within the corporate PAC community. The first was from Justin Dart, CEO of Dart Industries, and a personal friend of Ronald Reagan (though later also a friend and supporter of Bill Clinton). The second mailing was sent to all members of the Business Roundtable by Donald Kendall, CEO of Pepsico and chair of the Roundtable, with an accompanying analysis by Clark MacGregor of United Technologies. Dart's analysis was framed in more aggressively conservative tones, but both communications contained the same basic message: Corporations should reduce their contributions to liberal and moderate (mostly Democratic) incumbents, and be more "attentive to candidates' records on the broader, free-enterprise issues."[18] Kendall also decried the, "in my opinion, inflated role Washington representatives of some companies play in picking recipients of PAC funds"; implicitly he therefore urged CEOs to do more to set the direction for their PACs.[19]

These letters were circulated only during the middle of the 1978 election cycle. Corporations had already given many donations, and it undoubtedly took time for CEOs and boards of directors to consider the advice, change company policy, and then communicate this new policy to the company's PAC director and PAC committee. An analysis by *National Journal*, comparing 1978 corporate contributions before and after October 1, revealed dramatically different patterns in the two periods. Through September 30, corporate PACs gave 72 percent of their money to incumbents; thereafter, only 49 percent.[20]

The attempts to mobilize and unify the corporate community in support of ideological conservatism and an aggressive political stance began late in the 1978 election, but came to fruition in 1980. As one corporate PAC director told us:

There was a genuine movement, the closest thing I've ever seen on the part of business in this country, almost a phenomenon that occurred in that year and a half or two years of that particular election. It was a genuine virtual fervor. Let's go out there and we can do it, we can change the system. The Chamber of Commerce and NAM [National Association of Manufacturers] and everybody beating the drum.

Or, as another put it to us: "I think we just basically kind of got with the program and did what we thought a business PAC was supposed to do at that point in time." Around 1980 "was the big, really exciting time."

The change in behavior shows starkly in data on campaign contributions. As we noted earlier, ideological corporate PAC behavior is most evident in contributions to challengers. During the long period of Democratic congressional dominance (up to 1994, in the House), donations to Democratic incumbents were evidence of an access strategy, while contributions to Republican incumbents were ambiguous—they could have been motivated either by the candidate's incumbency and attendant power, an access-oriented consideration, or by the person's Republican values, an ideological consideration. Open-seat donations were also somewhat ambiguous.[21]

With few exceptions, corporate contributions to challengers are based on ideological commitments. Incumbents usually win: In most of the recent elections, over 90 percent of House incumbents and more than 75 percent of Senate incumbents won. Occasionally an incumbent is the underdog, but this almost requires that the incumbent be arrested for a sexual offense or be caught bribing someone. Some challengers are much longer shots than others, but contributing to a challenger is hardly ever a way of playing the percentages. Moreover, even if the two candidates are equally likely to win, the correct access strategy nearly always is to contribute to the incumbent. For example, in 1980 Al Ullman (Democrat–Oregon) was in a tight race with Denny Smith. Ullman, however, was chair of the House Ways and Means Committee, probably the single most important committee in the House, and certainly the committee of greatest importance to business. Denny Smith, the Republican challenger, ultimately won, but, as a first-year incumbent, he had little power to help his supporters. Had Ullman won, on the other hand, he would have been able to reward corporations that supported him, or even to penalize those that had opposed him. Contributions to challengers are thus a fairly unequivocal indication of corporate ideological commitment, a commitment strong enough for the corporation to run risks and face potential penalties.

Contributions to either Democratic or Republican challengers potentially indicate an ideological orientation. Some left analysts have developed a theory of corporate liberalism, an argument that "liberalism has been the political ideology of the rising, and then dominant, business groups."[22] Similar analyses are sometimes put forward by extreme conservatives.[23] If these views are correct, we would expect a substantial number of corporations to give significant amounts of money to Democratic challengers. While this is a possible ideological stance, in practice no corporation has adopted such a strategy.[24]

Corporations may be willing to ignore political party in contributing to established incumbents, but they are only rarely willing to give to a Democratic challenger, much less a liberal one. In both 1994 and 1996, corporate PACs gave less than 1.2 percent of their money to Democratic challengers, roughly the same as they gave in all other elections of the past twenty years.[25] Although, in theory, corporations could be ideologically liberal, in practice, none are (at least in terms of PAC contributions). Many corporations have made a pragmatic decision to support Democratic incumbents, but *no* corporation that makes substantial campaign contributions shows an ideological preference for liberals or Democratic challengers. If they are able to make a choice uncoerced by pragmatic access considerations, all corporate PACs apparently exclude the left half of the political spectrum. This is an unstated, but extremely important, ideological stance by even the most pragmatic of corporations.

Corporations that want to influence the overall composition of Congress in order to produce a more pro-business stance have no real choice: They must contribute to Republican challengers. Thus, the degree to which corporations engage in ideological versus access spending is best assessed by examining donations to such challengers. We measure this by looking at how many corporate PACs gave 30 percent or more of their money to Republican challengers during each election year. By this measure, the 1980 election emerges as a high point of ideological giving. In 1980, 88 of the largest corporate PACs engaged in an ideological strategy by directing more than 30 percent of their giving to Republican challengers, 6 times the figure for the next closest year of the decade, 1984, when 14 corporations did so.[26]

Studies indicate that campaign money influences election outcomes primarily through its effect on challengers. In order to be viable candidates, challengers must raise substantial amounts of money, something they are often unable to do. In 1980 the large group of ideologically conservative corporations vastly increased the flow of funds to Republican challengers, and many of these candidates won. The shift in business behavior was dramatic. Among races pitting Democratic incumbents against Republican challengers, in 1972 the Democratic incumbents received four times as much as their challengers, in 1976 twice as much, but, in 1980, the Democratic incumbents received only about the same amount of money as their Republican challengers.[27]

The shifting character of corporate political activity can be shown in another way, through the use of a quantitative technique known as network analysis. Analysts generally agree that *if* business is able to achieve political unity, it can be enormously effective; arguments revolve around whether, when, and to what degree business is politically unified (see Chapter 6). Network analysis seeks to determine whether there are groups of corporations with similar political behavior, and if so, what the characteristics of these groups and corporations are. We used one variant of this technique to analyze the overall pattern of corporate PAC donations for each election from 1976 through 1986.[28]

A significant shift takes place in the period between 1976 and 1980. In 1976 about one-quarter of all PACs were in some group with politically similar behavior. These PACs were spread among five different groups, the largest of which had only 9 members.[29] Though the technique we used allows a corporation to be a member of many different groups, only one corporation was in more than one group.[30] Most of the groups were based on a specific industry (railroads, utilities) or geographic region (California). Two groups were more pragmatic, or access oriented, than the norm, and three were more conservative, though even the conservative groups provided limited support to challengers.

By 1980, the picture had changed dramatically. Once again one-quarter of all corporations were in a group with politically similar behavior—but this time all of these corporations were in a single group (with 63 members), and there were no other groups. The corporations in this bloc came from all industries and regions, indicating that they had transcended any narrow basis for unity. The bloc with politically similar behavior contains the corporations that contributed heavily to conservative challengers. Politically, the bloc PACs differed dramatically from the PACs not in the bloc—for example, bloc PACs gave only 36.5 percent of their money to incumbents, while nonbloc PACs gave 68.7 percent. After 1981, there continued to be a single large conservative bloc, with no alternative groups of PACs with politically similar behavior, but the conservative bloc no longer aggressively tried for ideological change. Instead, it primarily supported conservative incumbents.

THE DEMOCRATS: TAKING CARE OF BUSINESS

The shift in business behavior is one key factor explaining the differential policy outcomes of 1981 and subsequent years. In 1980 and 1981, there was "a genuine virtual fervor." Far more corporate PACs gave substantial amounts to Republican challengers than had done so before. After 1981 business reverted to its normal (moderate, access) approach, in campaign finance and in political action more generally. Why did business change its approach after the 1980 election, becoming less aggressive, more willing to support moderate Democratic incumbents? Many factors undoubtedly played a part—the 1982 recession and the return of prosperity, reduced concern about government because of the implementation of deregulation, a fear of popular backlash, the difficulties of a declining world power in deciding on a coherent strategy, and—undoubtedly crucial—the fact that business had succeeded in getting its most pressing demands addressed. Some of the corporations we interviewed stressed their economic difficulties in the early and mid-1980s as the reason that their behavior changed: "I think we are a little bit more pragmatic now—because we have to be." As another explained:

> We were making money in 1980. It wasn't until later that the companies in [our industry] started really having serious problems and we had to look for all the help we could get from anybody. I think if you look at all the [industry] companies, basically they became much less ideological and much more concerned about their own problems.

We would stress another key factor: the Democratic countermobilization and—associated with that—the increasingly pro-business character of the Democrats. After the 1980 election, pro-business Democrats mobilized to persuade business that they deserved support. Tony Coelho, chair of the Democratic Congressional Campaign Committee, and perhaps the most successful Democratic fundraiser in the interval between Lyndon B. Johnson and Bill Clinton, led this effort. Coelho went to corporate PACs and told them, "You people are determined to get rid of the Democratic party. The records show it. I just want you to know we are going to be in the majority of the House for many, many years and I don't think it makes good business sense for you to try to destroy us."[31] Coelho is convinced that it was this kind of fundraising that helped revive the Democratic party and prevent a realignment: "What had happened, in 1980, we had our butts kicked. If the Republicans had been successful, they would have completed the job."[32]

Our data make Coelho's claim plausible. Corporate PACs did change their behavior dramatically between 1980 and 1984: They drastically reduced their efforts to defeat Democratic incumbents and they returned to a pattern of acceptance of the status quo. The corporate executive who had described 1980 as "a genuine movement" also offered an explanation for its not persisting:

CORPORATE EXECUTIVE: I think that certainly that experience has not been replicated since that point.

INTERVIEWER: Why not?

CORPORATE EXECUTIVE: For a variety of reasons, not the least of which is the impact which that election had on Democrats. [The Senator he used to work for] is a perfect example of that. Here's a guy who as a representative was conceived of as quite liberal, and now is conceived of and is a genuine moderate.

INTERVIEWER: Do you think that Democrats are more moderate since the 1980 election?

CORPORATE EXECUTIVE: No question about that.

The increased conservatism by Democrats, along with corporate willingness to coexist with pro-business Democrats, reduced the probability of a thoroughgoing partisan realignment.

For a brief period around 1980, a large proportion of corporations embraced a risk-taking, ideologically conservative, political strategy. Thereafter, however, most corporations returned to a pragmatic strategy of supporting incumbents to gain access: Business and the Democratic party moved toward each other. The Democratic party became more accommodating to business, and corporations became more willing to give to moderate Democratic incumbents.

Bill Clinton's election culminated and solidified this change. Clinton was one of the founders of the Democratic Leadership Council, a group that self-consciously supported "moderate," pro-business, Democratic policies, in contrast to what its members saw as the "too liberal" views of Michael Dukakis, Gary Hart, or Walter Mondale.[33] Clinton's campaigns and governance have been characterized by a mix containing some liberal initiatives and lots of conservative ones. Thus Clinton endorsed nondiscrimination against gays in the military, a significant tax increase for higher-income individuals, an executive order banning striker replacement by federal contractors, restoration of (limited) abortion rights, and a variety of other progressive initiatives. But he also supported the death penalty and a variety of "tough-on-crime" measures, immediately retreated from his support for gay rights in the military, pushed through NAFTA, and signed a draconian welfare "reform" bill. During the 1996 election, and to a lesser extent in 1992, the Republicans complained that Clinton was stealing their issues, that he had adopted their positions on all the key initiatives. And Clinton was hardly alone in this: The most serious threat to his nomination in 1992 was Paul Tsongas, who espoused what were, if anything, even more pro-business positions. In such a situation business can hardly lose. As Kevin Phillips reminds us, the Democratic party is the second-most procapitalist party to be found anywhere in the world.

As a result of these changes in the Democratic party, by the late 1980s most businesses no longer saw a major difference between the two political parties and no longer felt the need to keep pushing for further ideological change. As one executive said to us in 1989:

I don't really feel I have a party now. I think it is foolish for anybody in this business to profess an affiliation with a party. I don't think that is very healthy.

The extent of the shift is evident even in the behavior of those corporate executives who had changed the least, those who remained strongly conservative in both their beliefs and behavior. Only a handful of true believers remained, and even some of these were discouraged and weakening. In interviews we conducted at the end of the 1980s, one said:

> Part of it is disillusionment. We have given close to a million dollars and what good is it doing? We are losing all the time. Even though I know that we are going to keep plugging away at it because we have just got this philosophical bent and it's for the good of the country, and we are altruistic and everything else. It's not a change in direction. Not so strong as that. It's more of a tiptoeing into the realism that maybe we should support some of these people more.

At this same time, the PAC director at a major oil company reported: "We start to say, 'What difference does it make to us if somebody is 100 percent labor-rated when we are not a labor-intensive company?'" One of the most ideologically committed executives we talked with at that time remained firm in his convictions, but even he had changed. Earlier he had proselytized among other corporations, but he was no longer willing to do so. In the late 1970s, he explained, "We were very, very active. We were assiduous in trying to sell our approach to the running of business PACs." However, by 1989 that was no longer true:

> Back when PACs were first being created, I had a hell of a lot to say about it. I don't choose to do that anymore. . . . I consider my convictions to be important things, and I don't wish to discuss political convictions with the people who run those corporate PACs. I think the behavior of corporate PACs is absolutely fucking disgraceful, if that's not clear. And stupid and shortsighted beyond measure.

At the end of the 1980s, only one of the ideological executives we interviewed remained confident: "Despite the fact that we're alone and in the dark at this point in time, I'm not despondent that that's not ultimately going to pay off."

1994 AND REPUBLICAN CONTROL OF CONGRESS

This analysis may hold through the 1980s and the 1992 election, but the remarkable Republican victories of 1994 pose a challenge to a simple theory that business is crucial to conservative success. Shortly after the 1994 election, Walter Dean Burnham called it "very probably the most consequential off-year election in (exactly) one hundred years."[34] The election produced stunning gains for Republicans at all levels, state as well as federal. In House elections, Democrats lost 21 of 31 open seats vacated by Democrats, and 35 of 225 incumbents were defeated. Democrats were unable to defeat a single Republican incumbent and picked up only four open seats vacated by Republicans. This led to the first Republican majority in the House since 1953–54. The Senate shift was not so dramatic—8 Republican gains with no losses—but nonetheless sufficient to take control. At the state level, before the 1994 election, 38 percent of Americans lived under a Republican governor; after the election, 72 percent did.[35] "No Republican incumbent governor, representative, or senator was defeated."[36] The Republican gain did not depend on a passive stance during a time of economic (or other) difficulty—the economy was relatively healthy. In fact, Republicans boldly seized the initiative, making the campaign so much a national referendum on the "Contract with America" that Congress—and in particular the House and Speaker Newt Gingrich—was setting the national agenda.

We have argued that business mobilization was crucial to conservative successes in 1980. Given the massive conservative victory in 1994, one could reason backward and argue that the conservative victory "must" have depended on massive amounts of business money. This appears to have been Thomas Ferguson's logic. Shortly after the 1994 election, he compared the Democratic Congress of 1994 to the eruption of Mt. Vesuvius at Pompeii:

> Sudden, violent changes in an ocean of money are less visually dramatic than shifts in the Bay of Naples. But long before the Federal Election Commission unveils its final report on the financing of the 1994 midterm elections, it is already clear that in the weeks before the explosion that buried alive the Democratic Party, changes in financial flows occurred that were as remarkable as anything Pliny and his terrified cohorts witnessed 2,000 years ago: A sea of money that had been flowing reliably to congressional Democrats and the party that controlled the White House abruptly reversed direction and began gushing in torrents to Republican challengers.[37]

Ferguson's approach makes a neat, elegant theory: Conservatives win electoral victories if and only if they receive massive quantities of business campaign contributions. Unfortunately, however, this isn't true—and it's not the first time Ferguson's theory has not stood up to the available evidence.[38] We first present the evidence on business behavior during the 1994 and 1996 elections, accept that it runs counter to a theory of business as crucial to electoral change, and then develop a more sophisticated theory.

In the 1994 elections, corporate campaign contributions were more or less the same as they had been in 1992, or 1990, or any of the quiet years of the mid to late 1980s. Most corporations stuck to a pragmatic strategy of giving their money to incumbents, including many Democrats. As before, any corporation that gave 30 percent or more of its money to Republican challengers can be classified as pursuing an ideological strategy aimed at changing the political character of Congress. In 1980, 88 corporations met this ideological criterion, but only 4 did so in 1994, and only 1 in 1996. (The contrast is dramatically clear in Figure 1.)[39] Clearly corporate campaign contributions were *not* the driving force behind the Republican successes of 1994.

It is useful to compare corporate campaign contributions in 1980 to those in 1994, the two elections of greatest importance to conservatives. In 1980, Republicans had nearly a 2 to 1 edge over Democrats in corporate PAC contributions; in 1994, the split was almost even. The biggest difference is found in those races that would be most important to any push for a realignment. In races pitting Republican incumbents against Democratic challengers, both ideology and pragmatism argue that corporations should contribute to the Republican incumbent. In both years, therefore, these Republican incumbents had a huge advantage over their Democratic challengers: a 26 to 1 edge in 1980, a 66 to 1 edge in 1994, the main change being a reduction in the already-minuscule proportion of corporate money going to Democratic challengers. Open-seat races, where there is no incumbent, often allow a corporation to push for its ideological preferences without having to oppose a powerful and entrenched incumbent; contributing to such races is a relatively safe and cautious way to promote a political shift. In 1980, the Republican edge in such races was 7.2 to 1; in 1994, it was 3.6 to 1—still substantial, but only half as large.

The dramatic contrast, however, is found in races pitting Democratic incumbents against Republican challengers—precisely the races of most importance if there is to be a conservative and pro-business realignment. Entrenched incumbents have a huge advantage in visibility, experience, knowledge, resources, credibility—and funding. In 1980, overall, Democratic incumbents and their Republican challengers had a fairly level playing field in terms of corporate campaign contributions—the incumbent Democrats had a 1.1 to 1 advantage. (This is, of course, the overall average; in some races, the Republican had an overwhelming advantage, in others the Democrat had, and in some the money was divided relatively equally.) In 1994, Democratic incumbents had a better than 8 to 1 advantage over their Republican challengers in corporate PAC contributions. In many of

FIGURE 5.1
1980 WAS PEAK YEAR FOR IDEOLOGY
NUMBER OF IDEOLOGICAL PACS GIVING AT LEAST 30 PERCENT OF
DONATIONS TO REPUBLICAN CHALLENGERS

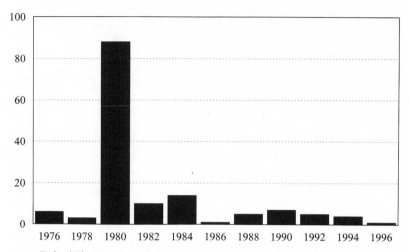

SOURCE: Federal Election Commission

the 1994 races, the Republican challenger did not have the corporate campaign contributions that would ordinarily be needed to mount credible challenges to his or her Democratic incumbent opponent—nonetheless, many challengers won. In 1980, Republican challengers received 28.6 percent of all the money contributed by corporations; in 1994, they received only 5.7 percent. Corporate funding cannot explain the 1994 Republican victories.

Much the same story could be told of the 1996 elections. For challenger and open-seat candidates, corporate PAC contributions in 1996 were very similar to those in 1994. Republican challengers received 5.7 percent of corporate money in 1994, and 5.6 percent in 1996; Republican open-seat candidates received 12.1 percent of total corporate PAC contributions in 1994 and 11.2 percent of this pool in 1996; and the (small) amounts to Democratic challenger and open-seat races were also very similar in the two years.[40] The big change between the two elections was in contributions to incumbents. At the time campaign contributions were being made to candidates in the 1994 elections, Democrats had controlled Congress for forty years, and that control seemed likely to continue, so an access strategy argued for contributions to Democrats; by 1996, the Republicans were in control and seemed likely to remain there. As a consequence, Democratic incumbents received 46.0 percent of all corporate contributions in 1994, but only 22.6 percent in 1996, while Republican incumbents received only 32.3 percent of the total corporate pool in 1994, but 55.7 percent in 1996.[41] In races pitting Democratic incumbents against Republican challengers, the Democratic advantage dropped from 8 to 1 in 1994 to 4.1 to 1 in 1996. This drop was the result of Democratic incumbents receiving less, not of Republican challengers receiving more.

IS BUSINESS THE KEY TO POLICY CHANGES?

One response to these findings would be to conclude that business political activity does not explain the key political shifts of the past twenty years. If the goal of a theory is to explain changes in electoral outcomes, then two elections—1980 and 1994—are test cases, and only one of them (1980) shows unusual business behavior. For electoral outcomes, the theory is only half-right, and a 50 percent score isn't impressive.

But we do not agree that election outcomes are the most important thing to be explained. The extent to which corporate actions hold the key to the political changes of the period from the mid 1970s to the late 1990s depends in part on what we mean by "political." Do we mean the party label for the people who sit in Congress and the White House, or do we mean the policies that actually get implemented? Most discussions focus exclusively on what percentage of the vote went to Democrats versus Republicans, or the number of officeholders from each party. But to be a "Democrat" may mean something very different today from what it did thirty (twenty, ten) years ago, and the same holds true for the meaning of "Republican." If Bill Clinton gets reelected by adopting much of the Republican agenda, this may be a personal triumph for Clinton and a noteworthy victory for those Democrats whose livelihoods depend on electoral success, but it may not change the programs and policies that structure daily life. We believe that the more important issue is which policies are adopted and the impact those policies have on the lives of people in this country and around the world, both now and in the future. Electoral success does not necessarily produce policy change.

On the one hand, our basic argument is simple; on the other, many readers may find it difficult to grasp because it is so contrary to most analyses of politics. Extraelectoral mobilization—in the 1960s, social movements, and from the 1970s to the 1990s, corporate political action—is the factor that best explains major shifts in policy; its impact is more important than election outcomes. Because this book is about corporate political activity in the period from the mid 1970s to late 1997, that will be the focus here, but a similar argument could be made concerning the influences of the social movements of the 1960s.[42] Corporate political activity can influence election results, but—as a host of studies have shown[43]—it can be even more effective when it operates directly on policy. Corporate campaign contributions are important in themselves (in terms of their influence on election outcomes), but are even more important as an indicator of the level, intensity, and character of the mobilization of business, a mobilization that is reflected in a range of other kinds of activities: think-tank funding, relations with unions, contributions to nonprofit groups, communications to stockholders and employees, investment and disinvestment decisions, lobbying, and the political mobilization of managers.

We are not especially interested in the labels ("Democrat," "Republican") attached to political office holders. What matters is the policies that get adopted, and understanding why policy shifts. To what extent does corporate political activity explain changes in policy outcomes? This can best be examined through a comparison of the periods following the 1980 and 1994 elections. In 1980, corporate campaign contributions indicate a unique degree of corporate political mobilization and an unprecedentedly aggressive push for ideological conservatism. In 1994 (and 1996), corporate campaign contributions indicate business as usual—that is, a preference for conservative policies, but no major push for change. If policy responds to business's extraelectoral mobilization, we would expect to find major policy shifts after the 1980 election, and much milder policy changes following the 1994 election—despite the fact that both elections involved similar conservative victories at the polls. And we do find exactly that.

The period after the 1980 election redefined what was seen as normal and expected, what values people held, and what the government was to do. This redefinition was in part cultural, but it also was embodied in a host of major policy changes, including:

◆ the most massive peacetime military buildup in history
◆ a huge tax cut, with a disproportionate share of the benefits going to business and the wealthy
◆ budget cuts in a wide range of nonmilitary programs, especially those that benefited the poor
◆ a dramatic rise in the size of the government deficit, in effect a result of the tax cut for the rich, but culturally and politically accepted as limiting the ability of the government to introduce any new programs
◆ a wholesale firing and permanent replacement of striking federal (PATCO)

workers, not because of individual acts of violence but simply because they had gone on strike

◆ an open attack on affirmative action and minority populations, exemplified by Reagan's "welfare Cadillac" stories.

Collectively, these actions altered the political and cultural framework, replacing the old New Deal understandings—government is responsible for economic prosperity, taxes should at least intend to redistribute income from the rich to the poor, and government programs are the solution to various problems caused by the market—with a new framework that presented government as the problem, not the solution. Tax cuts, not new programs, became the first emphasis; income inequality and "trickle-down" were the preferred ways to structure the economy. The government (and especially Reagan's team) carried out these changes, but government never acted alone. Observers were continually surprised by the success of the Reagan Revolution: The Democrats controlled the House of Representatives, and the American political system gives enormous advantages to any group trying to stall and prevent change; so the conventional wisdom, at least initially, was that Reagan would be unable to pass his program in anything approximating its full form. Instead, not only did it pass, but it did so with amazing speed.

A major reason for the success was solid business support for this program; our data on the unprecedented character of corporate campaign contributions are one indicator of that unity. Many of the changes were a result of "nonpolitical" actions. For example, it was business's aggressive stance toward labor that gave meaning and significance to Reagan's firing of PATCO (Professional Air Traffic Controllers) workers. The altered business stance toward labor dated back at least to the 1978 battle over labor law reform, and many of the other changes—military buildup, a change in Federal Reserve policy—had begun before Reagan's election. Contrary to the common perception, Reagan was not popular at the time he introduced these key changes (in 1981 and 1982), but was popular at a later point (in 1984 and 1985) when he was not able to pass his program.[44] The operative factor was not popular opinion, but business support and mobilization, though, over time, a range of cultural and media forces helped solidify an altered understanding of what was reasonable, normal, and expected. Popular support was thus a consequence, not a cause, of the new program.

A number of indicators give a sense of the magnitude of this shift, by far the most significant one since the New Deal itself. In the period from 1973 to 1980, the real interest[45] rate exceeded 2 percent only once (in 1976, at 2.6 percent). The rate in 1981 was 3.9 percent, and thereafter it stayed above 7 percent through 1986, dropping below 4 percent only once (in 1990, to 3.9 percent) through 1995. Strike data tell the same story: From 1969 through 1979, strike rates stayed above 950,000 in every year;[46] thereafter strike rates never reached 950,000, and they fell below 400,000 in ten of twelve years from 1984 on, as the lessons of PATCO and employer intransigence reshaped labor relations.

Now consider income data. From 1962 to 1981, in *every single year*, the bottom 80 percent of U.S. families received 59 percent of the nation's total income. (The variation is from 58.5 to 59.5 percent.) In 1982, as the new policies kicked in, that percentage suddenly dropped a full percentage point to 57.8 percent, and continued slipping throughout the 1980s to a figure of 53.5 percent in 1995.[47] All these indicators, and many others, show a sharp— indeed, startling—break in the period around 1980.

The 1994 election did not lead to a similarly significant policy shift. A shift always takes place in relation to a baseline. As the figures we've just presented indicate, the post-1980 baseline is conservative policies, attacks on the poor, a redistribution of income from almost everyone to the richest Americans, a movement away from racial equality, deregulation whenever possible, and a continuing budget-and-tax based squeeze on all social programs. Clinton's election and the 1992 to 1994 period did not mark a sharp break with the Reagan–Bush policies. It offered instead a continuation with some moderation, though we need to remember that the 1980–81 period redefined what constituted "moderation."

A significant shift from the post-1980 baseline would have required *either* a move toward liberalism—not on Newt Gingrich's agenda—*or* the successful imposition of policies that were drastically more conservative and did substantially more to attack minorities and the poor in order to aid business and the rich.[48] Newt Gingrich and his allies made every effort to accomplish exactly that. They had some success, but remarkably little, given the scope of their electoral victory and given that Clinton's preferred strategy is "always compromise." In many ways, the 1993–94 period was similar to the 1979–80 period in terms of congressional outcomes and conservative successes. In both periods, a Democratic president, operating with Democratic majorities in both Houses of Congress, introduced a moderate policy— labor law reform in 1978, a health policy in 1994. Both of these moderate policies met strong opposition from the right and were defeated as "too liberal" and "antibusiness." In both cases, the period ended with a smashing and unexpected Republican electoral triumph. A crucial difference, however, is that the 1980 conservative electoral triumph was backed by unprecedented corporate political activity. The best available indicator of this is our own data on corporate campaign contributions, data which show that corporations substantially increased their political unity, and unified to aggressively support conservative challengers. In 1994, business campaign contributions—and political activity more generally—demonstrated no unusual mobilization or preference.

We argue that this difference in corporate political activity explains why the electoral victories of 1994 did not lead to 1995–96 conservative policy successes on the scale of 1981. The Republican Congress tried to use the budget to force Clinton to accept their agenda; he resisted, and received far more support than Congress. At such a juncture, the situation can be framed either as, "What's wrong with Clinton? Why can't he listen to the clear voice of the electorate as expressed in the last election? Didn't he claim to be a New Democrat, not an old-fashioned defender of big government?" or as, "Why are Gingrich and the Republicans being so intransigent? Their extremist attempts are seriously interfering with the needed work of government and hurting business as well as others." Clinton, by and large, won this argument over framing. Solid business support for the Republican agenda could have altered drastically the terms of debate.

The 1995–96 Congress did enact one major and highly consequential law sought by conservatives: welfare "reform." This may have dramatic consequences far into the future, and it provides the main counterargument to our position—or an indication of its limits. It should be remembered, however, that in 1992 Clinton promised "to end welfare as we know it," and that Democrats as well as Republicans had for some time been attacking welfare and the poor. Moreover, although the bill is a disaster, it is unclear how sharp and extensive the actual changes will be. States and activist groups are already finding dozens of ways around the act.[49] By 1997 Newt Gingrich was insisting that welfare reform had been sabotaged, that new legislation was needed or "reform" would be subverted.[50] A second conservative victory in this period was the attack on affirmative action—but this came not so much by way of Congress, the president, or the policy apparatus, as it did through a public referendum in California. In some ways it is surprising that Congress did not do more to attack affirmative action, given the strength of popular sentiment against it. Also, it is worth noting that the second most important legislative act of the 1995–96 Congress was raising the minimum wage. That raise was directly antithetical to the new Republican platform, but it happened nonetheless, and happened (once again) because of an extraelectoral mobilization by a significant social force—a revived labor movement.

Nor did the 1994 elections serve as a harbinger of a fundamental electoral realignment. The Republicans did manage to hold on to their congressional majorities (at diminished levels), but in 1996 Clinton was reelected by a decisive margin. Business was largely unconcerned about the election: Certainly it was not engaged in an all-out-for-Dole-and-Gingrich mobilization. One indicator of this laid-back attitude is a *Fortune* magazine poll of the CEOs of major corporations taken during the spring of 1996: 40 percent of them believed that who was selected as chair of the Federal Reserve Board was at least as important as who was elected president.[51] In part, this is simply a recognition of the power of the Federal Reserve chair,[52] but if the Democrats had been running Jesse Jackson, we suspect the poll results would have been different.

Part of the reason corporate owners and executives were unconcerned about the election was Clinton's success in co-opting Republican issues. Politics had already been redefined. Rather than a pro-business party confronting a populist mobilization, the 1990s are better understood as a one-party—money-party—state, although the party contains two contending factions. In the wake of the 1994 election, Clinton's most important political task was to reassure business. Clinton's White House coffees have been considered exclusively in terms of their importance for fundraising. Perhaps as important as the money raised was the message to business: "I'm on your side, I want to hear what you have to say, and I will do my best to meet your needs if I can do so." Implicitly the message was: "Despite what might seem like a golden opportunity, this is not the time for you to push for a full-scale realignment." Sometimes what does *not* happen is as important as what does: Clinton's coffees may have prevented the emergence of an active corporate opposition, and that may have been as important to his election victory as the money raised. It is probably too early to evaluate the consequences of 1995–96 policy changes (especially of welfare "reform"). Based on what business did—and even more, on what it did *not* do—we predict that the 1995–96 period will *not* mark a sharp break with past trends in income distribution, labor success, interest rates, government spending, tax policy, or any other major area, with the possible—and very significant—exception of welfare.

The next chapter examines some of the underlying bases of business power, the factors that enable business to influence policy through a range of mechanisms in addition to campaign contributions, and thus help explain why policy shifted so much more in the period following the 1980 election than it did after the 1994 election.

◆ 6

PACS RUNNING IN PACKS

WE HAVE ARGUED THAT THE 1980–81 PERIOD DRAMATICALLY TRANSFORMED the direction of U.S. policy and that the impetus for this transformation was aggressive action (of all kinds) carried out by a unified business community. Campaign finance was one part of that, and it provides the best quantitative indicator of a change that actually involved a range of other behaviors. If this is so, we need to ask: How is this business unity and power developed? What underlying mechanisms make it possible for businesses to unify and act effectively?

Academic debates about business power usually center on the extent and character of business unity or division. A large group of academics, including many located in business schools and political science departments, admit much of what this book has argued: that businesses are enormously powerful, make huge campaign contributions and use them to gain access not available to other groups, advance interests different from those of the general population, and that they are not democratically run. Nonetheless, these "moderates" deny that business has much overall impact on the political system. A rather neat trick. How can they do it?

Their approach is to admit what they can't deny, and at the same time insist that none of this matters. Pluralists, as advocates of this position are called, admit business has far more *potential* power than any other group. They argue, however, that businesses are politically divided, so that the actions of one cancel out those of another, and the *net* impact of business is minimal, perhaps nil. Chrysler might favor air bags, while General Motors might be strongly opposed to them. The auto companies might want steel imports to lower prices, but the steel companies might prefer protectionism.

For at least the last thirty years, the central question in academic debates about business political power has been whether or not business unifies to promote a common agenda. Many pluralist contentions have been decisively refuted, so their case now rests primarily on the claim that business has no clear and uniform political interest. If the various parts of business pursue differing political agendas, then one part of business counterbalances another, and business's total political impact is much less than it might be. Robert Dahl has argued that a group's power depends on *both* its potential for control (in which business scores very high) and its potential for unity (in which business is said to be low). "Thus a group with relatively low potential for control but a high potential for unity may be more politically effective than a group with a high potential for control but a low potential for unity."[1] For pluralists, business is the quintessential example of this: "Business groups often conflict with each other as much as they do with their rivals in the labor, consumer, and environmentalist movements."[2] Theodore Eismeier and Philip Pollock, III have made this point specifically for corporate campaign contributions:

The diverse reactions of business to the rise of the positive state have in part been the product of cleavages within the business community. Regulated versus unregulated, region versus region, small versus large, exporters versus non-exporters—these and other divisions have created a lively pluralism in business politics, often pitting corporate interests against each other as much as other groups.[3]

If the pluralist argument is correct, then business has little cumulative power. If corporations are pitted "against each other as much as [against] other groups," then one cancels out the other, and no corporation can have much effect. It goes without saying that unity can never be total, with all corporations and all executives thinking and acting in concert. The issue is always: What is the degree of unity or division?

Unfortunately for pluralism, this is another case of a beautiful theory confronting an ugly fact. Elegant as the theory may be, its factual premises just can't be supported. Congress is generally considered the area where pluralists make their best case. Here, if anywhere, each company promotes its own interests in opposition to those of other businesses. In this chapter we contribute to a long-running political and academic debate by providing additional evidence that business is usually politically unified, even in congressional activities.

Our earlier quantitative analyses of computerized records of all corporate donations indicated this was so, but the interviews helped us understand how this unity is achieved. One of our quantitative articles analyzed donations by *all* large PACs (those that gave over $100,000 in 1984): labor, environmental, nonconnected ideological, and trade association as well as corporate.[4] It revealed an exceptionally sharp split—a unified business–Republican group on one side, and a labor–women–environmentalist–Democratic group on the other. Though this confirms common sense, it also strongly refutes those pluralists who argue that business is as divided against itself as it is opposed to labor and environmentalists. Another article, which examined donations by only the largest corporate PACs, showed that corporations nearly always unify to support one of the two candidates in a race. In about 3 out of 4 races, business can be classified as unified, giving at least 9 times as much to one candidate as to the other; in 1 out of 5 races it provides predominant support to one candidate, giving him or her from 2 to 9 times as much as the opponent; and in only 1 race out of 15 is business divided (accepting a split of 2 to 1 or closer as evidence of division).[5] A complicated computer simulation led us to conclude that PAC officers may disagree with their counterparts at other corporations, but the unstated rules forbid public disputes, and only reluctantly will one business directly oppose another.

The first half of this chapter examines how business achieves this political unity. Its basis is a fundamental set of underlying material relations—loans from the same banks, sales and purchases from one another, interlocking boards of directors, and common interests in accumulating capital and avoiding government initiatives that might restrict business power.[6] These underlying material relations, which are simultaneously social relations, make it possible for corporate officials to create a common culture that structures their understandings, interpretations, decisions, and actions. Corporations share information, ask each other for money, do each other favors, work together on campaigns around specific issues, and use humor and good-natured ribbing to coerce other corporations to maintain unity. We agree that candidates do not need to worry about an isolated donor, even if the company is enormous and the potential donation the maximum legally allowed. They *do*, however, need to be concerned about "PACs running in packs."

Business power derives in part from this ability to achieve political unity on most issues. Even more important, however, is business's control of the economy, a control that is neglected in many analyses of power. We examine it and its implications in the last part of this chapter. Corporations control a host of decisions *unless* and *until* the government specifically intervenes. Control of the economy also gives business vast resources for influencing society in a host of "non-political" ways. No campaign finance reform proposal can realistically hope to fix the problems of our current system unless it takes into account the vast power business exercises in other realms.

◆ BUILDING BUSINESS UNITY

LEARNING ABOUT ISSUES

If each company learned about congressional races and proposed legislation separately, pluralism would be on strong ground. A few sources of information *are* company specific. For example, sometimes a company individually researches candidate positions on the legislation of most importance to their firm. But most information comes from a generalized "business community," a shared network of contacts and information.

One basic source of information is simple: "We read constantly; till our eyes come out of our heads. We read all the dailies, and industry publications, and news journals, and special publications, and we are constantly looking for things." Another executive put the emphasis on newspaper reading:

> I read nine newspapers a day. I read two or three extra papers on Sunday. I subscribe to things like the *Political Report*, put out by Stuart Rothenberg, which is an excellent report. I read *Congressional Insight*. I read *National Journal* and *CQ*. I read [several industry-specific journals].

Many of these publications are intended for a large audience, but others are industry specific or intended only for government relations specialists. Shared reading helps create a common basis of knowledge and similar orientations.

A second source is the lawyers, lobbyists, and consultants whose own business is to provide information, ideas, and influence to corporations.

> Our principal outside counsel is Willkie, Farr and Gallagher, and they often call us up and talk about an issue and bring it to our attention. Plus half the law firms in Washington call us up to tell us about things because they want our business. We have a huge constituency of law firms and the like that we have worked with in the past, or that do little bits and pieces for us, or that hope to do so, and they tell us about things because they hope there'll be business in it for them.

A telephone industry official echoed him:

> We have an extensive, extensive list of consultants and publishers who

make money off the phone company. On my desk there are *Communications Week, Communications Daily, Telephone Magazine,* and God knows how many others. Who are out every day with what is going on. Full-time reports, daily to weekly to monthly, just on our industry.

Consultants and industry publications can't make money by servicing a single company; they need to sell the same information and provide the appropriate services to as many companies as possible.

Use of a paid consultant or lobbyist can greatly reduce the task facing a corporation's government relations unit, while ensuring the corporation has a chance to get its views included:

It's important to us to know what's happening. It's a significant part of any major entity's business. What happens to small businesses that don't get involved is they get told what legislation is and have to respond to it, and don't get enough time to get their input into the legislation ahead of time. We're trying to save ourselves the trouble of changing the system and rechanging it, by being involved from the beginning.

Unless you read every piece of legislation and every amendment that comes to it, you could miss something important. We could assign someone to that task full time but it's much easier for us to contract that out to someone else. So out of 3,000 House bills I only had to read 200 and track 110.

A third source of information is communication from members of Congress and their staffs.

Members and their staffs call us up. Even if they are part of the problem they call us to warn us, "We're planning to do this or thinking about doing that and it might have an impact on you." We've worked with lots of these people before, we've done them favors and we will again in the future, and they do us favors by keeping us informed. Plus, many of them are friends one way or another.

This is one of the few major sources of information that is not necessarily shared. A member of Congress may have a special relationship with a particular company and call only it. Of course, members as well as consultants may want to make money out of as many companies as possible, and a sympathetic phone call to fifteen different companies in the same industry could produce a bonanza of donations from grateful PAC officers.

A fourth source of information is fundraisers. As discussed in Chapter 2, fundraisers are first of all an occasion to deliver some money and get noticed by a candidate, but they are also an opportunity to meet the government relations officials of other corporations, the lawyers, consultants, and lobbyists that corporations hire, as well as other members of Congress and their staffs.

> You see a staffer who you haven't seen. You run into somebody—you want him to know you have been there, because you are going to try to see him. You run into one of your counterparts in another company who you haven't seen in two months and you want to talk to him about issues. You run into people from out of town who you don't see a lot. It's a whole composite.

Most fundraisers are in Washington, but the same principle applies to other cities. We asked a corporate executive based in Texas, one who rarely goes to Washington, whether Texas fundraisers were similar to those in the capital:

> Sure. You see the same kinds of people. It's a chance to not only see the candidate whoever he is, but see your friends from other company PACs or trade associations or whatever. Every once in a while you run into one that's a little different. Sometimes it might be some business person has the reception in their home. It's a smaller group of people and probably a higher level of people in the business, so you get more CEOs than PAC operative-type people.

Ideological corporations, who are less tied in to the Washington fundraiser circuit, have other ways of getting together. Most frequently mentioned were the Chamber of Commerce and the Business–Industry Political Action Committee, with BIPAC receiving especially favorable notice. In our 1986 mail survey of corporate PACs, about 40 percent indicated that they consulted with BIPAC; it continues to be the most important such group, though there is a plethora of others.[7] BIPAC holds forums to introduce promising conservative candidates to corporate campaign finance officials; these gatherings are even attended by many unequivocally pragmatic corporations. For example, an executive for a highly regulated industry told us that "Bernadette Budde [head of BIPAC] does a heck of a job. I have gone in the past to her meetings, simply to know who's got a chance or what the score is." Executives of ideological corporations were even more enthusiastic: "We support BIPAC, their educational arm. I think that's the greatest source of information that we have."

Some other groups serve many of the same purposes. A few companies rely heavily on the Republican senatorial committee and the congressional committee for their input, although that's not necessarily so helpful because, of course, they are slanted and, of course, they are biased. They have their job to do. But they would help us out a lot more if they'd be a little more objective, and tell us more of a straight story.

One corporate official, although reporting that "compared to what I am used to or compared to what I know should be, I would say we are relatively isolated," nonetheless noted that "I know all the staff members at NAM [National Association of Manufacturers]. I know quite a few staff members at the Chamber [of Commerce]." One company contributes "one, two, five, twenty thousand a shot" to various single-interest organizations such as the Coalition to Stop the Raid on Corporate America. For ideological corporations whose managers attend fewer Washington fundraisers where they rub elbows with all the other business executives, events like the BIPAC forums offer a chance to get together with like-minded corporate officials from a range of different businesses.

Fifth, finally, and above all, corporate government relations officials learn what is happening by socializing with each other and with other key players in any and every way they can. Fundraisers are one important institutional mechanism, but there are a host of informal occasions: golf games, lunches, dinners, parties, phone calls, chance meetings in the halls of Congress, at the theater, or at charity events. One vice president, who is not based in Washington but spends a great deal of time visiting there, explained to us, "Washington is a constant networking of various levels, various circles that come together in different degrees." As another vice president said:

Talk's cheap and worthless, and everybody's got an opinion; politics is all this town thinks about. We talk to each other all the time: "Are you giving to Henry or to Steve?" or "You ought to be giving to Henry or Steve." Obviously I call up my friends in the industry and say, "Look, if you have to give to a Democrat, you ought to be supporting Dukakis instead of Lautenberg," or I'll get a call, "Will you please sign your name to a letter for Steve Symms because he was so good on the catastrophic bill. He really needs some support." So, sure, I'll do that. We have meetings. I have meetings coming out my ears.

Corporate government relations officials even have an association specifically for discussing how to operate a PAC—the National Association of Business Political Action Committees, or NABPAC. It seemed that practically every person we interviewed had at one time or another been on the board of directors of NABPAC.

I am on the board of directors of the National Association of Business PACs. Now nobody invents the wheel, but in this group there can be sharing of information. In terms of how to best solicit employees, brochures, things like that. What you should ask an employee, for $5 a pay period or $10 a month, what is a good number? What do top executives give? . . . So these types of things you discuss.

At some relatively early point in their careers, evidently most had found it to be very helpful and continued to think fondly of it, though senior people tended not to remain so actively involved.

Networking is more than simply talking to each other at events and through formal organizations; it includes lunches, golf, and phone calls to friends.

> I've been in this town since 1963, and I started off working for a senator. I worked in the government doing congressional liaison—made a lot of friends, a lot of guys, and I have a lot of respect for them. There's guys I talk to, not on a daily basis but on a weekly basis, whose opinions I don't take because they are goofy, but I enjoy talking to them.

It also includes helping one another out by sharing news articles, documents, copies of bills, and the like.

> People are constantly sending me articles. I try to keep up within my own purview of friends by finding as many interesting articles as I can and passing them around when I have a chance to.

PAC directors out in the hinterlands (that is, anywhere outside Washington) are expected to be experts on their region:

> I have to be the source of intelligence on these races. If I know you as a PAC director in a particular state, and if I want to know the situation in that state, I would like to be able to call you and ask your opinion.

Only government relations and PAC personnel are likely to network about candidates, but people in other divisions of the corporation are talking to their counterparts about actual or proposed policies. The consciousness and involvement of operating-unit employees can be an important source of information:

> INTERVIEWER: And how would you learn about something that specifically was going to clip your company but not Shell?
>
> CORPORATE EXECUTIVE: Because we have an environmental department and a tax department and it is highly likely that those kind of things would crop up in those kinds of areas. They have networks of people that do the same things in other companies. They participate in the trade associations. They receive publications on a daily basis. I get some of this but mine is more generic. Theirs is real specific. And so they find out about the stuff.

ASKING ONE ANOTHER FOR MONEY

Government relations officials not only share information and learn about the candidates and policies, they also actively solicit donations from one another as part of their efforts to help their "friends" in Congress. This process is one of the least visible and most difficult to study. For soft money donors, for example, various levels of honorary membership (Team 100, Republican Eagles, Senatorial Trust, Congressional Forum) can be achieved not just by directly making a ($250,000) contribution, but also by raising that much in donations from others. The political parties are obsessed with cultivating these (nonofficeholder) individuals who raise money from others, but no information on this is reported in any public record—and, at one fundraiser, reporters were arrested for trying to observe who was sitting at the big-money tables.

Giving a candidate money is the basic token of entry, the means of establishing a relationship. But if a member of Congress has helped you out, or if you'd like to do more than just make a contribution, the next step is to serve on the member's steering committee, which is both an honor and an obligation. Each member of the steering committee is responsible for selling a certain number of tickets to the member's fundraiser. Usually that is the committee's only function. Some steering committees are much larger than others; they can require members to sell a few or many tickets. Once you are asked to serve, it is important to fulfill your obligations and sell the requisite number of tickets.

It's going back to what I didn't like to do in the beginning—that's begging guys for a lot of money. Only this time I can call the guy: "Joe, can you give me $250 for Congressman X? Come on please, he's a good guy." "Well, what's good about him?" Well you know, you spend a half-hour schmoozing. Two weeks later he says: "Remember I helped you with this guy. Well, I want you to help me with this guy." "He's a terrible jerk." "That doesn't make any difference—you've gotta help me: I helped you." Then you go back to your PAC committee and say: "I need $250 for Joe Jones," and they say, "What? Why?"

Here, the donation is a gift not so much to the candidate as to the other corporation, helping it to build a relationship with a member. One business can ask another for favors in ways not open to candidates themselves:

I get calls, "Jack, we want you to give some money to Gephardt." Had this call two days ago. "Marty, I don't want to give any money to Gephardt. His failed presidential campaign—I don't want to give any money to that." "No, it's for his congressional campaign." "Marty, you've done some things for me, I'll do one for you. If it's really necessary, if you need another body there, I might." In other words we'll do favors for one another. We're always calling each other to ask them to give.

These two comments illustrate that, when one corporate executive calls another to ask for a contribution, the discussion is likely to be honest, with the two executives raising problems that could never be discussed with the candidate him- or herself. In these discussions corporate managers learn a

lot about each other as individuals, about one another's corporations—
their wants, needs, problems, successes, failures—and, of course, what candidates have (or have not) done for other corporations. Word quickly spreads
about whether a member can be trusted to deliver. In order to operate
successfully, government relations officers must be willing and able to do
favors for one another; any corporation that did not participate in these
networks would be cut off from valuable information and would find it
difficult to build a special relationship with a member. The networks of
deals and obligations are such that, at any given time, a major player is
likely to owe and be owed favors by dozens of other corporations.

Although some people and some corporations actively seek opportunities to serve on steering committees, most consider it a necessary chore to
be avoided if possible. We asked one corporate executive if he served on
steering committees:

> We would like not to, and I try to avoid it as much as I can, and so
> does everybody else in our government operation. I'd avoid it if I could
> get away with it, but you can't always do that. Sometimes you have to
> serve because the member—he's a friend of yours. He's known you for
> ten years, and he says he wants you to be on his steering committee.
> You try to say, "Well, it's a company policy not to." But there are guys
> who are friends of yours who won't understand your saying, "I would
> rather not." They'll say, "I've helped you and you've helped me, so you
> go out and help raise some more money."

A corporate executive could of course tell a member, "I'd rather not; it's
inconvenient for me." But that dramatically increases the possibility that
the next time the corporation wants a favor the member will reply, "I'd
rather not; it's inconvenient for *me.*" To maintain the gift-exchange network,
participants have to be willing *and able* to participate and reciprocate.

A corporation can help a member even more by taking responsibility
for organizing a fundraiser for him or her.

> Senator X is a fraternity brother. Well, he's on the Y committee. He's
> somewhat important to our industry, but not critical. He's right on
> the edge, so I gave a fundraiser for him. Well, I had to get on the
> phone and call some people.

These fundraisers are typically for an industry or other specialty group.
This means that one company in the industry is getting extra credit with
the member for having taken the lead; other companies are thus helping to
strengthen their competitor's position. This might not be a company's first
choice, but, nonetheless, it is likely to participate:

> I think everybody obviously is trying to promote themselves and their

companies. But most of it is cooperative things. . . . I don't say just because they are doing the fundraiser, I am not going to go. I will say this, if we belong to an association that's sponsoring a fundraiser, and at the same time one of our competitors is having one, I would say we go to the one at the association and not to the competitor's.

This is obviously a very moderate statement; the remarkable fact, especially from the perspective of pluralist theory on business political competition and opposition, is that a company is *ever* willing to attend a fundraiser sponsored by a competitor.

Corporations support each other for a whole host of reasons. Support need not be based on a specific shared commonality, such as industry, region, capital intensity, or multinational orientation. Statistical analyses examining these factors find they have a modest impact.[8] Corporations give in common not only because of specific interests, but also because of a generalized sense of being part of the same social world, which can be activated by any one of a host of specific connections. The ties among PACs thus create a loose overlapping network, much like the interlocking networks among boards of directors.[9] These reciprocal networks obscure any industry-based relationship that might exist. Perhaps paper companies are particularly concerned about the Agriculture, Nutrition, and Forestry Committee, while savings and loans care primarily about the Banking, Housing, and Urban Affairs Committee. The statistical record of donations may show that both paper companies and savings and loans gave to members of both committees, but it will not indicate which donations were initiated by direct interest and which were given as reciprocal favors to the other corporations.

In this world, a corporation's ability to have political influence and leverage often *depends on other corporations as much as it does on politicians.* A corporation that is a major participant in the traffic in donations[10] is in a position to exercise a great deal of leverage. Such a corporation can offer a member much more than $5,000: It can raise many times this amount from its friends in the corporate PAC community. Equally important, it can vouch for the member and provide introductions to other corporations. Obviously, the member then has to make the right moves to build a positive relationship, but the introduction is invaluable. In effect, the corporation uses its network to evade the limits on the maximum legal donation.

Corporations don't make demands on each other, they make requests. And many of these requests are turned down. A donation is not guaranteed just because a corporate executive calls to say, "I gave $1,000 when you asked me to, now you have to give $1,000 to the person I pick." The candidate's characteristics are important. If Corporation A asks Corporation B to contribute to a powerful pro-business candidate such as William Thomas, Bill McCollum, or John Dingell, Corporation B's PAC is giving money to someone it is probably pleased to support. That doesn't mean that Corporation A could expect Corporation B to be willing to contribute to Bernie Sanders (Socialist–Vermont). The support of a respected PAC officer of a major corporation can do a great deal to advance a potentially marginal candidate such as Dick Gephardt—but Citibank itself would have trouble selling tickets to a Bernie Sanders fundraiser (not that there is any indication it's about to try). As one PAC Officer said, "They give me money, sometimes I'll give them money—but not to Metzenbaum or Kennedy." Of course, most of the time a corporation is only willing to ask for help on behalf of candidates who have helped them out and are at least willing to do favors for business. Participating in these exchanges "gives us a friendly network to reach out and get funds for specific candidates we have a real interest in and anxiety to help." Other companies don't always contribute,

[but] more often than not they will, especially for a company of our size and reputation and the size of our PAC and our credibility. More often than not they will participate because they look to us for similar support from time to time.

While "more often than not," corporations do participate, their participation is always contingent and voluntary. Several executives stressed that "everybody runs their own show. Nobody outside my corporation's gigging me about how I give money." Or, as another put it, "We turn down a lot of fundraising invitations from various industry-type PACs. The tail doesn't wag the dog; we make our own decisions." Sometimes the very same people who told us about giving money to "some jerk" simply because another corporation had asked them to do so also insisted that:

I don't think I've ever been concerned with what another PAC did about something. There's a service who will tell you what other PACs are doing, who other PACs are giving to. I don't care, and so I don't buy it. What they do in no way influences what I am going to do or anything I am going to spend.

Both sides of the coin are crucial: Corporations often help each other by donating to someone they don't care about (or actively dislike), but they do so *voluntarily*, as a *favor*, not because they are being ordered to do so. This is another form of loosely structured gift relationship, which creates obligations but permits room for maneuver in any individual instance.

Most favors and help result from government relations officials serving on candidate steering committees. But top executives also are involved in business networks that lead to contributions to candidates, either in response to requests from other corporate executives or as the incidental product of other forms of business networking. In one interview, the PAC committee chair ran through a partial list of noteworthy involvements for just a few of the corporation's top executives: The CEO is a member of the Business Roundtable and of the mayor's most important commission; formerly he was president of the industry trade association. Next year another executive will be chair of a different trade association. Other executives are members of the boards of several leading charities and officers of state and local trade associations. These executives, as well as others, are individually active in "the political arena, sometimes on the Democratic side of the aisle, sometimes on the Republican."

> All these things give you exposure to people who want you to help them financially run for public office. So our top executives are frequently requested to make contributions to political candidates individually, which they pass on to the PAC to make or consider making in their behalf. We [in government relations] frequently ask them to lend their support to get their friends to help the candidates we are interested in, and their friends in business ask them to do things like that. They are constantly asked, as are we, by our friends in other companies through our knowledge of them, through our trade associations where we work together on various legislative matters, to support Jones in your state who is running for Congress.

Although the corporation normally honors requests from the top half-dozen officers, this is not invariably the case:

> Sometimes we've got a problem because one of our executive officers has been asked to be on the campaign committee to raise money for Jones, and the next thing you know we have a request to give Jones $1,000. And we say right on the form, executive officer XYZ is on Jones's campaign committee to raise money for this event. And somebody says, "I don't care if he is." So we have arguments. We try to support them if we can, but there are times that we don't.

Another company with recommendations from top executives reported that:

> The PAC is not the biggest thing on their mind. They are running a $10 billion business and not worrying about a $60,000 PAC. But when the issues tend to come up, what happens is at a cocktail party or a social function, they will bump into a congressman or a senator will hit them.
>
> Usually it's a nuisance. They will say, "So and so asked me if we can give him something. Do you think we can do something for him?" We would hope that they will always say, "I'll get back to you" or, "Call

Bill or Stan" [the key government relations people]. But they don't, they say, "Oh yes, we'll do something."

So what happens is then we got to go and try to whittle down what the candidate thinks is a grand promise. Because he knows the president of the company or he met the president of the company.

So most of them, the sharper candidates, are going to realize that it's going to come back to us anyway. But once in a while you get a couple of guys who are nervous enough or anxious enough or really worried about losing that they will not take the usual kind of cooldown, so you might spend a couple grand a year that you would have preferred to spend otherwise. They don't cost us tens of thousands.

Corporations also make donations because their customers have asked them to do so. One executive reported, "The more serious issue, the times top executives really care, is if a client asks them to have us contribute to a candidate. I would guess about 10 percent of our contributions are at the request of a client." Although this is an unusually high proportion, others report similar experiences:

We supply [another giant company]. They'll contact our executive senior V.P. who heads up that business segment and say, "This is what's going on. This is real important. This issue is real important to us, and as a supplier to us it should be important to you too. Would you consider a contribution to [this candidate]?"

One executive who told us about such donations regarded them as a form of corporate service for customers. In at least one instance, however, the request to contribute to a candidate came from the CEO of the company's bank and was made directly to the company's CEO. This request was made at a far higher level than most of the customer requests, yet the company solicited had no legislation immediately pending, and the candidate was not facing an election contest. This implies a truly impressive level of business (and candidate) coordination. Presumably, the corporation was first identified as a noncontributor, and then an effort was made to find the right executive to request the donation. It's hard to imagine what would give more leverage than a request from the CEO of the corporation's bank.

CAN INDUSTRY COMPETITORS WORK TOGETHER?

Pluralists stress the opposition among businesses. Even though it is clear that companies routinely work with many other companies, a pluralist could plausibly argue that companies oppose the actions of their direct competitors. Exxon might cooperate with General Motors or Dow Chemical, but that doesn't mean it could bring itself to work politically with Mobil, Shell, or Texaco. Although this theory has surface plausibility, it is absolutely wrong. The companies *most* likely to work together are those in the same industry who compete directly with each other.

> In our X division, we are major competitors with a company called Y. You couldn't get more competitive—we're suing each other all the time. We hate each other, but I have a very good relationship with them down here and often we work together on the Hill for certain bills. The [provision] in the Z bill was something we worked on together because it benefits us, even though in that business they have more of a share than we do. So when we're down here, we're working on issues that impact all of our companies, even though we all want to make money in competition with the other guy. But when we're petitioning the government, our interests are very similar, and that's why we have the [industry trade] association. You obviously want to work a coalition if you can. So we'll have industry fundraisers.

Important political activity takes place in and around industry trade associations, and these campaigns often have both pragmatic and ideological dimensions. A company may have pragmatic reasons to fight for a change that benefits the entire industry, but a change that affects a major industry such as oil or banking has the potential also to be an important issue for all of business. Industry trade associations bridge the gap between "company" and "classwide" rationality.[11] This kind of politics involves fighting for something much broader than the interests of a specific company, but narrower than the interests of business as a whole. Trade associations have many functions—public relations, information gathering, research, occasionally some kinds of marketing—but government relations is certainly a major focus, a fact that is reflected in their concentration in Washington.

When an entire industry mounts a campaign, the degree of coordination, and the political impact, can be impressive. One state had several times considered and rejected a change in its banking regulations. A bank executive explained how the industry finally won.

> We said, this is the year to do it. We've got to have an influx of capital or the banks are really going to be in trouble; we're already in trouble anyway. The legislature is going to be more open to this than in the past, so let's form an alliance and get going.

> We hired a lobbyist. The [state] association hired a lobby team, one of the top ones in the state. And we let them direct us and use us as necessary. One of the things we did in conjunction, we started a survey in this company that we did in all of our offices across the state. We

sent our managers a list and said, how well do you know these legislators? And coded it and put it in a PC so we had a contact list statewide, who knew each state representative. We used that quite extensively.

We went through at the beginning of that legislative session and we
assigned a contact to every legislator. We said, okay, you're going to be
the contact. Here's some information. Here's why we're for it. Here's
all the pro and con arguments. And a lot of this of course was developed by the Banking Association and other groups. It was an education process that we put our people through . . . and some of our
people, frankly, had to be convinced; people at the smaller banks, because they were saying, "Now wait a minute, that doesn't sound like a
very good idea." But for the most part we did a pretty good job of that.

And we used that network quite extensively to the extent of gener-
ating a typical letter-writing campaign, which we did. A lobbyist might
call me up and say, so-and-so from X is all of a sudden undecided, she
needs someone to call her up and reassure her. And I'd pick up the
phone and call [a manager] and say, can you call [this legislator] and
reassure her about it. It was a good effort, it really was.

This account mentions most of the elements of many successful business
political campaigns: an entire industry united for a particular change, acting together through a trade association, using outside consultants and
allowing them to direct and coordinate the campaign, beginning by convinc-
ing or coercing their own managers, using the contacts of each manager to
further the change, and ultimately succeeding. The undecided legislator in
this example probably received at least one call from each of the several
banks promoting the new legislation, and many of the calls probably came
from people she already knew.

Omitted from this account is the process whereby the industry itself
came to agree on a solution. Typically, this is the first step in the process. It
may take some time and involve some difficulty to resolve internal disagreements, but before the issues are brought into the public arena they are
resolved inside groups restricted to the business community.[12] Occasionally an industry is simply allowed to make the decision itself within parameters established by Congress. In the insurance industry, taxes on assets hit
mutual companies harder, and taxes on profits hit stock companies harder.

So what usually happens is, and it's happened now two or three times
in a row when Congress wanted to change the law. This is a gross
oversimplification, but the way it happened in 1959 and in the early
eighties Congress said, Look, we are getting 3 billion bucks from you
guys. We want 3.5 billion. You figure out how to write the law, which

fairly gets it from everybody. And if you can't, we will do it, not for you, but to you.

Although industry trade associations are usually important, some of the largest companies scorn them:

Most associations that represent those companies that are in the same business you are almost have to look at the lowest common denominator when it comes to handling issues. They have to make sure they don't offend anyone or step on anyone's toes, and very often they can't become high profile. And we need to be high profile on certain issues. We just dig our own way and we are big enough to make these decisions. If we don't like what's going on, we go it on our own.

While "small" companies—like this oil company with sales in the billions—must rely on the trade association, they also have to watch out for their own interests:

We have to depend on trade associations that we are members of to take the lead on that stuff because we just don't have the staff. What we try to watch for on the state level and the federal level are issues that affect us as a company that don't affect anybody else. Because most of the time you've got your ARCOs and Exxons out there working on the same stuff that you are interested in. But at any rate, because of the oil, most of the time that is the situation. So you have to look for little peculiar stuff that would really zap your company and nobody else.

Trade associations don't always work effectively, and the members of an industry can't always agree. One company that operates in several different industries noted:

It's through the industry association that we usually take positions on public issues, as opposed to our working something out bilaterally with someone else. We would all work together to come up with an industry position if that were possible. If that weren't possible, then we would all work separately.

But this same company also reported:

It depends on the industry. In the X industry, for a long time, the companies were all at odds with one another, and they couldn't seem to get together on any public policy issue. There was no strong association. [Our subsidiary] walked out of the association because it had become dominated by our competitor. Now there's a new association in which the major companies are amicably working together on issues concerning the industry. So now, at this point, we have pretty good cooperation.

Sometimes the members of one industry agree, and work together in opposition to another industry. Our interviews offered only two examples of this: one, the local phone companies against the long-distance carriers; the other, a gas and electric utility opposing each other. However, these counterexamples of businesses opposed to one another appear trivial compared to the examples of business cooperation. We have tried to include *every* instance of businesses opposed to each other mentioned in our interviews. These add up to a single trade association that for a time functioned ineffectively because of conflict between two major companies, but now has "pretty good cooperation"; a gas and electric utility quarreling over what our informant estimates to be about one million dollars a year; and disputes among the different kinds of phone companies. In contrast to this short list, we found dozens of other examples, many of which indicate that companies that "hate each other," are "suing each other all the time," and are each other's major competitors nonetheless work together well in Washington. They cooperate in promoting the same policies, sponsoring joint fundraisers, and in general behaving as a unified bloc.

BUSINESS UNITY BEYOND THE INDUSTRY

Political unity on an industrywide basis, whether or not coordinated through the trade association, is the most common form of political coalition, but corporations also unify on other bases: a similar marketing approach, form of financing, pension arrangement, source of raw material, ultimate client, and the like.

> On other types of legislation, on tax legislation affecting 936 companies in Puerto Rico—we're allies with any other 936 company. We're working with [our top two competitors]—we're not competitors, then.
>
> In the marketplace we're competitors, but when it comes to the halls of Congress or the halls of the legislatures, we are allies more than we are opponents. It is bottom-line oriented, but it's not who has the biggest share of the market. It's all of us being able to sell our products in a healthy environment, so then we can compete for market share.

Unity need not be based on a specific shared attribute. A general sense of shared commonality is the hardest to explain and specify, but it is perhaps the most important basis for unity. Corporations have a common structural position; PAC officers share a social world and culture. The top executives of the corporation are tied together through common stock ownership, bank loans, board of director interlocks, membership in policy associations, and socialization. Company CEOs frequently show an amazing degree of agreement; for example, a spring 1996 poll reported that 96 percent of them wanted Alan Greenspan to serve another four years as chair of the Federal Reserve.[13] The government relations officers are members of the same few associations, spend their lives attending the same kinds of events and functions, meet each other fifty times a year at fundraisers, legislative committee hearings, restaurants and clubs. They talk to each other on the phone, read the same journals and materials, and get information from the same places. Even their disagreements occur within a larger framework of ideological consensus and personal trust. People have friends and acquaintances in common. Years ago they may have worked for the same senator or House member, or for the same federal agency. When they want to pressure each other, they can do so gently through humor and banter that affirm their common position even as they express displeasure with a specific action:

> INTERVIEWER: If you did give to Metzenbaum, would someone call you up and say what are you doing?
>
> CORPORATE EXECUTIVE: Yes, they might. I've said that to other people: "Why? Why? You're cutting off your nose."

Mild humor is fine, the kind of teasing that makes you uneasy enough to avoid a course of action that might bring about a barrage of similar remarks, but none of this joshing involves outright hostility or serious pressure:

> You get offhand remarks: "What did you give to that pain in the ass for?" "Your pain in the ass is my salve." You get that sometimes. Nobody's ever called me on the phone to seriously badger us for having done something, but you might say something in passing.

These kinds of innocent exchanges are enforcement mechanisms that preserve a generalized business unity. They allow one corporation to express displeasure with another, but only in the acceptable context of humor.

Corporations may at times choose to go it alone, but for even the largest and most powerful it is a considered choice, and it is a point of pride that they are willing and able to do so:

> We've gone against the wind or against the grain on a number of occasions, and it doesn't cause us any particular grief. We supported a congressman from [state] back in the seventies and eighties by the name of X. It was in those days a Democratic district. We had a facility with almost ten thousand employees in it. He didn't particularly vote down the line on all issues we felt were important, but he did recognize we were a major employer and a force in his district, and he always had an open mind and was very helpful to us. Sometimes if he couldn't be with us on an issue, he was very helpful in the procedural aspect of Congress. And as a powerful figure in Congress, he was influential to

help out there, and we had a great deal of support from our employees, and we supported him. I'd venture to say X didn't get a lot of corporate PAC money when he was in the House of Representatives.

INTERVIEWER: Did other businesses have any trouble about that?

CORPORATE EXECUTIVE: Oh yes, people will good-naturedly give you a little barb or a catcall. Other PACs would, or sometimes candidates would. They would say, "What are you giving to that guy for," but again we don't try to tell other people how to run their PACs. We think we have enough expertise and enough people who know what they are doing, and I guess we have enough self-confidence that if other people tell us how to run our PAC, that's their freedom, but we are not necessarily going to listen to them.

This highly pragmatic corporation was proud of its willingness to go against the grain—to contribute to a powerful Democrat who did his best to help them out and was extremely popular with the ten thousand company employees he represented! The grain it was going against is a generalized sense that corporations shouldn't give to liberals, and this member was not just a moderate but a genuine liberal.[14]

These organizations and this common culture create a situation where "it's pretty easy to see if you are in the mainstream or if you are not"; associated with this is an array of pressures for conformity. Usually this is the primary meaning of business unity: a generalized sense of common orientation and purpose, with subtle pressures on those who step outside the mainstream. The sense exists that businesses ought to support one another, even if the issue has no particular significance to their corporation:

You have to put [our company] not only in [this industry and that industry] but also in the broader service sector. Occasionally there are differences between the service sector and manufacturing, but, generally speaking, the goals we seek are consistent with the free enterprise system. Plant-closing legislation just passed. We would oppose that just as the NAM did, Chamber of Commerce—we're members of both of those—so even though manufacturing would be most heavily concerned about plant-closing legislation, we too in the service sector are concerned. You will always find divergence of opinion on specifics, but, generally speaking, I think we are all consistent in our support of the free enterprise system.

In this instance the company played a largely passive role on the issue, but in other cases corporations are mobilized to fight a key issue, and even those who would be willing to accept a proposed bill nevertheless maintain business solidarity by taking an active stance against it.

For example, in the labor law reform fight discussed in Chapter 5, unions expected most major employers to support the bill, or at least to stay out of the fight. It seemed that pragmatic corporations ought to be able to live easily with the bill—perhaps after winning a few "minor adjustments." Inside the business community, opinion was in fact divided, with major employers who had good labor relations arguing that business should let the bill pass without making a major effort to fight it. The turning point was a decision by the Business Roundtable: Its policy committee voted 19 to 8 to oppose the bill.

> Subsequently, even those corporations that had favored neutrality lobbied actively against the bill. GE, perhaps the strongest supporter of neutrality, sent its plant managers to Washington to lobby their representatives.[15]

The congressional outcome might have been different if a sizeable fraction of the major corporations had supported the bill, or even had let it be known that they wouldn't mind if it passed. Corporate success in this struggle depended on the ability of business to unify, and the willingness of those on the losing end of the vote to reverse themselves and work hard for the position they had voted against.

◆ CONTROL OF THE ECONOMY

Business's power is magnified and reinforced by its political unity. The bedrock of its power, however, is the pervasive economic inequality in our society, and the domination of the economy by business. Corporations do not get their political power solely from campaign contributions. We need to examine the full range of business power in order to understand the obstacles to campaign finance reform.

LEVELS OF INEQUALITY

Discussions of inequality in the United States usually focus on income, and the inequalities of income *are* substantial. In 1995, 1 out of 5 families had an income of less than $19,070, the average (median) family had an income of $40,611, the top 5 percent had incomes of more than $123,656, and the top 1 percent of households had average (mean) incomes of more than $400,000.[16] For every dollar in income received by households in the bottom fifth of the income distribution, 13 dollars were received by households in the top fifth.

But the inequalities of *wealth* are far greater.[17] The top 10 percent of the nation's families control more than two-thirds of the national wealth;[18] the top 1 percent control 42 percent.[19] The top 1 percent thus controls substantially more wealth than the bottom 90 percent of the population.

These disparities are enormous, not simply because the wealthy have several Porsches and Mercedes while others drive beat-up Chevys or Fords. They are enormous because some people, wealthy people, own the factories and offices where many of the rest of us work. The very rich own productive assets as well as consumption goods. In consumption, there are only gradational differences: Everyone has some, the issue is only how much. In production, there are fundamentally different relationships: Some people own assets and give orders; others work for a wage and obey orders.[20]

The primary power of the wealthy is not exercised by individuals or even by families. Power in our society is based in institutions, not individuals, and the power of wealth is channeled through corporations. There are more than 200,000 industrial corporations in the United States, but all companies are *not* created equal: The 500 largest industrials control three-quarters of the sales, assets, and profits of *all* industrial corporations. More than 250 of these companies had revenues of more than $5 billion.[21] Similarly, in the service sector, 500 firms control a disproportionate share of the resources. The dominance of these corporations means that a handful of owners and top executives, perhaps one-hundredth of one percent of the U.S. population, or 25,000 individuals, have the power to make decisions that have a huge impact on all of our lives.[22] Collectively these people exercise incalculable power, making decisions with more impact on most of our lives than those made by the entire elected government.[23]

Consider for a moment those decisions that virtually everyone in our society agrees should be made by business. Consider, for this exercise, only those decisions on which there is broad bipartisan political agreement; exclude anything that would generally be considered ethically or legally dubious and anything where a significant fraction of elected officials dispute business's right. Exclude, as well, any actions that are taken only through business's influence on government, and confine your attention to the decisions made in operating businesses. Remember that any decision made by "business" is primarily determined by the 25,000 individuals at the top of the corporate ladder, since their companies control about three-quarters of *all* corporate sales, assets, employees, and profits.

BUSINESS DECISIONS

What are some of these decisions? A brief and partial list indicates their scope:

Decisions about employment

- the number of people employed
- when to have layoffs
- the number of hours people work
- when work begins in the morning and ends in the afternoon
- whether to phase out full-time jobs and replace them with part-time, lower-wage, no-benefits jobs. In 1997, UPS workers and the Teamsters Union successfully contested the company's increasingly heavy reliance on part-timers, but it was big news that a union even attempted to raise the issue, much less that they were able to win.
- whether or not there is overtime, and whether it is compulsory
- whether to allow flextime and job-sharing
- the skill level of the jobs. Does the company make an effort to use lots of skilled workers paid good wages or is it always trying to de-skill positions and replace skilled workers with unskilled?
- the educational (and other) requirements for employment. Are certain educational levels *necessary* in order to be hired, or are they simply helpful? Are exconvicts or former mental patients eligible for all jobs or only some? What about the handicapped?
- whether the firm de facto discriminates in favor of men and whites or makes an active effort to recruit and promote minorities and women
- workers' rights on the job. For example, do they have free speech? A worker at a Coca-Cola plant was given a three-day suspension (without pay) because his wife brought him a lunch with a soda from Burger King, at a time when Burger King sold Pepsi. It is totally legal to penalize an employee for this or many other such actions.
- job safety. In one of the most extreme examples, a worker was killed while performing a dangerous task. Almost immediately thereafter another worker was ordered to do the same job, and refused because he said conditions were unsafe and had not been remedied. The company fired him for this refusal, and the Supreme Court upheld the firing.
- (within limits) whether or not a union is recognized; whether the union and the workers are treated with dignity and respect; how bitterly and viciously the union is resisted.

Investment decisions

- decisions about whether to expand a plant, and if so, which plant to expand
- whether to merge the corporation and "downsize" workers. Recently, a number of corporations have laid off thousands of employees, blighting

communities and individual lives, at the same giving huge bonuses to the top executives.

◆ whether to contract out jobs

◆ whether to close down a plant; when and how to do so. Virtually no one questions a company's absolute right (in the United States, not in Europe) to shut down if it chooses to do so, no matter what the effect on the workers and communities.

◆ where to open new plants. The company has every right to bargain for the best deal it can get. Deals can include tax abatements and implicit agreements to ignore labor or pollution laws.

Product and marketing

◆ the products produced, including whether to introduce a new product and whether to discontinue an old stand-by

◆ the design, both functional and esthetic

◆ the relative attention to different considerations: in a new car, how important is styling? sex appeal? fuel efficiency? safety? durability?

◆ the quality of the goods produced. Are they made to last, with high standards throughout, or are they just made to look good in the store and for the first month of use?

◆ the price for which goods are sold

◆ the character of the advertising used to promote the product. Does it stress the significant features of the product, or distract through sex and extraneous symbols?

◆ the amount spent on advertising—90 percent of the commercials on prime time television are sponsored by the nation's 500 largest corporations[24]

◆ the places where ads appear—in left-wing journals? in right-wing journals? on television? on which programs?

Community and environment

◆ the level of pollution in the workplace: air, heat, noise, chemicals, and so on

◆ the level of pollution in the outside environment. Beginning in the 1970s, for pollution both in the workplace and in the larger community, the government set maximum limits for a few items, but companies are completely free to do better than these standards. No government regulation prevents companies from setting and meeting tougher standards of their own devising. For example, in July 1991, a railroad tanker car derailed, tumbled into the Sacramento River, ruptured, and spilled pesticide. The pesticide was not listed as a regulated substance, and therefore the railroad was not required to carry it in a double-hulled tanker, though it could have chosen to do so. Though the pesticide was unregulated, it *was* strong enough to kill virtually all the fish in the river, formerly famous for its trout.[25]

◆ the degree of consideration for the community: Does the company make an effort to be a good neighbor? Does it contribute to local charities?[26] Support local initiatives?

This by no means exhausts the list of decisions that companies are allowed to make. Not only allowed to make, but expected and, in many cases, required to make. There is some regulation of business decisions at the margin, with possible regulation for issues such as: Can a company pull up stakes and leave town with no more than a day's notice? Can it dump raw wastes in the river? Can it make dubious claims in its advertising? For the most part, however, corporations are free to make decisions about their economic operations. *If the government fails to act, big business can do as it wishes.* The access process can be so successful because a corporation is not usually asking for an explicit transfer of government funds, but asking "only" to be allowed to continue to make economic decisions on the basis of its own short-term interests without regard to their effect on other members of the society. The corporation's government relations operation can succeed by winning delays, using the access process to craft special language that permits the specific corporate practice to continue, getting the regulations drafted in the way most favorable to the company, or reducing enforcement and penalties for violations. Weak or ineffective government—or at least, weak and ineffective enforcement of certain regulations—serves corporate interests almost as effectively as pro-business regulations. Thus there are three times as many fish and wildlife inspectors as there are inspectors to enforce all workplace health and safety regulations. This is one reason Gingrich and the Republicans thought they would have support if they refused to pass a budget and "closed down the government" in late 1995.[27]

THE PINTO GAS TANK

What does this mean in practice? How does business economic control interact with government relations and political action? Thousands of examples could be chosen, either from cases where business decisions seem thoroughly sensible or from those where they do not. Since power is most visible when it appears problematic, we illustrate business decision making with the Pinto gas tank, an example chosen primarily because some excellent reporting has managed to bring out facts that usually stay hidden.

In the late 1960s, Lee Iacocca, at the time president of Ford Motor Company and fresh from his triumph with the Mustang, fought to have Ford produce subcompacts. What ultimately became the Pinto was rushed into production in order to meet competition from the imports. Iacocca insisted that "the Pinto was not to weigh an ounce over 2,000 pounds and not to cost a cent over $2,000."[28] Business defenders can reasonably argue that approximately these limits were determined by the competitive market; in this sense, while Iacocca made the decision, it was heavily constrained. These constraints are real and important, but they still leave a great deal of room for maneuver.[29]

This point is illustrated by what happened as design and production proceeded, and "crash tests revealed a serious defect in the gas tank." Dowie reports that in Ford's own tests every crash at more than 25 miles per hour resulted in a ruptured fuel tank, unless the car was structurally altered.

When it was discovered the gas tank was unsafe, did anyone go to Iacocca and tell him? "Hell no," replied an engineer who worked on the Pinto, a high company official for many years. . . . "That person would have been fired. Safety wasn't a popular subject around Ford in those days. With Lee it was taboo. Whenever a problem was raised that meant a delay on the Pinto, Lee would chomp on his cigar, look out the window and say 'Read the product objectives and get back to work.'"[30]

In the "good old days" before about 1965, the odds are that no one would have learned that the Pinto had a dangerous and defective gas tank design, because the overwhelmingly dominant safety focus was on drivers. Almost certainly the fact that Ford made explicit decisions to save money by letting the defective gas tanks kill people would not have emerged. The issue of the cars themselves simply wasn't discussed until 1965, when consumer activist Ralph Nader burst on the scene with *Unsafe at Any Speed*[31] and then led a campaign for federal regulation of auto safety. In the altered political climate of the 1970s, the federal government was supposed to regulate auto safety. Ford was no longer allowed simply to make these decisions for itself; the decisions now became matters of public policy. It is in such situations that the access process becomes crucial. Corporate PAC and government relations officials work to prevent the government from making "hasty" and "ill-informed" decisions. By providing Congress and government regulators with relevant information and lobbying them for "sensible" regulations, corporate government relations specialists try to limit the "damage" that government does through "inappropriate" regulations.

In this particular case, Ford and its allies delayed the implementation of gas tank safety regulations for eight years. During that period Ford was free to continue to make its own decisions, guided by its own conception of what was best. Because business makes the decisions unless and until government specifically enacts a law or regulation to limit business "freedom,"[32] Ford did not have to secure passage of the legislation it wanted, much less public support for its position. It needed only to delay, weaken, and frustrate Congress and regulatory agencies.

One of the tools Ford used was a "cost–benefit analysis" calculation of whether it made economic sense to prevent gas tank fuel leakage accidents. By Ford's calculation, safe gas tanks would save 180 burn deaths, 180 serious burn injuries, and 2,100 burned vehicles each year. Ford calculated the value of human life as $200,000 per death, $67,000 per injury, and $700 per vehicle, for a net benefit of $49.5 million from this regulation.[33] However, by Ford's estimate, the cost of saving lives and injuries was far higher: $11 per car or truck, and, with annual production of 11 million cars and 1.5 million light trucks, the cost would come to $137 million per year. This cost–benefit analysis (like many others) was biased and subject to manipulation. Others estimated there would be ten times as many burn injuries as Ford projected and that accidents could be prevented for far less than the $11 figure Ford used—not to mention the small matter of the value of a human life. But Ford's chief "safety" official included the analysis in documents submitted to the Secretary of Transportation arguing against new regulations. This kind of memo would not be used in an advertising campaign ("Ford has a better idea—Let em burn"), but it is relatively standard fare for government relations lobbying. While this cost–benefit analysis was probably the most outrageous of Ford's lobbying tactics, Ford found many additional ways to delay regulation, by submitting reams of evidence, insisting additional studies were needed, coming up with new arguments at each stage in the proceedings, and always delaying its response until the last possible day.

From one perspective, this delay meant the needless loss of human lives, but from the perspective of corporate government relations, it did an effective job of defending company profits. In retrospect, Ford would probably have been better off if it had been less successful in fighting the regulation. When Ford was ultimately forced to fix the problem, it managed to do so for only about $1 per car (not the $11 it had projected in its cost–benefit analysis).

Meanwhile, the dangers of the Ford Pinto became widely known, and burn victims sued the company. Juries learned that Ford had consciously decided to let people burn and die rather than spend somewhere between $1 and $11 per car to prevent fuel tank fires. Jurors valued human life somewhat more dearly than did the Ford Motor Company, and victims received substantial settlements. (Today companies are trying to deal with this "problem" by limiting the right to sue companies and restricting the amounts that can be received for such injuries.)

SPENDING THE MONEY

Direct decisions about day-to-day operations are the foundation for business power. But those who control production also receive the profits and can decide how they get spent. This implies choices about the kind of society we should have and the activities that should be supported. For example, national advertising expenditures were $161.86 billion in 1995.[34] This amounts to $647 per person—more than the total annual income per person in many countries of the world.[35] Total spending on advertising (per year) is well over fifty times what we spend on elections (every other year), and is well over half of total spending on public elementary and secondary education.[36]

The dollar amounts are huge; the impact on our culture no less so. An average television viewer spends well over four hours a week watching commercials.[37] Whatever advertising's effect on sales of specific products, the continuous implicit message—buy, buy, buy; you are what you own; consumer goods can make you sexy, respected, a good mother—necessarily shapes every member of this society, whether we accept these values happily or attempt to reject them. In choosing presidential candidates, television ads ("Where's the beef?") provide the memorable lines, so that our choice of a president is influenced by a snappy hamburger ad. Many of our best minds devote themselves to promoting toothpaste and soap powder, not to mention tobacco and beer. Advertising shapes the culture when it "only" promotes the merits of Presta-Glop over Ultra-Goo toothpaste, but corporations spend increasingly large sums on advertising that is not tied to a product. Some of this is simply meant to convince you that Octopus Industries is a good neighbor and citizen, that you should forget the lung cancer and drunk driving associated with their products and focus instead on their support for the Bill of Rights (or the Olympics, Statue of Liberty, and the rest). But much of it specifically promotes political positions. Corporations, or wealthy individuals and foundations that derive their money from business, are also primary sources of funding for many charities, for essential elements of higher education, and for think tanks. Most attempts to develop policy proposals are funded by business, and while there is no direct control over the findings of these studies, business obviously tends to support analysts with a past record of recommending the kinds of proposals business likes to see.

Consider what this means, in practice, for advertising. Big corporations are perfectly clear: They won't advertise in magazines that run stories criticizing the company's business. A striking example of this is the tobacco industry. An American Cancer Society representative noted, "What's very dramatically absent from women's magazines—and some news magazines—are articles about tobacco, the rising rate of women smoking, and the resulting health problems."[38] A study in the *New England Journal of Medicine* concluded, after comparing magazines that did not carry cigarette ads to those that did, that the no-ad magazines were almost twice as likely to carry articles on the dangers of smoking. Most magazines censor themselves in order to avoid losing advertising revenue, and this process is becoming more explicit and blatant. At *Harper's*, ever since Nuveen canceled a major ad, the ad director and the publisher have become "more and more involved in the editorial process, killing articles and pictures on the grounds that advertisers would object." Chrysler's advertising agency notified magazines: "Each and every issue that carries Chrysler advertising requires a written summary outlining major theme/articles appearing in upcoming issues"; and this must be provided sufficiently in advance so that Chrysler can cancel its ads in any issue containing information it doesn't want the public to have. A Los Angeles television station fired a reporter for his stories on auto safety; a Duluth newspaper fired its consumer affairs reporter for stories on selling your house without a real estate agent. A survey of investigative reporters found that "74 percent said advertisers had tried to influence the content of a news story in the last three years—40 percent said the advertiser succeeded."

CONFRONTING BUSINESS POWER

A corporation's political power does not depend simply on its own campaign contributions. A member of Congress evaluating a company's request for a multimillion-dollar tax loophole does not simply balance a $1,000 campaign contribution against a $50 million tax giveaway. Because business is politically unified and tied together in overlapping informal networks, helping this one corporation can develop a reputation for the member as someone who is willing (and able) to help out. Such a reputation can lead to donations from companies (and individuals) that the member barely knows.

The member's decision on whether to support the company's request is not based exclusively on campaign finance. Probably more important is the corporation's role in the economy. The member may well resent the fact that the company is proposing a sleazy tax deal. But the company may implicitly (or explicitly) be threatening that if it doesn't get this giveaway, it will close the factory and move production overseas. A similar logic applies to environmental regulations: The company may have a plausible, though suspect, analysis proving that a proposed regulation cannot be met without closing a plant. Although companies frequently lie and/or err in these claims, the company's control over the economy influences a field of power that constrains the member's decision more surely than any campaign contribution.[39]

Campaign finance proposals cannot ignore the power relations in the larger society. Many reform proposals are intended only to punish the occasional maverick, while ratifying the ability of money in general to dominate political decisions. Other reform proposals attempt to use Band-Aids to deal with cancer. Even a lot of Band-Aids won't do the job. We need to go another way, and that is the course we propose in the next chapter.

◆ 7

SCANDAL OR SYSTEM?

THE 1996 ELECTIONS INVOLVED MASSIVE CAMPAIGN FINANCE ABUSES—but so had every previous election. Although 1996 was substantially worse than usual, the sharpest change from the past was the 1996–97 media attention to, and congressional investigation of, the issue. Much of the hype was silly and/or fraudulent, with politicians acting shocked that anyone would ever do *x, y*, or *z*—even if they themselves have routinely done *x, y*, and *z*. One possible response to these scandals and investigations would be to recognize that the problems are fundamental and widespread, so that meaningful reform requires a basic change of the system, not minor tinkering. Few significant political figures have embraced that conclusion, but it is the solution we propose here. An alternative response is: "Let's find a couple of scapegoats, punish them, then make a few cosmetic changes in the areas that have attracted the most attention. That will leave the basic framework untouched and allow us to proceed more or less as in the past." This strategy—the de facto policy of virtually every member of Congress—works best if the scapegoats are clearly marked out as different from ordinary donors and politicians.

The scapegoat donor has been foreign money, presumably on the rationale that it's fine to have democracy bought off and manipulated by American businesses and rich people, but it would be terrible if foreigners did so. The slogan for this might be, "Corruption for Americans!" The scapegoat politician, at least as of this writing, appears to be Vice President Al Gore, with President Bill Clinton as understudy. The problem with taking a scapegoat from Congress is that he or she could point out that dozens—probably hundreds—of other members had done the same things. The president

198 ♦ DOLLARS AND VOTES

and vice president, however, can be presented as different. The president doesn't make so good a scapegoat as the vice president since he will not run for office again.

This chapter investigates the 1996 election scandals, puts them in perspective, and then considers reform, both the pseudoreforms that are widely discussed and what meaningful reform would require. The most promising development in decades is the emergence of state ballot initiatives with the potential to totally transform the system. Going directly to the voters might lead to change—professional politicians have a long history of publicly favoring reform and then finding ways to bury it in committee.

CLINTON AND GINGRICH AS REFORMERS

In the 1992 election, Bill Clinton promised not only "to end welfare as we know it," but also to end big-money domination of politics. In his first Inaugural Address, he returned to the issue: "Let us resolve to reform our politics so that power and privilege no longer shout down the voice of the people." Clinton hasn't changed his mind since: At least in public, he continues to support reform. In June 1995, Clinton and Speaker of the House Newt Gingrich appeared together at a New Hampshire senior center, where Clinton said: "I would love to have a bipartisan commission on it [campaign finance reform]. It's the only chance to get anything passed." Then Gingrich joined: "Let's shake hands right here in front of everybody. How's that? Is that a pretty good deal?"[1] During the year that followed, no commission was ever named, and none of the hundreds of campaign finance reform bills introduced in Congress made it to a floor vote. In his 1997 State of the Union address, Clinton "challenged" Congress to give him a campaign finance reform bill to sign by Independence Day. Clinton—while failing to appoint Federal Election Commissioners who would enforce the law—continued to insist that Congress do something, even threatening, in September 1997, to keep Congress in session until it voted on a bill.[2] In Congress, dozens of members sponsored their own reform legislation—great publicity for a reelection campaign—but somehow none of the legislation made it as far as a committee vote, until a sudden change in late September brought legislation straight to the floor without having gone through committee. Even then, however, congressional leaders made it clear that they were committed to killing the legislation. Their failure to pass legislation is not the result of public opposition: Campaign finance reform remains popular with the voters. If voters were the key to public policy, the campaign finance system would long since have been changed, and NAFTA (North American Free Trade Agreement), business's favorite, would have been defeated; instead, Clinton made NAFTA his priority and quietly buried campaign finance—with the full cooperation of a Republican Congress.

1996 DEMOCRATIC SCANDALS

Campaign finance violations in the 1996 election were the most serious since Watergate. "What we saw in this election cycle was nothing less than the breakdown of the campaign finance system," said political scientist Anthony Corrado. "The system we created in the 1970s essentially collapsed. . . . It's the Wild West out there. It's anything goes."[3] The system collapsed in a dozen different ways, with every rule being bent past the breaking point and politicians assuming they didn't need to worry about enforcement, from soft money to issue advertising to reporting requirements.

Most of the attention, at least initially, focused on foreign soft money contributions to the Democrats—especially Asian contributions. A headline after the first day of Senate hearings on campaign finance read: "Chinese plot on campaign funds seen."[4] The chair of the Senate Governmental Affairs Committee, Fred Thompson, trumpeted the news: "I speak of allegations concerning a plan hatched during the last election cycle by the Chinese government and designed to pour illegal money into American political campaigns . . . to buy access and influence in furtherance of Chinese Government interests." The publicly available evidence did not substantiate this claim, but Thompson—a potential Republican presidential nominee in 2000—continued to insist it was true. Unfortunately, he said, he could not reveal the secret information that would prove his charges,[5] information that Democratic members of the committee had seen and most had found unconvincing.

The cast of characters brought before the 1997 Senate inquiry or featured in the news came primarily from this "Asian connection": John Huang, Charlie Trie, the Riadys (Mochtar and James), Johnny Chung, Wang Jun, Buddhist nuns, and others. There is little doubt that millions of the dollars raised by Huang and Trie came from sources other than those listed on FEC-required documents. Trie is infamous for turning in two manila envelopes containing $460,000 (in cash) supposedly collected from penniless Buddhists, while Huang's donors included those with untraceable addresses, several with identical handwriting (and misspellings!), and a few who were dead. Johnny Chung is best known for explaining that "the White House is like a subway: You have to put in coins to open the gates."[6] The Democrats have been embarrassed into returning $1.6 million of the $3.4 million that Huang raised and $645,000 that came through Trie.

Both Huang and Trie are longtime friends of the Clintons from their Little Rock days, as are the Riadys, the family that controls the Indonesia-based Lippo Group, a $12 billion conglomerate with large investments in China and Hong Kong. The Riadys and Lippo appear at the center of the web of connections that makes up this foreign influence scandal. More than $1 million in soft money can be traced from the Riadys—through various entities—to the Democrats, and nearly two-thirds of the foreign money returned had come from this one family. Huang was the head of the Lippo bank in Los Angeles before serving as deputy assistant secretary of trade in the Commerce Department and later, after a "marathon lobbying campaign" by the Riadys, as Democratic National Committee (DNC) vice chair. Pushing for Huang to move his connections closer to the White House—including top-secret security clearance—were James Riady, the son of Lippo's founder and a friend of Bill Clinton, and Joseph Giroir, a former law partner of Hillary Clinton turned Riady lobbyist.[7] Huang, the former Riady employee, visited the White House ninety-four times and met with the president fifteen times. The Riady-Clinton ties were extremely close, offering the Riady family and associates extraordinary access to the president and other top U.S. officials.

Although the primary focus was on donations that directly or indirectly came from companies and individuals based in Asia, almost as much attention was accorded aggressive fundraising by Clinton and Gore. Tens of millions of dollars were raised from those attending White House events, such as "coffees" and sleepovers in the Lincoln Bedroom, with the donations typically arriving shortly before or after the White House visit. According to FBI agent Jerome Campane, "Ninety percent of those who attended the coffee sessions donated money to the Democrats and 40 percent did so within a month of the event."[8] White House spokesperson Michael McCurry, however, maintains: "The question is whether the president directly solicited funds during these occasions, and he did not."[9] Legal technicalities aside, it is clear that potential donors were encouraged to believe that their contributions would produce access, and that access was in fact delivered. A summer 1995 letter signed by party cochairs Senator Christopher Dodd and Donald Fowler indicated that a contribution of $100,000 or more would get a donor meals with President Clinton and Vice President Gore, as well as a Democratic National Committee (DNC) staff member assigned to assist with their "personal requests."[10] Fowler, the chair of the DNC during the election, explicitly admitted arranging access for big donors and defended the practice,[11] by insisting only that his principle was to provide access "for a supporter, some of whom are donors and some of whom are not," and that "whatever they contributed or didn't contribute had nothing to do with my actions in that regard."[12]

Clinton and Gore also made fundraising calls from the White House. The then–White House counsel, Abner J. Mikva, clearly believed this to be illegal, since in 1995 he issued a directive that "no fundraising phone calls or mail may emanate from the White House or any other federal building."[13] By late 1997, White House counsel Lanny Davis was defending the opposite conclusion.[14] Vice President Gore claimed that his credit card fundraising calls from the White House were legal, repeating seven times in the course of his public comments: "My counsel tells me there is no controlling legal authority that says there was any violation of any law."[15] Gore claims that the money was not raised "directly," as the transaction took place at the receiving end of the phone call. "I never asked for a campaign contribution from anyone who was in a government office," said Gore. The legal issues are extremely murky: The law in question dates to 1883 (before telephones), is part of the act that created the modern civil service, and was intended to protect federal employees from being asked for contributions in exchange for patronage jobs; it is unclear whether the law has ever been applied to a case like Gore's or Clinton's. If Gore solicited exclusively for soft money contributions, those are probably not covered by the law (soft money, by definition, is all the money that is not regulated by law). The Democratic party, however, in a quest to increase the amount of hard money available to spend directly promoting President Clinton, divided large donations into two parts, putting as much as possible into hard money accounts and the remainder into soft money accounts. Gore and Clinton may or may not have known this was happening, but it potentially changes the legal standing of the activity.[16] Similar concerns apply to some of Clinton's phone calls, though he appears to be less vulnerable.[17] The release of videotapes of Clinton fundraisers—tapes which the White House had long insisted did not exist—further embarrassed the Democrats. Numerous Republicans denounced both the apparent cover-up and the activities revealed on camera, but for the most part the tapes were boring and framed in the vague terms that dominate these exchanges—that is, as gifts, not explicit exchanges—thereby avoiding any legal liability. A Republican lawyer said "I would be flabbergasted if there was any criminal action," adding "I would even be highly skeptical of any civil action by the Federal Election Commission."[18]

None of this led to any significant action. In October 1997, Congress voted down all campaign finance reform legislation, and in December, Attorney General Janet Reno decided not to appoint an independent prosecutor.[19] Republicans responded with outrage, but public attention rapidly moved on to other issues. Further revelations are likely, and there is still the possibility of a special prosecutor. That seems to be the main accountability that Clinton and Gore dread, because the history of special prosecutors shows that, once appointed, they always find violations.[20]

ONLY THE DEMOCRATS?

Most of the attention focused on abuses by Democrats—perhaps because Republicans controlled Congress and thus set the agenda for the congressional investigations. The Democrats may have been the worst offenders: Most rich people favor the Republicans, so the Democrats always have to stretch hard to raise money, and in doing so may be more likely to accept dubious arrangements. But the Republican record was nothing to brag about. The Republicans, too, have their "Asia connection." Haley Barbour, as chair of the Republican party, solicited a $2.2 million loan guarantee from Hong Kong businessman Ambrous Tung Young of Young Brothers in the final days of the 1994 campaign. The loan was ostensibly to keep the National Policy Forum (NPF) afloat, but the think tank's separation from the Republican National Committee (RNC) was a "fiction," according to former NPF president, Michael Baroody. Baroody, in his resignation letter, wrote about Barbour's desire to raise money from foreign sources: "I told you . . . that you were right about the possibility foreign money could be raised, but thought it would be wrong to do so. . . . The idea, nevertheless, seemed to hold some fascination."[21] The NPF used $1.6 million to pay money it owed the RNC, money that the RNC, in turn, immediately funneled into about twenty state Republican parties around the country.[22] Two years later, the NPF defaulted on the loan, sticking Young with a $700,000 loss but sparing the Republicans at election time 1996 from reaching into campaign funds to pay off the debt.[23]

Representative Dan Burton (Republican–Indiana), chair of the House Government Reform and Oversight Committee in charge of investigating campaign finance illegalities, is embroiled in two foreign-money scandals of his own. The FBI is investigating reports that Burton "shook down" a lobbyist for the Pakistani government, threatening to cut off contact with the lobbyist when the $5,000 Burton requested did not surface.[24] A U.S. Department of Education official, in another case, claims Congressman

Burton pressured him to delay eligibility standards for foreign medical schools involved in the U.S. student loan program. This exchange happened less than one week after Burton had received the second of two $1,000 donations from the president of a Caribbean medical school and his wife. Just months later, Burton, our crusader for campaign finance rectitude, asked the medical school's president to admit his daughter and to help his son-in-law get a job.[25]

For Republicans, as for Democrats, foreign money is only one part of the picture. Simon Fireman, a vice chair of Bob Dole's campaign finance committee, was penalized $6 million—split between Fireman personally and his company—for avoiding the $1,000 limit on individual campaign donations by persuading his employees to contribute, with a guarantee that they would be reimbursed from an overseas fund. By using his employees this way, Fireman funneled $120,000 in illegal contributions to Dole campaigns, the 1992 Bush–Quayle campaign, the Republican party, and even a group supporting Representative Joseph Kennedy (Democrat–Massachusetts).[26] The penalty, the largest ever imposed by the FEC, might just as well have been for stupidity, since Fireman could have contributed this amount in soft money and avoided legal hassles. Needless to say, given that Fireman is a white business owner, no one even considered a prison sentence for these multiple, carefully planned, legal violations.

Republicans as well as Democrats may need to return money already received. Auditors for the Federal Election Commission contend that Republicans violated rules about convention funding, and recommended the Republican party return $3.7 million, more than the total amount the Democrats have had to return for the 1996 campaign.[27]

The Republican National Committee has been explicit about what large donations buy. For $250,000, a "season ticket holder" is promised "the best access to Congress" and "the party's inner circle," including "support personnel in Washington DC" and private meetings with GOP leaders.[28] For $175,000 over four years, you become a member of "Team 100" and get to meet with high-ranking Republican officials and "international Team 100 business missions."[29] For $10,000, a Senatorial Trust rewards contributors with "intimacy" and "one-on-one interaction with Republican senators."[30] At the $5,000 level, you can become a GOP "Presidential Roundtable" member, which according to Senate Majority Leader Trent Lott's fundraising letter, entitles you to "plenty of opportunities to share your personal ideas and vision with some of our top Republican leaders."[31]

For other reports of Republican scandals, we need go no further than the members of the congressional campaign finance probe committees. Senate

Majority Whip and former National Policy Forum board member Don Nickles (Republican–Oklahoma) expressed shock and dismay at President Clinton's use of the White House for fundraising, but in 1990 he signed a fundraising appeal for a reception at the official residence of Vice President Quayle.[32] In a similar vein, Senator Robert C. Smith (Republican–New Hampshire) left a message on the wrong answering machine in 1995, revealing his request for campaign funds from his Senate office in violation of Senate rules.[33] In January 1997, Dan Burton (Republican–Indiana) became the head of the House committee investigating the ways political money is used to gain special access. Three weeks later he was playing golf in the Pebble Beach National Pro-Am Tournament, courtesy of an invitation from its sponsor, AT&T. Burton had long sought the invitation: "Over the past several years, whenever I talked to anybody at AT&T, I told them that if they ever had a chance, I'd like to play in that tournament." In fact, he said, "Since I was a kid, I've always watched it and wanted to play in it."[34] In addition to investigating big money's influence on the political process, Burton's committee will award "at least $5 billion in long-distance and local telephone and telecommunications contracts with the government."[35] Presumably the tournament positioned him to serve as an effective critic of White House ethics.

Many violations are bipartisan, including:

KIDDIE CASH. Contributions of more than $1,000 from "students" in FEC records have increased fourfold since 1980. Senator Edward Kennedy (Democrat–Massachusetts) set the record for such collections with $65,000 in the 1993–94 election cycle.[36] Fred Thompson raised $25,000 from children as young as nine years old in his 1994 Senate campaign.[37] The on-line magazine, *Slate*, reports FEC records reveal that:

> At least 25 and perhaps 50 of the top 400 political donors last year (two in the top 10) were joined by one or more children or grandchildren, from preteens to grad students, in giving to their favorite candidates. These top givers earned four White House sleepovers, eight White House coffees, two trade missions, and four memberships to the Republican Party's Team 100.[38]

Children are being used to expand the amount their parents can give to candidates and parties. Vinod Gupta, a $50,000 Democratic contributor, shows how it's done. His seventeen-year-old son told *USA Today*: "Dad makes these donations in my name," after dipping into his son's trust fund.[39] But some of these wealthy youngsters are fighting back. Two of Texas billionaire Harold C. Simmons's daughters sued their father for using their trust funds as "his own personal checking account." FEC records show the Simmons family contributing over $315,000 to Republicans since 1993. Tens of thousands, the daughters claim, came from their trust accounts to candidates and causes they often opposed. It seems Harold persuaded his daughters to sign blank political contribution letters under threat of losing their inheritance.[40]

"LAZY" BOOKKEEPING. How hard can it be to get a name, address, occupation, and employer name for a money donor? As discussed in the soft money chapter, for individual (not corporate, union, and the like) donors, each party obtains information for only about one-quarter of the contributors. This makes it difficult or impossible to discover the source of the campaign contribution. A policy of laziness keeps the money flowing without interruption. For instance, when the Wiriadinatas, an Indonesian couple with permanent residency status in the United States, contributed $425,000 to the Democratic party from November 1995 to June 1996, their donations were unquestioned, even though the couple had never made contributions in the past. The Wiriadinatas were later subpoenaed by the Senate inquiry into campaign finance. Amy Weiss Tobe, DNC press secretary, explained the look-the-other-way policy: "It's not the practice of the DNC or the fund-raising staff to interrogate donors about the source of funds used to make a contribution. If someone gives a donation for the party, we don't ask them what kind of car they drive or how big their home is."[41]

DOES IT MATTER?

Much of this focus on campaign finance is not only hypocritical, but seems self-consciously intended to shift attention away from the real problem—a *system* whose day-to-day operation necessarily involves creating advantages for those with wealth and power—to a focus on a few individuals and a limited number of technical abuses. The main attack on Vice President Gore, for example, focused on the phone calls he made to solicit contributions, and specifically his making some of these calls from the White House. Virtually every member of Congress makes phone calls to solicit contributions, and many of them routinely do so two or three days a week, often for half the day. We have no firm quantitative evidence on how frequently these calls are made from congressional offices, but if every senator or representative who had made such calls were punished, the only way Congress could muster a quorum would be to meet at the jail. Suppose Gore had walked across the street to make the calls: Would that change anything significant?

Or consider the so-called China connection and Clinton's links to the Riady family. Did the Riadys get favorable policy decisions in return for their contributions to the Clinton Democrats? When he campaigned for the presidency, Clinton opposed Most Favored Nation (MFN) trade status for China, given the country's post–Tiananmen Square human rights record. Documents show that in 1993, Mochtar Riady, James's father, urged Clinton to reverse his decision.[42] In 1996, James Riady called on Clinton to expand trade with China. Clinton granted Most Favored Nation status to China against the recommendations of the State Department and then planned to exchange visits with Chinese leaders in both 1997 and 1998.

Did the Riadys buy better investment conditions for Lippo?[43] Did China subvert the U.S. political system through a sinister use of $2 million? At least four points need to be made. First, despite every effort by the congressional committees, no convincing evidence of Chinese government involvement was produced. In a world of transnational corporations, of course the Riadys had business connections to China. By the same logic, we could show General Motors to be an agent of Germany, or Chrysler of Japan. Second, if it were possible to show that the Chinese government put $2 million into the 1996 U.S. elections, how much influence would this give them? It would be less than 1 percent of the soft money raised and less than one-tenth of 1 percent of total election spending. Altogether, subsidiaries of foreign-owned businesses contributed soft and PAC money totaling $12.5 million in 1995–96, and two-thirds of that went to Republicans; in total this money is less than 1 percent of election spending.[44]

Third, many of the same people who are outraged at the (remote) possibility of (minimal) Chinese involvement in U.S. elections vehemently support U.S. intervention in elections in other countries. In the 1980s, for example, the United States spent more than $4 million on influencing Nicaraguan elections. In order to spend as much *per person*, the Chinese would have had to put $300 million into the U.S. elections—and to spend as much in relation to per capita income, the Chinese would have had to put in $6 billion.[45] As the *New York Times* reported:

Congress routinely appropriates tens of millions of dollars in covert and overt money to use in influencing domestic politics abroad. The National Endowment for Democracy, created 15 years ago to do in the open what the Central Intelligence Agency has done surreptitiously for decades, spends $30 million a year to support things like political parties, labor unions, dissident movements and the news media in dozens of countries, including China.[46]

The endowment openly gave $3 million for the 1990 Nicaraguan election, "some of which," the Times reports, "was used to bolster Violeta Barrios de Chamorro, the presidential candidate favored by the United States."[47]

Fourth, and perhaps most important, the furor over foreign money is part of a current wave of U.S. xenophobia that blames our problems on foreigners and ignores the actions of U.S. business. If Clinton supported Chinese democracy when running for election, and then reversed himself and granted China trade privileges, the explanation for the turnabout has a lot more to do with huge U.S. multinationals than it does with the Riadys, who are big players by many standards but minor compared to the top U.S. firms. Consider the ad hoc Business Coalition for U.S.–China Trade, "a $1 trillion bloc of 55 major U.S. companies committed to free trade, including General Motors, Mobil, Exxon, Caterpillar, United Technologies, Boeing, Cargill, Philip Morris, Procter & Gamble, TRW, Westinghouse, IBM, and a few dozen more."[48] On the eve of the June 1996 vote for China's Most Favored Nation trade status, the Center for Responsive Politics estimated that these businesses gave over $20 million in PAC money to members of Congress in just one year. Robert Dreyfuss may have summed up the situation best: "China doesn't need to lobby the U.S. government—it has the Fortune 500."[49]

◆ REFORMING THE SYSTEM

Everyone is talking about campaign finance reform. But what kind of reform? The answer varies. If the problem is occasional abuses by renegade fundraisers, then the only change needed is a system of improved enforcement; and if the major recurring abuse is accepting (indirect) Asian money, the solution is to scrutinize—if necessary, to harass—any Asian American contributor.[50] If the problem is that the public has (momentarily? irrationally?) lost faith in the system, and now sees democracy for sale, then the solution is to address the most visible symbol of this—soft money—and make cosmetic changes elsewhere, loudly proclaiming that this is a thorough reform. For campaign finance insiders—a tiny fraction of the population, but crucial for policy decisions—the problem is that politicians are having to work too hard to raise money. The solution is to find some way to reduce the cost of campaigns (typically, through limited free television time), while seeing to it that the margin of success continues to depend on campaign contributions from big-money donors, which is, after all, the system that put these politicians into office. Most campaign finance experts analyze the issue in ways generally similar to the political insiders. Academic "expertise," and certainly media punditry, generally depends on possessing views certified as "reasonable" by those with power—that is, by politicians, the media, business, and big-money campaign contributors. For most members of the American public—and for us—the problem is an entire system that is institutionally corrupt, that coerces politicians to put dollars over voters, that buys off democracy. The solution, therefore, must be a complete overhaul and the introduction of a fundamentally new system.

THE PURPOSE OF REFORM

A naive observer might think that campaign finance reform is about reforming campaign finance. Nothing could be more mistaken. The voters want to reform the system. Politicians have a variety of other priorities. In order, they are probably as follows:

CONTINUING TO GET RE-ELECTED. From the politicians' perspective, their own election is proof that the current system works—or, at least, their own election shows that talented individuals with noble ideals often win. In order to be elected, politicians must be master fundraisers; they are therefore likely to conclude the money primary serves a useful purpose.

MAINTAINING GOOD RELATIONS WITH BIG CONTRIBUTORS. Supporting real reform would offend these contributors, and that's a huge risk, since politicians assume that whatever "reform" is enacted, the system will continue to be dominated by big money, and reelection will continue to depend on the support of these donors. Moreover, most members hope that when they leave Congress they will make a lot more money. That nearly always means going to work for business, either directly (as an employee) or indirectly (as a lobbyist or consultant).

MAINTAINING THE LEGITIMACY OF THE SYSTEM. For those with power, up to a point a cynical and alienated public has as many advantages as disadvantages, since it means that politicians and business are left to run the system themselves. However, if too many people conclude the system is rotten, that creates the potential for mass mobilization demanding a fundamental change in the system. That's a risk that neither politicians nor business wants to run. During the 1930s, Joseph P. Kennedy declared, "I felt and said I would be willing to part with half of what I had if I could be sure of keeping, under law and order, the other half."[51] In order to forestall the possibility of again facing such a situation, many of the rich and powerful—and even more politicians—are concluding that some kind of change, one that can plausibly be sold as reform, would be at least useful and is perhaps necessary.

GAINING PARTISAN ADVANTAGE. Some sources of money strongly favor the Republicans, other sources favor the Democrats. If there is to be "reform," each party concludes that regulation needs to be tightened for the money that goes to the other party. In the 1996 election cycle, the Democrats raised almost as much soft money as the Republicans; the Republicans had small but significant advantages for both PAC and individual contributions. Republicans receive almost no labor money; coincidentally, they are convinced that labor (despite its comparatively small scale and marginal status) is the worst offender, and hence the area most in need of new regulation.

ACHIEVING REAL REFORM. Many politicians are committed to democracy. Their understanding of what that means, and their visions of how to achieve it, may differ from our own, but a great many members of Congress—though by no means all of them—would like to see reform, as long as it doesn't drastically reduce their chances of getting elected, hurt their relations with big-money contributors, or hurt the chances of their political party.

SERIOUSLY CONSIDERED REFORMS

In the wake of the 1996 election, only one reform proposal was taken seriously and given a realistic chance of being enacted—the McCain-Feingold bill, sponsored by Republican Senator John McCain (Arizona) and Democratic Senator Russell Feingold (Wisconsin), and thus a bill with bipartisan credentials. (McCain, currently the Senate's most visible campaign finance reformer, was one of the "Keating Five"—senators who, in the late 1980s, accepted large donations from Charles Keating and interceded for him with federal regulators; Keating's savings and loan subsequently went bankrupt, costing taxpayers more than $2 billion.) Although "McCain–Feingold" was always the focus of debate, the bill's provisions changed frequently. In September 1997, Feingold acknowledged that "the question of what will be in the bill is still very much up in the air."[52]

The fluid and shifting character of campaign finance discussions makes it impossible to focus on a single package of compromises. Many of the "reform" packages include proposals to permit *more* latitude for certain kinds of contributions, and as always with Congress, the devil is often in the details. It is, however, useful to consider some of the proposals that are widely discussed and that are likely, in one or another form, to be incorporated into any reform legislation:

LIMIT INDIVIDUAL DONATIONS. Individuals are now limited to $1,000 per candidate per election and $25,000 total per year, but a number of state ballot initiatives have sought to decrease contributions to as low as $100 per person per candidate. The simplicity of the $100 (or $200 or $300) limit is appealing and the logic of the approach—"limit what rich people can donate to an amount ordinary people can contemplate"[53]—tends to win votes. Lower courts, however, have several times (District of Columbia, Missouri, and Oregon) rejected the $100-limit proposal on the grounds that it interferes with free speech.[54] Aside from the legal obstacles, the consequences aren't clear: It would certainly help to create a Congress of millionaires who funded their own campaigns and would encourage "independent" spending; it might also lead to a form of contribution brokering, where key individuals lined up $100 contributors.[55]

LIMIT PAC DONATIONS. The current limit of $5,000 per candidate per election enables a PAC to give $10,000 to a candidate who faces both a primary and general election. The intent of both the current law and the proposed reforms is to limit the size of the donation to an amount so small that it couldn't influence a member's behavior.

Chapter 3 on access explains the misconception underlying this proposal. Even with today's limits, a single PAC donation is rarely large enough to make a member change a vote on a major, visible, contested issue. Therefore, the proposal won't change much in this regard. Relatively small donations, however, are sufficient to gain corporate PACs access to members to win "minor" wording changes that the public never hears about. The average corporate PAC donation in 1996 was $1,313 to House members and $1,942 to senators. Many proposed revisions would not touch these access donations. Moreover, if the limit were reduced to $500 (one-tenth of the current limit), the likely consequence would simply be an expansion of the steering committee approach (discussed in Chapter 6). Corporations that wanted access would join a member's steering committee, get ten other corporations to give the $500 limit, and earn credit with the member for raising $5,000. The total amount corporations gave and members received might not change at all.

BAN CORPORATE, LABOR, AND TRADE ASSOCIATION PACS. This ban was pro-

posed by President Bush in 1989. More recently, it became a part of one of
the many versions of the McCain–Feingold proposal endorsed by President Clinton in 1996. Assuming it could withstand legal challenges—which
is far from certain—one principal effect would be to cause a switch from
PAC giving (relatively easily monitored) to individual or soft money donations (much harder to track).

As powerful as they are, however, PACs account for only one-quarter of
the funding for congressional campaigns.[56] Assuming PAC money might
actually be abolished and not turn up in other forms of contributions, that
still leaves 75 percent of congressional campaign money untouched.

BAN SOFT MONEY. Great! Let's do it. This significant reform has wide back-
ing and may actually pass. But then the issue of political inequality remains. The problem of unequal political influence resulting, in part, from
a privately funded campaign system existed long before the soft money
scandals and certainly will not go away if soft money is abolished. A return
to the campaign finance system of 1990 or 1988 is not, to our minds, the
goal of reform.

LIMIT SPENDING. To hold down the cost of campaigns, limits could be set
on the total amount a candidate could spend during a campaign. The Supreme Court has outlawed spending limits, however, unless they are part
of a plan where candidates voluntarily accept public funding in exchange
for agreeing to abide by a spending limit. Even if this hurdle could be
overcome (and with the current composition of the Supreme Court that
seems unlikely), spending limits without additional changes would turn
out to be an incumbent-protection program. Why? Incumbents have important built-in advantages—name recognition, a chance to make news
through their actions, free postage for congressional business, money to
hire staff (some of whom will work in the district servicing constituents),
and so on. Therefore, in order to beat an incumbent, a challenger needs to
be able to spend a substantial amount of money. If maximum campaign
spending is legally set at a low figure, incumbents will be virtually impossible to dislodge. This is contrary to what most supporters of this provision
probably anticipate.

GIVE TAX CREDITS FOR DONATIONS. This type of reform is intended to empower ordinary citizens by giving them extra money to make campaign
donations. In Minnesota and Arkansas, for example, individual contributors can receive tax credits of up to $50 ($100 for couples) per year for
campaign contributions. The small government subsidy is unlikely to make
much difference to either donors or candidates. Only 4 percent of the people

in the United States make any campaign contributions at all, and $50 is probably not enough to entice many more into becoming donors. Moreover, any tax-based policy will be utilized more by the affluent than by the working class. Federal candidates get 80 percent of their money from contributions of $200 or more. Less than 1 percent of the U.S. population makes donations of this size. The experience in Minnesota is illustrative: 62,000 individual tax filers applied to the state's refund program in 1995, down from 72,000 in the 1994 election year—compared to a state population of 4.4 million.[57] The danger is that tax credit for political contributions ends up being a tax reduction for a select few.

PROVIDE TV TIME. Walter Cronkite and many others advocate providing candidates free or reduced-rate television time, for which candidates could be required to run longer, positive, message ads. This reform appeals as a measure of public financing that (supposedly) doesn't need to be paid for by Congress or the taxpayers, although in practice it's almost certain that television stations would be compensated with some hidden-from-the-public benefit. Straight public financing permits candidates to decide how to use their money; free television time coerces campaigns to become more television-centered and less concerned about personal contacts. Moreover, television is significantly more important at the presidential level than at the congressional: House incumbents spent 25 percent of their reelection money on broadcast advertisements and challengers 35 percent.[58]

THE DONORS' PERSPECTIVE

The primary players in discussions of campaign finance reform are the politicians, with a subsidiary role played by outside reformers. The donors, the people who give the money, are usually invisible during these debates, but they add a valuable perspective. Begin with big-money individual contributors, those who gave $5,000 or more to federal elections, and compare their views to those of the general public. Both groups agree that members of Congress decide what to do based on what their political contributors want (among big donors, 61 percent agree; among the public, 71 percent agree)—that's why the donors are giving the money. But on many issues the two groups sharply disagree. Six out of ten big donors think free trade agreements create jobs; six out of ten members of the public think free trade agreements cost U.S. jobs. More than four out of five members of the public, but only a minority of big donors, agree that "average working families have less economic security today, because corporations have become too greedy and care more about their profits than about being fair and loyal to their employees."[59]

Now consider the people who run PACs. Most of our interviews with corporate executives were conducted at the end of the 1980s. The larger issues then were nearly identical to those of today, though the focus at the time was on PACs (Political Action Committees) rather than on soft money, with most reform efforts aimed at abolishing PACs—just as today the key goal is abolishing soft money. The executives in charge of campaign finance weren't worried then about abolishing PACs, and they aren't worried now about abolishing soft money. We were surprised to learn how many were at least indifferent to reform:

◆ If PACs were done away with tomorrow, I don't think we'd care too much.

◆ I'd love to see PACs closed down.

◆ If we got out of the PAC business tomorrow, maybe a lot of people would say "great."

◆ The company doesn't take positions, but personally I am strongly in favor of election reforms.

Only a minority expressed those views. A strong majority of corporate executives wanted to keep the existing system, arguing that, otherwise, "it goes back under the table" and "there will be all kinds of scandal."

It is so much better now it is all out in the open. You walked in to me and you laid out exactly what our company has been doing, who we've been giving to, and everything else. I think that that's marvelous, and that's the way it should be.

"A TOOL AND NOTHING MORE"

Corporate executives don't worry about the prospect of campaign finance reform because campaign contributions are only one of many ways of accomplishing their purposes, reform does not seem imminent, and even if it does come they expect things to continue in much the same way. Their first reason for feeling sanguine is a belief that campaign contributions are only one of many tools available to them, and not necessarily the most important.

◆ A lot of companies think their PAC is more powerful than it is. I dare say we wouldn't be in any worse shape if we didn't have them.

◆ We don't need a PAC. There was a time we needed it, but now business gets a fair hearing, and so we don't need PACs, we'll get a fair hearing, anyway.

◆ Some PACs really get an overblown idea what it does. I always find that the type of person who is fresh out of the corporate headquarters or fresh out of the Hill thinks that PACs are more important than they are. After you get to see what they can do and what they can't do, you realize the sun does not rise or set because of the PAC system.

◆ I think PACs can do a few little minor things—help staff people like myself get entrée, open doors, things of that sort which may help us do our job a little easier. But the bottom line is you still have to have your arguments and your substance correct and you do have to be persuasive.

The point that corporate executives are making here is probably *the* most fundamental fact about any proposed campaign finance reform. As the previous chapter argued, business attains its power primarily through its control of the economy and its privileged position in American society. Campaign contributions are only one part of the total picture. For certain purposes they are a key part, but even if business made absolutely no campaign contributions, it would still have a vast array of other resources.

Let me tell you something. If I couldn't do the job without PACs, I shouldn't be in the job. It is a tool and nothing more. But I've got all sorts of other tools. And the biggest tool I've got is experience. And also you know I talk to a lot of guys who become congressmen long before they become congressmen. You talk to them, you help write speeches for them and other things. There's other tools to help people. Some guy might be a lot more impressed if you took him into your plant and met five thousand workers than he ever would be if you give him $1,000. There's all sorts of ways to help guys without money. Now I'm not saying tomorrow I'm going to do away with it.

UNDERLYING PRINCIPLES

The dominant view of how campaign finance should operate is a regulatory model. Wealthy individuals and corporations are allowed to use their money in any way they want, unless there is a specific prohibition or regulation. Anything not specifically covered by the rules is permitted. Because money can be used in a million different ways, and because it is very unequally distributed, the people and organizations trying to uphold and enforce existing rules tend to fall behind those looking for ways to evade the rules.[60] As one executive told us, if one form of contribution is ended, that won't stop corporate influence; instead, "it would take a little different avenue, a different tack. . . . There are ways around it. The system is dynamic. By the time they change it, it's too late."

Campaign finance can be thought of as similar to a balloon. If people and PACs pump money into it, it will expand. Regulators occasionally push on the balloon to try to make it go down. With some effort they can push the balloon down in one place—but that just makes it billow out farther somewhere else. If people focus only on the area of the balloon, that has been pushed in, they conclude that the reform has worked. However, if you look at the back of the balloon it becomes evident that it has swollen even larger somewhere else. This regulatory model of campaign finance reform will not work. Some alternative strategy must be found.

Every campaign finance system implicitly condones or encourages certain outcomes while prohibiting or discouraging others. "Every way of seeing is also a way of not seeing."[61] Campaign finance proposals draw attention to certain features of the current political system while ignoring others. Underlying each proposal is an assessment of what kind of world is desirable; the variations among proposals reflect differences in people's visions of how society should be organized and governed. These visions are not necessarily articulated or self-conscious. The explicit rhetoric may offer a strikingly different image of the intent of the proposal. But the place to begin any examination of a campaign finance system is to consider the kind of political order it both creates and requires.

The current disarray in the campaign finance system means that only one rule is left: public disclosure. One reform—an end to soft money—is widely supported, based on a general agreement that there should be some limit on the amount that any one donor can give to any one candidate. The end of soft money, accompanied by no other change, would return the campaign finance system to the world of about 1990, prior to the beginning of the soft money explosion. A ban on soft money, with the return of donation limits, has two consequences. First, it limits the power of an individual or company to control one or more members by making them financially dependent on a single donor. If the existing rules are enforced, no member can be too dependent on any particular donor. Therefore, the member never finds it in his or her financial interest to support a single maverick in opposition to the rest of business. This limits the ability of a maverick to use government action to override the market and the private actions of businesses. Second, this also limits the ability of a member to extort money from a campaign contributor. Since the maximum legal donation is not large, even if a donor feels compelled to contribute, a small amount will satisfy that obligation.

More important is what this system does *not* try to do, the practices and conditions it does not attempt to regulate. No attempt is made to limit the total amount an organization may give or a candidate may raise and spend. The implicit claim is that it is possible for a democratic society to have enormous economic inequalities, but nonetheless allow the use of money to influence politics. This can be accepted because of the belief that a set of rules for the appropriate uses of money can successfully ensure that inequalities in the economic realm do not influence the political process. Even though the economy is said to require and thrive on inequality, whereas the polity depends on equal say and representation, no conflict is seen between these two realms and the principles underlying them. We, however, believe this to be the key structural contradiction that must be faced by any plan to reform campaign finance, and we therefore address the issue.

ECONOMY AND POLITY: CONTRADICTORY PRINCIPLES

Our society takes private property, the "free" market, and the buying and selling of anything and everything as givens; it accepts the idea of someone owning a book, an idea (through a patent or copyright), a contract for a person's services, an animal, or a tree. With few exceptions, the person (or corporation) who owns these has the right to do anything and everything with them. If a corporation has the patent on a process that would substantially improve a product, but lower company profitability, the corporation is under no obligation to use the patent—or let anyone else use it—even if it would make the world a better place. If you buy a house with a dozen large, pleasant shade trees, many over one hundred years old, it is your "right" to chop them all down as soon as you become the legal owner, with no regard to the effects on the environment, your neighbors, or those who will come after you.

Enamored as we are with buying and selling as the best way to handle virtually any problem, and with private property and the "free" market, these concepts are not considered good policy in the political realm. "The best Congress that money can buy," to use Will Rogers's phrase,[62] is a pretty terrible Congress, because some things aren't supposed to be for sale. In fact, it is illegal to sell some things (marijuana, but not tobacco or alcohol), and some actions are regarded as noble if done for disinterested motives, but are illegal if done for cash. Thus, members of Congress are supposed to help their "friends" and constituents, to shape legislation to serve their interests, but it is illegal to explicitly offer to sell either a legislative outcome or even their best efforts to produce such an outcome. It is similarly illegal to offer to (directly) pay a member of Congress for such services. Doing so is called bribery. In the economic marketplace the people with the most money are supposed to have more impact than others, but in politics each person is supposed to have one and only one vote, and explicitly buying and selling political influence is taboo. Instead of directly buying and selling, corporate PACs give gifts to members, creating loose but nonetheless binding networks of obligation.

The disjuncture our society creates between politics and economics is at the heart of this book. Economic democracy is regarded as not just impractical, but somehow immoral. It is "obvious" that people can't and shouldn't vote to determine how their workplaces are run. Even democratic combinations of workers to negotiate with owners—that is, unions—are regarded with skepticism, and tolerated only if they stay weak and limited. The only "efficient" way to operate a "private" enterprise is by having the owners have dictatorial powers; these powers are then used to create bureaucratic systems to control recalcitrant employees.[63] Economic democracy would be the worst form of socialism: hopelessly utopian, totally unworkable. At the same time most people feel it is equally obvious that democracy is the best, in fact, the only acceptable, form of government. In politics, democratic procedures are not regarded as inefficient or utopian; instead they are viewed as imposing certain short-run costs, but for enormous long-run benefits. Virtually everyone in the modern United States firmly holds *both* that the economy must be operated on the basis of "free" ownership of "private" property, with those who have the money in control of all key decisions, *and* that the polity must be based on "one person one vote," with money not allowed to exercise a disproportionate influence.[64]

No contradiction is seen between these two beliefs, held with equal surety. We, however, argue that these two practices *do* contradict one another; it is difficult or impossible for a society with enormous disparities of wealth and income to maintain equality in politics. As long as people with money are allowed to use it to influence politics, those with the most money will have disproportionate influence both on election campaigns and on the shaping of public policy. The fiction may be maintained that every person's vote counts equally—in fact, the people with the most wealth may insist on this loudly and vehemently—but the reality is that "money talks," and those who have the gold make the rules. This is the underlying problem that must be confronted by any attempt at campaign finance reform. If this issue is not addressed in some way, the almost certain outcome of any reform is that rather than ending the ability of money to influence politics, one specific practice will be prohibited, and one or more new practices will emerge.

THE AIMS OF REFORM

One of the corporate executives we interviewed explained why he'd be opposed to abolishing private money in campaigns: "I think the members would be less accessible because I think they might start running it strictly for the votes." That, of course, is precisely the point. For us, it is the hope; for him, it was the fear.

We prefer a system where members of Congress run "strictly for the votes" rather than for the money, and where members are concerned with what the majority of their constituents want, not with the wishes of big contributors. Below, we outline our proposal for campaign finance reform. That proposal has four principal aims:

The first and primary aim is to do as much as possible to see to it that each individual has equal representation. Those with wealth and power should not be able to use them to gain extra influence. We therefore wish to create equality in campaign funding, making it more difficult for corporations to use campaign contributions to gain access to or influence over candidates.

Second, the system should be as democratic as possible. If congressional incumbents are practically unbeatable, then democracy operates only once a generation, when a member dies or chooses to retire. Throughout the post–World War II period, incumbents have been almost certain of reelection. In 1988, for example, the figure was 98 percent,[65] and even in the 1994 upheaval more than 90 percent of the incumbents running for reelection won. Moreover, in most years more than 90 percent of members ran for reelection, so that a very high proportion of House members have stayed from one term to the next.[66] It has not always been so. In the nineteenth-century turnover was far higher. The rate of members staying from one term to the next was below 50 percent for seven straight elections beginning in 1842, and above 60 percent for only two elections between 1832 and 1884.[67]

Any reform of the campaign finance system should aim to increase the number of competitive races. Studies indicate that the problem is not overspending by incumbents, but underspending by challengers.[68] In order to run a competitive race, challengers need to be able to spend enough money to get their message out to voters. Challengers who can raise enough money to do so are usually competitive; challengers who are drastically outspent can rarely make the race competitive. In 1988, in better than 4 out of 5 races (81.4 percent), one candidate spent more than twice as much as the other. Only 3.2 percent of these races were competitive (that is, decided by margins of 10 points or less, e.g., 55 percent to 45 percent). In the remaining 1 out of 5 races the underfinanced candidate had at least half as much money as the funding leader. A much higher proportion of these races were competitive—about 4 out of 10 (39.1 percent). Therefore, a reform proposal needs to ensure adequate funding for challengers.

Third, members of Congress should spend their time on issues rather than on fundraising. "Half of all senators surveyed by the Center for Responsive Politics and almost one-quarter of the House members said that the demands of fundraising cut *significantly* into the time they devoted to legislative work. Another 12 percent of the senators and 20 percent of the House members said fundraising had some effect on legislative time."[69] Moreover, members should spend time on *major* issues, not on writing individual exceptions to legislation for actual or potential campaign contributors.

Finally, the system should maintain these characteristics over time. Lots of smart, powerful, and sharp operators will do their best to subvert the system. If they are allowed to do so, they will undermine every positive feature of the reform.

Our goals for campaign finance reform are not shared by corporate executives or most members. Public statements aside, most members don't want to be in competitive races. Corporate personnel think it perfectly appropriate for wealthy individuals and organizations to use money to get additional access and influence. They want members of Congress to have to raise money privately, because then members will provide preferential access to corporations. Former Senator Rudy Boschwitz (Republican–Minnesota) institutionalized the practice. Those who contributed $1,000 or more received special blue stamps to place on their envelopes; lesser contributions entitled people to other-colored stamps; and noncontributors had to take their chances. Letters were opened and replied to according to the contribution level; Boschwitz called this "a nifty idea."[70]

PUBLIC FINANCING

The regulatory model of campaign finance is doomed to failure. As long as our society continues to have vast inequalities of wealth, income, and power, the people with the most money will be able to find ways around restrictive rules. Virtually all current proposals are intended to limit the ways in which money can be funneled into campaigns. It is extremely difficult to impose limitations, because however many rules and barriers are erected, the ingenuity of the rich, or their hirelings, will always find ways to evade the regulations. Clinton's Deputy Chief of Staff Harold Ickes explains, "Money is like water. . . . If there is a crack, water will find it. Same way with political money."[71] Moreover, virtually no meaningful penalties are imposed on those caught violating the rules. As a result, the regulators are always one step behind the evaders and shysters.

The alternative approach is to cut the Gordian knot of restrictions by instituting public financing of election campaigns. In the early 1990s, such proposals seemed utopian. In 1992, we argued that Congress and the president would not institute public financing unless a popular movement put a gun to their heads. As we predicted, Washington didn't budge, but state-level referendum campaigns may do what Congress would never do. In 1996, Maine voters adopted a public financing system, and Public Campaign, a new organization dedicated to taking special interest money out of elections, is spearheading a movement around the country to bring about public campaign financing, one state at a time, if necessary. Real reform, with full public financing, is no longer a utopian dream—it's on today's political agenda. Other proposals are of course possible, but Public Campaign's model law is an excellent framework, *and* it has helped mobilize and coordinate a major grassroots campaign. Our discussion therefore focuses on this proposal.

Public Campaign, and its Clean Money Campaign Reform (CMCR), are—at least for now—bypassing Congress, which has shown an amazing ability to sidetrack and frustrate reform efforts, and focusing instead on state-by-state efforts, most notably by putting referendum questions on the ballot. By taking the issue directly to the voters in a ballot referendum, it's possible to pass a full reform proposal. The normal legislative process is highly likely to bury reform in committee and then change "just a few" details in order to make the proposal "more realistic"—that is, to be sure that special interest money continues to provide a decisive margin in most contests.

State level campaigns necessarily mean that there will be minor variations from one place to another. And any effort to present a campaign finance proposal confronts a dilemma: Readers want enough detail to be sure the proposal is viable—that it won't encounter an insoluble contradiction—but don't want to be bogged down in minor provisions of interest only to technocrats and political junkies. In its broad outlines, Clean Money Campaign Reform limits campaign spending, prohibits special interest contributions to those candidates who participate in the system, provides public financing for participating candidates, and guarantees a level playing field. The system is completely voluntary. Here's how CMCR will work for candidates who choose to participate:[72]

QUALIFICATION. To qualify, candidates must collect a specified number of signatures and $5 qualifying contributions, and these must come from registered voters in the candidate's state or district. The required number depends on the office sought, with higher offices requiring more signatures and contributions. In all cases, however, the number is set at a modest level that any viable candidate should be able to achieve. Five dollars is high enough to be sure that people won't support a candidate frivolously and unthinkingly, but low enough that virtually anyone could make the commitment. It's obviously much harder to collect $5 contributions than signatures, and the number of required contributions might need to be adjusted based on experience with the law, but a tentative starting point would be to require 1,000 contributions for a congressional candidate. (Congressional districts usually contain about 500,000 people.)

In order to prevent permanent campaigning, the qualifying signatures and contributions cannot be collected until three months before the primary, and must all be turned in by one month before the primary. Candidates are permitted to raise a limited amount of seed money from contributions of $100 or less. That money—perhaps totaling $10,000 to $20,000 for congressional candidates—can be raised before the qualifying period; if candidates raise more than that amount, the excess must be turned over to the Election Commission; if they spend more than that amount, they are not eligible for Clean Money campaign financing.

Today, many candidates (and most ballot initiatives) pay to get the signatures needed to qualify for the ballot, hiring low-wage workers to do the work. It goes without saying that no candidate can pay workers to collect their Clean Money qualifying contributions, and each contribution must be accompanied by a receipt identifying the contributor and certifying that he or she knew this money was to help this candidate qualify for Clean Money campaign funding.

One of the attacks on Clean Money Campaign Reform is likely to be that taxpayers will be forced to shell out for weak and silly candidates. Senator Mitch McConnell of Kentucky, for the past several years the Republican leader in the battle against campaign finance reform, argued against public funding—any public funding—on these grounds:

> If we extend [public financing to congressional] races, every crackpot who got up in the morning and looked in the mirror and said, "gee, I think I see a congressman" is going to be able to reach into the federal cookie jar and get some of those tax dollars.[73]

In practice, of course, as things stand today, crackpots can run for Congress—or the presidency—as long as they are rich crackpots, while candidates like Sally Robeson, the fictional candidate with whom we opened this book, are often excluded. Crackpots would not be able to collect one thousand $5 contributions during a sixty-day period; Sally Robeson would find that far simpler than making it through today's money primary.

PRIMARY FUNDING. Candidates who meet CMCR requirements will be guaranteed a set amount of money from the Clean Money fund, provided that they agree not to raise or spend any private money—even their own—during either the primary or the general election. Federal candidates will also receive a specified amount of free and discounted television and/or radio time.

GENERAL ELECTION FUNDING. Qualifying candidates who win their primaries, and qualifying independent candidates, will be guaranteed an additional set amount from the Clean Money fund, as well as additional free and discounted television and/or radio time.[74]

One major question is obviously: How much money should be provided to candidates? Voters who are disgusted with politics might want a low amount, but, perversely, setting a low figure is a way of protecting incumbents: In order to overcome incumbents' name recognition (and staff advantage), challengers need to be able to spend a substantial amount of money. On the other hand, CMCR candidates would not face any fundraising expenses. Setting public funding at 20 percent below the amount spent in competitive races in previous years will likely offer challengers enough to win; it will also control the overall cost of elections.

LEVEL PLAYING FIELD. What happens if one of the candidates in a race decides not to enter the Clean Money system and instead collects massive amounts of special interest money? Clean Money candidates facing such opponents are entitled to a limited amount of matching funds (beyond the normal amounts available to all CMCR candidates); those funds are also available to candidates who are targeted by independent expenditures.

This last provision is a vital element of a workable public finance proposal. The Supreme Court has ruled that any spending limits must be voluntary, which in practice has meant "accepted in exchange for public funding." Candidates who accept public financing need a guarantee that they can't be outspent by their opponent. Without this provision, the special interests could simply work to see that the amount available per candidate is very low. If public financing provides less than half of what is needed to run a viable campaign, then anyone relying exclusively on public financing is almost certain to lose, and candidates would once again be beholden to the special interests. Having successfully subverted meaningful public financing, business will then turn around and say this outcome proves that the people oppose public financing and love special interests.

If candidates using public financing are guaranteed that they can match the spending of their special interest–financed opponents, most of the reason for private fundraising will be undercut. As a result, nearly all candidates would accept public funding. Although PACs and individual donations would continue to be theoretically possible, general election candidates would not want their money, because, if they accepted it, they would not be eligible for public financing, and private funding would not enable them to outspend their opponents.[75]

OBJECTIONS AND ARGUMENTS AGAINST

EXPENSE. The first and most obvious objection likely to be raised to such a system is expense. The best response is simply to accept the figures offered by Senator Mitch McConnell (Republican–Kentucky); in arguing that there is no campaign finance problem, he "said Federal campaign spending last year [1996] amounted to $3.89 per eligible voter, 'about the price of a McDonald's value meal.'"[76] That's not much to take big money out of politics. McConnell's figures are lower than our own calculations, but the principle remains: for $10 per person per year we could guarantee funding for all candidates at all levels (federal, state, and local).

A public financing proposal costs nothing from the perspective of American society as a whole; it simply shifts the expense from private sources to taxpayers. That does *not* mean, however, that taxpayers will pay more. Quite the contrary. Why are "private sources" (largely business) making these contributions? In order to cut their taxes. If their taxes go down, who makes up the difference? Consider just one example of this: In 1955 corporations paid 27.3 percent of all federal taxes, but in 1995 they paid only 11.6 percent.[77] The reduced contributions by corporations meant that individuals paid more. Total federal tax revenue in 1995 was $1,355 billion. If corporations had paid the same share of taxes in 1995 as in 1955, they would have paid an additional $213 billion, enough in that one year to provide public financing for both House and Senate elections for well over a century.[78]

These savings could be multiplied by eliminating any of a long list of special interest tax breaks. Moreover, as the Ford Pinto example in the last chapter illustrates, many special interest benefits cost taxpayers "nothing"— at least nothing that shows up in a Treasury statement. The survivors of those people who burned to death in Pintos, the parents of mutilated and handicapped children, would nonetheless tell you that society paid a cost for the failure to require safe cars. Therefore, for 99 percent of the population, our proposal does not cost money—it saves money.

TAX CHECKOFF. Some will argue that if we are to have public financing, the money should be raised through a voluntary checkoff on tax returns. Experience with this system for presidential elections, it will be argued, indicates that the public does not support public financing of elections.

The voluntary checkoff system is extraordinary, and in our opinion, it is intended to subvert public financing. *Nothing* else the government funds depends on voluntary checkoffs. If building the B-2 relied exclusively on taxpayers voluntarily designating money, how many bombers would we build? We believe that public financing of elections should be paid for in the same way everything else is—out of general revenues. Let voluntary taxpayer checkoffs be used for the savings-and-loan bailout.

RED TAPE. A third objection to Clean Money Campaign Reform might be that it would involve red tape and bureaucracy. In fact, CMCR would reduce the red tape in the current system. At present, candidates need to keep careful records of both receipts and expenditures. Receipts are the most difficult to monitor and record, but with public financing there would be no need for a record of receipts (after the initial qualifying period). Public funding of presidential candidates has operated successfully with a minimum of paperwork.

WOULD REPUBLICANS USE IT? For over a decade, Republicans have steadfastly opposed public financing; the 1991 Senate action on this provision was by a straight party-line vote, and in 1997 only four Republicans—but all forty-five Democrats—supported the McCain–Feingold bill, which included free television time, a limited form of quasi-public financing. Republican opposition is important in two senses. The first is in trying to get the proposal passed. The other is the question of whether Republicans would use public financing if it were available; if they did not, the system would have a partisan character that would undermine its intent. Experience with the presidential public finance system is, however, reassuring. Every Republican nominee for president has accepted public financing, and Republicans have accepted federal money for their nominating conventions.[79] Public pronouncements are one thing, action quite another. If the money is available, Republicans will take it.

THIRD PARTIES. Clean Money Campaign Reform permits third-party candidates to qualify for public funding. Some will see this as a strength of the proposal; others will be concerned that it will permit extremists to get public financing for their campaigns. This is sure to be one of the arguments used against the reform, but it would clearly be discriminatory to privilege the Democrats and Republicans—and to qualify any candidate will have to demonstrate support by collecting signatures and $5 contributions from registered voters inside their district.

WILL IT LAST? A final objection is that even if the system sounds good, those with wealth and power will find a way to corrupt it and evade the rules. We agree: Constant vigilance will be needed to keep this from happening, and implementation of the system would have to be accompanied by other changes to plug existing loopholes and prevent the emergence of new ones. But one of the most important aspects of CMCR is that it contains a built-in safeguard to keep it effective: Each candidate has enough money to communicate his or her message and to warn voters about attempts to evade restrictions or launch unfair attacks.

No change will be meaningful unless the rules are enforced. The Federal Election Commission has become a joke because it is unwilling or unable to uphold the law. For example, presidential candidates have spending limits for each state primary. In 1988 in Iowa, the Democratic winner, Richard Gephardt, exceeded his spending limit by almost $500,000, and the Republican winner, Robert Dole, exceeded his by $306,000. It was more than three years before the FEC completed its audit of these campaigns—long after the presidential nominations were decided.[80] The FEC is often unwilling even to *investigate* complaints.[81] Abuses need to be exposed to public scrutiny even if they ultimately go unpunished. It should not take a majority of votes to pursue an investigation, but only a one-third minority, and reports of those investigations should be publicly available. Congress prefers to move in the opposite direction, making it more difficult for the public to file complaints against members of Congress: "Republicans in the House pushed through a change in ethics rules today [September 18, 1997] that would bar outside groups from lodging an ethics complaint against a House member."[82]

A new system needs to be implemented in which party loyalists (who invariably vote a straight party line, leading to tie votes and no action) are replaced by people committed to upholding the law. No matter how good the system that is installed, if every loophole receives official authorization, and no violation is ever punished, then the system will quickly fall apart. We need commissioners prepared to take abuses seriously, act swiftly, impose penalties, and seek criminal sanctions. If corrupting Congress and the democratic system isn't a serious offense, what is?

Soft money would have to be abolished and independent expenditures controlled. Abolishing soft money is, in principle, relatively simple.

FREE SPEECH. Controlling independent expenditures—without interfering with free speech—is more difficult, but it is not impossible. For example, under current law, issue advertisements do not come under federal regulations unless they specifically recommend voting for or against a candidate. Ads escape regulation unless they use the magic words "vote for" or "vote against." Under the 1997 McCain–Feingold bill, anyone placing an "issue ad" that appeared within sixty days of an election would have two choices: omit the candidate's name, or meet the disclosure and donation-limit rules that apply to normal campaign expenditures ("hard money").

The American Civil Liberties Union (ACLU) has, with much internal dissent and controversy, attacked many attempts at campaign finance reform, including the Maine Clean Elections Act. We are unequivocally in favor of free speech, but the class bias around this issue is striking. The primary proponents of the "campaign contributions as free speech" argument are the same Republican conservatives who usually lead the attack on free speech. Companies can require their workers to attend "captive audience" meetings to be lectured on the evils of unions; neither workers nor unions have the right of reply. If workers speaks up for the union, the company can exclude them from the next meeting. Workers, quite literally, do not have the right of free speech, at least not on the job. The ACLU accepts this; it's a nonissue. On the other hand, a major issue for the ACLU is any law that would simply require the *disclosure* of who is paying for "independent" issue advertising—when rich people speak, the ACLU doesn't think we have a right to know who is speaking.[83] Two explanations of this are possible: The ACLU is illogical, or rich people are entitled to more free speech than workers.

ABOLISH ALL RESTRICTIONS. Newt Gingrich and Trent Lott, the Republican leaders in the House and Senate, argue that the election system does not need less money; on the contrary, it needs more. We should, they say, abolish all limitations and restrictions other than public disclosure.[84] We wonder whether next year will bring an even bolder initiative: Allow members of Congress to sell their votes to the highest bidder. The logic is impeccable: Free enterprise demands it, anything else is unwarranted government interference.[85]

ARGUMENTS FOR

The arguments in favor of this system are more powerful, but they may be more briefly presented. Elections would be far more competitive. Although

SCANDAL OR SYSTEM? ◆ 227

challengers would still have less name recognition than incumbents, they would have enough money to mount credible campaigns,[86] and for the first time challengers as a group would have as much to spend as incumbents.[87]

Special interests could no longer use campaign money to increase their access and win benefits for themselves. It is not only that a member would not be indebted for a past donation. Members would also know they would never need to depend on a future donation and could never gain a campaign advantage by soliciting or accepting such a donation. Corporations would continue to have substantial clout based on their wealth, power, and respectability, their ability to maintain a staff of lobbyists, their advocacy advertising, their networks, connections, and friendships. But *one* of their major special interest weapons would have been eliminated.

The guarantee of public funding for campaigns would give members of Congress more time to spend on legislation and on keeping in touch with constituents who are *not* campaign contributors. As one of the two corporate executives who supported public financing said:

I am looking to take off the back of the politician this terrible concern he has of raising money. He spends too much time raising money. He spends too much time thinking about raising money. And I think if you turned around and gave him that time back—even if he didn't use it for legislation—even if he used it to think—we'd all be better off. When I first came to Washington as a kid, Congress wasn't in from July through January. They closed up for the whole summer months. These guys went home and got to see their people and thought a lot more about what was going on, and they came back better people for it. Now they have to spend all their time raising money. They have to spend all their time involved in enormous amounts of work that are not productive.

TAKING IT TO THE STATES

A public financing reform plan would eliminate or drastically reduce the impact of special interest money, would substantially increase competitive elections, and thus turnover among members of Congress. But is this realistic? Dick Cheney, at the time a Republican representative from Wyoming, and later Bush's secretary of defense, offered a memorable no: "If you think this Congress, or any other, is going to set up a system where someone can run against them on equal terms at government expense, you're smoking something you can't buy at the corner drugstore."[88]

Cheney's view is probably correct—it seems impossible that Congress will ever pass these reforms. That's the beauty of Public Campaign's state-by-state effort and their focus on ballot referendum questions. *Any* set of elected officials is likely to amend and compromise reform until it no longer brings much reform, but referendum questions are decided directly by the voters. The wake-up call was in Maine in 1996, when voters passed the Maine Clean Elections Act by a 56 to 44 percent margin. Seven months later, Vermont's state legislature, by lopsided votes, passed Clean Money Campaign Reform. In early 1997, the Connecticut House fell just two votes shy (73 to 75) of public financing for statewide offices. In November 1997, Massachusetts activists collected far more than the required number of signatures, guaranteeing that in 1998 voters will be able to decide the issue. Public Campaign, headed by Ellen Miller—formerly the head of the Center for Responsive Politics, the leading group monitoring campaign spending—received $9 million in funding from various foundations and is working to promote drives for ballot initiatives or legislative change in North Carolina, Georgia, Arizona, Idaho, Missouri, Massachusetts, New York, and Michigan. In Wisconsin, the coalition to promote public financing is called Elections not Auctions.[89]

If politics were an old-fashioned melodrama, we could say, "As soon as the issue goes directly to the voters, they will be sure to vote to take money out of politics." Unfortunately, it's not likely to be that simple. Entrenched interests—including most politicians in office, most of the media, and virtually every business—have a stake in seeing to it that the people with money continue to have more access, and more leverage, than average voters. The moneyed interests will not easily give up their privileges.

The public is confused about campaign finance issues. Responses to opinion polls vary dramatically, depending on how the issue is posed; this is in marked contrast to environmental issues, for example, where no matter how unfair the question, the public still favors taking care of the environment. It is easy to point to poll results that demonstrate broad support for taking money out of politics. For example, a poll commissioned by the Center for Responsive Politics found:

> Money and politics is seen as a systemic problem, not one associated with a particular party or elected officials. Seven in ten (71 percent) people believe the Republicans and Democrats are about equally likely to engage in questionable campaign fundraising these days, even though the recent media spotlight has been on the activities of Bill Clinton and the Democratic Party. . . . Money is widely assumed to give the rich and powerful special access to members of Congress. Three-quarters (77 percent) of Americans believe that major campaign contributors

from outside a congressional representative's district are granted more opportunity to make their views known on important issues than the people he or she was elected to represent. Furthermore, this is not a case where people tend to criticize Congress but not their own representative. Fully two-thirds (67 percent) think their own representative in Congress would listen to the views of outsiders who made large political contributions before constituents' views.[90]

Those results accurately reflect one important aspect of public sentiment, and help explain why 89 percent of the public thinks the campaign finance system needs fundamental change (50 percent) or needs to be completely rebuilt (39 percent). At the same time, however, 43 percent believe that public financing of campaigns would not reduce the influence of special interests,[91] and 72 percent opposed "financing political campaigns out of tax money."[92] This last is opponents' most effective argument: Do you want your tax dollars to pay for candidates' mud-slinging ads?[93] These ambiguities and contradictions in public sentiment help explain why the Maine ballot initiative won by a relatively small margin, despite the media focus on Clinton's fundraising abuses.

Two options are possible: full public financing of elections or continued domination by moneyed interests. At present, the public is unhappy with both of these. Another option appears attractive, but is, in fact, illusory: Continue private financing but "with effective regulation." It remains to be seen whether the advocates of public financing can persuade voters that, despite their reservations about public financing, it is the only realistic alternative to our current system. If those with wealth and power can get their act together, they will support a cosmetic pseudoreform that will, they hope, undercut demands for true reform.

If a campaign for real reform builds major public support, business will fight back on two fronts. First, it will mount a campaign to change public opinion. Corporations will commission in-depth studies to find out what parts of the proposal have the most and least support, then will focus as much attention as possible on those aspects that make the public uneasy. Academic experts will be hired to prove that the proposals wouldn't work. The mass media will run numerous interviews with "taxpayers" who are angry that their money is being used, against their will, to pay for mud-slinging and negative campaign commercials. Members will loudly insist they are happy to see anybody at anytime and will be photographed seeking the opinions of poor and middle-income constituents. Every attempt will be made to undercut support for reform through what Domhoff has called the "ideology process."[94]

At the same time—for anything *except* a ballot initiative—business will undertake a second approach, developing "minor" modifications that sound harmless but in practice gut the proposal. They will open loopholes that can be expanded at a later time when public attention is focused on other issues.[95] Corporations will aim to create a system where candidates need special interest money because it provides benefits not available in any other way, paying for the television ads that provide the margin of victory in a competitive election or for an increase in the member's effective personal income.

CONSEQUENCES

If Clean Money Campaign Reform were passed, it would lead to major changes in three areas: in the character of Congress as an institution, in the politics of the candidates elected, and in the power of business.

THE CHARACTER OF CONGRESS. The slowest and most minimal change would probably be in the character of Congress. In the current situation, a large fraction of what Congress does is serve as a peculiar sort of Ombuds office. Senator William Cohen estimates that "as much as forty percent of staff time is spent in casework."[96] Rather than spending their time on formulating legislation or evaluating general policy, members use political criteria—especially past or future campaign contributions—to make a host of relatively minor administrative decisions. Despite the generic use of the term "special interests," a large majority of these decisions are made for, and at the behest of, business. In some cases, the administrator at the regulatory agency or executive office is "persuaded" to adopt the member's interpretation—a persuasion that often depends on fear their agency's budget will be cut if they don't go along. In other cases, what ought to be a minor administrative decision is written into law, an extremely clumsy approach that provides little flexibility for adapting to changing circumstances. This is not the purpose for which Congress was intended, and it is a perfectly awful way to decide regulatory and policy details.

A large proportion of all these political interventions into administrative decisions are made in response to (or in hopes of) business campaign contributions. If members knew they could rely on public funding, this would remove one major incentive to engage in this process. With a little luck, over time, this might return Congress to the job of writing legislation and formulating general policy. At present, the typical congressional contest is decided on the basis of who is best at delivering pork barrels and putting in the fix; the edge almost invariably goes to the incumbent, whose seniority provides extra leverage. If Congress focused on policy issues rather than minor details, election contests might be decided on the basis of candidates' stands on the issues and on whether they had fresh ideas to contribute. In this case, quite a few current members would be in deep trouble, but the country as a whole would be better off.[97]

POLITICAL CHANGE. Public financing would also lead to a change in who would win elections, and in the political stands they would take. In our interviews we found that corporate PAC directors believe virtually every member of Congress is prepared to "be reasonable" and "help them out." If there are members with a different view, they have either learned to keep quiet about it, or they have been effectively silenced and are generally unable to interfere with the special benefits corporations win through the access process. Members go along in order to raise money themselves and to keep corporations from sending floods of money to their challengers.

The conventional wisdom is that public funding would help Democrats and hurt Republicans. Certainly support for such proposals is more common among Democrats than Republicans, one indication of their own assessments of who would benefit. Perhaps this is so, but if Democrats were the main beneficiaries, they would not necessarily be the Democrats currently in Congress. As G. William Domhoff, Walter Dean Burnham, Thomas Byrne Edsall, and others have argued, today's Democratic party has a split personality.[98] Republicans get lots of money from business, and virtually none from labor, women's groups, or environmentalists. Democrats, by contrast, get significant amounts of money from business as well as labor. In 1988, Republicans received $29.7 million from corporations and only $2.7 million from labor. Democrats received $26.4 million from corporations and $32.7 million from labor. As a consequence, the Democratic party has a split personality, and business (but not labor) has leverage with *both* major parties. The advantages of public funding would be greatest for those Democrats who are not able to raise money from business. That is, public funding would be of much more benefit to candidates such as Jesse Jackson or Paul Wellstone than it would be to Charles Robb or John Dingell. As a consequence, the character of the Democratic party might shift, and business-oriented Democrats might find themselves a beleaguered minority.

BUSINESS POWER. Finally, public funding of congressional campaigns would reduce the power of business. Not eliminate it: While campaign finance is *one* important tool business uses to influence politics, it is not the only one.

If full public funding were instituted and all loopholes were plugged, thus establishing a level playing field for campaign finance, business would still have a privileged position. Large corporations would continue to:

1. Dominate the economy and be able to make hundreds of key decisions influencing people's lives (and therefore, their votes).
2. Fund think tanks to prepare analyses and reports advancing a business point of view.
3. Collect and provide information that the government doesn't have (often information that business fights to keep the government from getting).
4. Be able to hold out the prospect of lucrative future employment for the member and/or key staff aides.
5. Maintain large staffs of lobbyists.
6. Communicate directly with stockholders.
7. Control access to employees for political and other purposes.
8. Engage in advocacy advertising.
9. Frustrate policies through a refusal to cooperate.

And in a host of other ways, to shape the character of the society—the options available and the costs and benefits associated with them.

PEOPLE POWER. If corporations would continue to be so powerful, is there any point in fighting for campaign finance reform? Is it possible to win against so much might? And if we did win, would anything really change? That these questions need to be addressed is one of the strongest indications of business hegemony. Once people believe that it isn't possible to change the system and that the struggle to do so can only lead to grief and frustration, the power structure has won more than half the battle.[99]

Real social change is possible. In the early 1960s, poor and vulnerable African Americans transformed Southern race relations. Thousands of nameless people put their lives on the line; many made enormous sacrifices. Their struggles have not (yet) brought equality, but they did end the Southern racial caste etiquette system, and they brought a resurgence of black pride and awareness. A similar story could be told of the women's movement—which itself owes a considerable debt to the black movement.

A less dramatic struggle more directly linked to corporate power makes the same point. In the early 1960s, auto safety was presented as depending entirely on safe drivers. Ralph Nader raised the heretical idea that perhaps cars were also a cause of accidents—and had the data to prove it. General Motors responded with a vicious campaign, even hiring detectives to dig up dirt on his private life.

Did Ralph Nader's campaign totally transform U.S. society and the power of business? No. Did it have any real effect on people's lives? Absolutely. In 1965, for every 100 million miles driven, 5.3 people died in automobile accidents. If that rate had still applied in 1994, an additional 80,000 people would have died in auto accidents.

People sometimes argue that such reforms only make the system more stable and resistant to change. Perhaps that is true in some instances. In other instances, what Andre Gorz called a "non-reformist reform" provides immediate benefits to people *and* makes it easier to win future reforms. Did the auto safety campaign Nader launched produce a significant change in the way people think about business? Yes. Did it make it people more or less willing to consider additional reforms? Obviously, much more willing.

We would argue that Clean Money Campaign Reform is also a "nonreformist reform." It proposes a reform that can be won, and one that if won will substantially weaken business power. By itself, will it transform American society? No. Will it have an impact? Yes. Will the end of corporate campaign contributions and the emergence of public financing make it easier or more difficult to make future political changes? Clearly, easier. Will continued struggle be necessary to elect good people and to fight business power? Certainly. Will electoral politics be enough? No. Business exercises power on many different fronts and that power must be opposed on every front.

Today, more than at any time in the last two decades, real social change is on the agenda. Campaigns for public financing of elections are one element of that, but by far the most important is the revival of the labor movement. The new leadership of the labor movement—John Sweeney, Richard Trumka, and Linda Chavez-Thompson—is committed to building a labor movement that is a *movement*, not just a bureaucracy. One small part of that is the AFL–CIO's recent decision to support public financing, which represents a dramatic shift from its long-standing opposition to any system that diminished the importance of labor political action committees. Far more important are its efforts to seek and build alliances with other social movements, to stand up not just for trade unionists but for all working people, and to take as its first priority organizing new workers, not just servicing those already in unions. Just as business operates on many fronts, so must a movement for social change. A revived labor movement is one encouraging sign, but it cannot succeed if it stands alone. In order to contest business power, we need to commit ourselves to many other sorts of struggle: for the liberation of women, people of color, gays and lesbians; to create alternative media and sources of information; to build our own think tanks; to transform schools, colleges, universities, and teaching.

NOTES

◆ CHAPTER I: FOLLOW THE MONEY

1. *Boston Globe*, November 8, 1996, p. A26.

2. *New York Times*, September 3, 1997, p. A18.

3. In 1976, 48 percent of House members' campaign receipts came from individual contributions of less than $500; in 1988, only 27 percent did ("Money and Politics: A Special Report," *National Journal*, June 16, 1990). In the 1996 elections, this remained nearly constant at approximately 28 percent (FEC online www publication).

4. For quotations in this and the preceding paragraph, see, "Money and Politics," *National Journal*, p. 1448.

5. "Money and Politics," *National Journal*, pp. 1462, 1460.

6. *Boston Globe*, February 14, 1996, p. 11.

7. *New York Times*, November, 1, 1996, p. A1.

8. Boschwitz, quoted in Brooks Jackson, *Honest Graft: Big Money and the American Political Process* (New York: Knopf, 1988), pp. 251–252. Emphasis in book. (Obviously, the secret memo didn't stay secret.) Boschwitz's 1990 strategy backfired. He discouraged the most "promising" Democratic candidates, but Paul Wellstone—a true long shot by all accounts—beat him, despite Boschwitz's 4 to 1 spending advantage. In the 1996 rematch between the two candidates, Wellstone outspent Boschwitz and won handily.

9. "Members" is the term most often used to refer to what once were called "congressmen." The term has the advantage of being gender neutral, and can refer either to senators or to House representatives. It will be our term of choice in this book, though some corporate executives still use the older form, so it will appear in some quotations.

10. Quoted in Elizabeth Drew, *Whatever it Takes: The Real Struggle for Political Power in America* (New York: Viking, 1997), pp. 19–20.

11. David Donnelly, Janice Fine, and Ellen S. Miller, "Going Public," *Boston Review*, April–May 1997. Larry Makinson, "The Big Picture: Money Follows Power Shift on Capitol Hill" (Washington, D.C.: Center for Responsive Politics, 1997, www.crp.org).

12. www.fec.gov.

13. William Greider, "Whitewash: Is Congress Conning Us on Clean Air?" *Rolling Stone*, June 14, 1990, p. 40.

14. Greider, "Whitewash,", p. 40.

15. Margaret E. Kriz, "Dunning the Midwest," *National Journal*, April 14, 1990, p. 895.

16. Kriz, "Dunning the Midwest," p. 895.

17. Not long after revision of the act, Mitchell left the Senate and became a

lobbyist; today one of his clients is the tobacco industry: a different kind of clean air issue.

18. Quoted in Greider, "Whitewash," p. 40.

19. Greider, "Whitewash," p. 41.

20. Margaret E. Kriz, "Politics at the Pump," *National Journal,* June 2, 1990, p. 1328.

21. See Chapter 3 for evidence bearing on how Waxman might have been persuaded—in particular the statement that "I can get to Waxman for $250." Information in this paragraph is from Kriz, "Politics at the Pump," pp. 1328–1329.

22. See Chapter 2 for a discussion of GM's special efforts to lobby women state legislators.

23. Why can't industry just come out and name its groups "Polluters for Profit" or the "Coalition for Acid Rain Preservation" (CARP)? All quotes in this paragraph are from Carol Matlack, "It's Round Two in Clean Air Fight," *National Journal,* January 26, 1991, p. 226.

24. *Washington Post,* January 16, 1991, p. A17.

25. *New York Times,* April 16, 1996, p. A16.

26. *New York Times,* June 22, 1997, p. 17.

27. *Wall Street Journal,* June 6, 1997.

28. *New York Times,* June 22, 1997, p. 17.

29. Matlack, "It's Round Two," p. 227.

30. *Boston Globe,* November 21, 1991, p. 17.

31. *Boston Globe,* November 21, 1991, p. 17.

32. *Boston Globe,* November 20, 1991, p. 4.

33. *Washington Post,* June 17, 1997, p. A1.

34. *Washington Post,* June 17, 1997, p. A1.

35. Richard E. Cohen, "Two Dems Are on Familiar Battlefield," *National Journal,* September 6, 1997, p. 1742.

36. Markinson, "The Big Picture."

37. While most new CEOs do not ask for any changes in PAC behavior, their right to do so is not contested. One PAC official identified himself as a conservative Republican who had attended the 1988 Republican National Convention as a delegate. Until recently the PAC had followed roughly that same orientation, but he told us that the PAC was going to become much more bipartisan due to the accession of a new CEO with strong ties to the Democratic party. As a loyal corporate employee (who wanted to keep his job), he strongly endorsed this shift.

38. His reference is to a bygone era.

39. Leonard Silk and David Vogel, *Ethics and Profits* (New York: Simon & Schuster, 1976), p. 43.

40. For more detail, see Dan Clawson, Alan Neustadtl, and Denise Scott, *Money Talks: Corporate PACs and Political Influence* (New York: Basic Books, 1992), pp. 15–17.

41. Occasionally during the interviews people would use some version of "don't quote me on that." These statements meant only: Don't quote me by name, don't identify my company. When we were in any doubt about this, we checked at the end of the interview. In a few instances, executives asked us to turn off the tape recorder so they could make comments completely off the record. Unfortunately we can't report those remarks.

42. To determine "the largest corporate PACs" to include, we sorted all corporate PACs from the largest to the smallest, then went down the list until we had included enough PACs to account for 60 percent of all corporate PAC donations. We did this for each election. For the elections from 1976 through 1988, if a PAC qualified for any one year we kept it in for all other years. For later years we included only those needed to account for 60 percent.

43. *Washington Post*, February 12, 1997, p. AI.

44. Their views on this, as on other issues, are sometimes complicated and contradictory, and at other points in the same interview the respondent might take a different position.

45. Steven Lukes, *Power: A Radical View* (New York: Macmillan, 1974).

46. Theodore J. Eismeier and Philip H. Pollock III, "The Retreat from Partisanship: Why the Dog Didn't Bark in the 1984 Election." In *Business Strategy and Public Policy*, ed. Alfred A. Marcus, Allen M. Kaufman, and David R. Beam (Wesport, Conn,: Quorum Books, 1987) pp. 137–147.

47. Thomas Wartenberg, *The Forms of Power: From Domination to Transformation* (Philadelphia: Temple University Press, 1990), pp. 66–67.

48. Wartenberg, *Forms of Power*, p. 74.

49. In Japan CEOs get an average of $300,000, or 17 times as much as workers. For an analysis of CEO pay, and information on how to get details on the pay for specific CEOs, see *America@Work* (May/June 1997), published by the AFL–CIO.

50. Quoted in Kevin Phillips, *The Politics of Rich and Poor: Wealth and the American Electorate in the Reagan Aftermath* (New York: Random House, 1990), p. 32.

51. Antonio Gramsci, *Selections From The Prison Notebooks of Antonio Gramsci*, ed. and trans. Quintin Hoare and Geoffrey Nowell Smith (New York: International Publishers, 1972).

52. Susan Harding, "Reconstructing Order through Action: Jim Crow and the Southern Civil Rights Movement." In *Statemaking and Social Movements: Essays in History and Theory*, ed. Charles Bright and Susan Harding (Ann Arbor: University of Michigan Press, 1984), pp. 378–402.

53. Or if talking to whites in circumstances where they felt secure in articulating their real feelings.

54. Betty Friedan, *The Feminine Mystique* (New York: Norton, 1963).

55. While tenure is often presented as a guaranteed job, this has to be qualified considerably. Tenure is a strong (though not absolute) guarantee against being fired for voicing unpopular views. Dismissal for cause is always possible; tenure does not protect someone who fails to meet her or his classes or is convicted of some sort of malfeasance. The most serious limit to tenure, however, is (appropriately enough for this book) financial.

56. Geraldine Bednash, "The Relationship Between Access and Selectivity in Tenure Review Outcomes." Ph.D. diss. University of Maryland, College Park, 1989.

57. At most of the better institutions of learning, very much including the universities of Massachusetts and Maryland, tenure is based primarily on publishing. Being a good (or outstanding) teacher by itself would never be enough to win tenure, unless supported by an "acceptable" level of scholarly productivity.

58. Any junior faculty who expressed contempt for this process and refused to play the game, much less anyone who publicly identified the senior faculty as outdated and of poor quality, would be even more likely to be terminated.

◆ CHAPTER 2:   GIFTS

1. *New York Times*, September 22, 1991.

2. This is the number of political action committee contributions from all sources in the 1996 election; if we included individual contributions, the number would be even higher.

3. Philip Stern used this as the title for his book (New York: Pantheon, 1988).

4. This approach also has to deal with a major problem: If campaign donations are bribes, why do most of them go to candidates who are already sympathetic to the company's position?

5. Newhouse News Service/*Ann Arbor News*, April 29, 1997.

6. Martin Schram, *Speaking Freely* (Washington, D.C.: Center for Responsive Politics, 1995).

7. We are indebted to Bill Domhoff for proposing this idea to us, developing a number of stimulating insights, and suggesting some readings. Obviously he is not responsible for our specific formulations.

8. In fact, in most cases it would be illegitimate (and perhaps illegal) for a clerk to give you a better or worse price because you were nasty or nice.

9. See also Shakespeare's famous lines from *Timon of Athens*, quoted by Marx in *The Economic and Philosophic Manuscripts of 1844* (Moscow: Progress Publishers, 1844/1959), p. 127:

> Gold? Yellow, glittering, precious gold? . . .
> Thus much of this will make black white, foul fair,
> Wrong right, base noble, old young, coward valiant.
> . . . This yellow slave
> Will knit and break religions, bless the accursed;
> Make the hoar leprosy adored, place thieves
> And give them title, knee and approbation
> With senators on the bench . . .

10. Arlie Russell Hochschild, *The Managed Heart: Commercialization of Human Feeling* (Berkeley: University of California Press, 1983).

11. Naomi Gerstel and Harriet Engel Gross, "Women and the American Family: Continuity and Change." In *Women: A Feminist Perspective*, ed. Jo Freeman, (Mountain View, Calif.: Mayfield Publishing, 1989), pp. 89–120; Jessie Bernard, *The Future of Marriage* (New York: Bantam, 1973); Nancy Folbre, "The Rhetoric of Self-Interest and the Ideology of Gender." In *The Consequences of Economic Rhetoric*, edited by Arjo Klamer, Donald N. McCloskey, and Robert M. Solow (Cambridge: Cambridge University Press, 1988) pp. 184–203; Arlie Hochschild, *The Second Shift: Working Parents and the Revolution at Home* (New York: Viking, 1990); Marcia Millman, *Warm Hearts and Cold Cash: How Families Handle Money and What This Reveals About Them* (New York: Free Press, 1991).

12. J. Thomas Scheff, *Being Mentally Ill: A Sociological Theory* (New York: Aldine, 1966).

13. Theodore Caplow, "Rule Enforcement Without Visible Means—Christmas Gift Giving in Middletown," *American Journal of Sociology* 89 (1984): 1310.

14. Marcel Mauss, *The Gift: Forms and Functions of Exchange in Archaic Societies* (New York: Norton, 1925/1967), p. xiv.

15. Mauss, "The Gift," p. 1.

16. Caplow, "Rule Enforcement Without Visible Means," p. 1307.

17. The text presents the general case, but several qualifications could be made. Many products contain a warranty; some offer a service contract; and the sales personnel almost always intend to create a friendly atmosphere that will ensure repeat business.

18. Alvin Gouldner, "The Norm of Reciprocity: A Preliminary Statement," *American Sociological Review* 25 (1960): 161–178.

19. Judith Rollins, *Between Women: Domestics and Their Employers* (Philadelphia: Temple University Press, 1985), p. 190.

20. Francis Wilkinson, "Rules of the Game: The Senate's Money Politics," *Rolling Stone*, August 8, 1991, p. 33.

21. Barry Schwartz, "The Social-Psychology of the Gift," *American Journal of Sociology* 73 (1967): 4.

22. Mauss, *The Gift*, p. 10.

23. Schwartz, "Social-Psychology of the Gift," p. 1.

24. For example, groups supporting gay and lesbian rights sometimes have difficulty getting members to accept their contributions.

25. Mauss, *The Gift*, p. 11. Former senator (and majority leader) George Mitchell reports, "Some of the most vigorous criticism I got and the worst chewing-out I got was from people whose contributions I returned. . . . People really called me up and gave me hell: 'What's the matter, isn't my money good enough for you?'" (Schram, *Speaking Freely*).

26. Cited in Philip M. Stern, *The Best Congress Money Can Buy* (New York: Pantheon, 1988), p. 63.

27. Stern, *The Best Congress*, p. 63.

28. *Washington Post*, March 2, 1997.

29. Quoted in Herbert E. Alexander, *Money in Politics* (Washington, D.C.: Public Affairs Press, 1972), p. 157.

30. In theory, a corporation could ideologically support liberals. None of the largest did so.

31. While this is a simple measure, our research indicates it is highly correlated with various more sophisticated measures. See, for instance, Dan Clawson, Alan Neustadtl, and James Bearden, "The Logic of Business Unity: Corporate Contributions to the 1980 Congressional Elections," *American Sociological Review* 51 (1986): 797–811; Clawson and Neustadtl, "Interlocks, PACs, and Corporate Conservatism," *American Journal of Sociology* 94 (1989): 749–793.

32. By large corporate PACs we mean the 173 that together accounted for 60 percent of all corporate PAC contributions: 78.6 percent of them gave at least 70 percent to incumbents, and 56.1 percent of them gave at least 80 percent to incumbents. Many open-seat donations are also pragmatic: The corporation gives to the likely winner hoping that an early contribution will lead to extra gratitude and help build a long-term relation.

33. At one of the corporations we interviewed, all PAC contributors, not just the PAC committee members, receive copies of this information.

34. Schram, *Speaking Freely*.

35. However, friendship rarely stands alone. In this case, the PAC officer sounded the candidate out about an issue crucial to the company's survival. The candidate

had (understandably) never thought about the issue before, but agreed to consider the issue carefully should she be elected.

36. These managers appear to be following not "company rationality" but "subsidiary rationality."

37. See Dan Clawson, Alan Neustadtl, and Denise Scott, *Money Talks: Corporate PACs and Political Influence* (New York: Basic Books, 1992), pp. 75–79 for examples.

38. *Wall Street Journal*, August 4, 1997, p. A20.

39. A study found that "51 Senators and 146 House Members were founders, officers, or directors of tax-exempt organizations." See Richard Cohen and Carol Matlack, "All-Purpose Loophole," *National Journal*, December 9, 1989, p. 2981.

40. *New York Times*, September 1, 1996, p. 32.

41. To complete the picture, Haley Barbour, chair of the Republican National Committee, had even more problems, in his case, with foreign donations; see Chapter 7.

42. *New York Times*, December 25, 1996, p. A11.

43. *New York Times*, December 5, 1996, pp. A1, A21.

44. Note that the amount of money a publisher spends to promote a book will influence its sales. A publisher could run extra ads for a politician's book, even if it didn't make economic sense in terms of gains in sales, intentionally losing money in order to increase the politician's royalties.

45. *New York Times*, November 12, 1990, p. A18.

46. *Washington Post*, September 24, 1997, p. A1.

47. See *New York Times*, March 13, 1997, p. A25; also October 27, 1996, p. 27.

48. *New York Times*, March 23, 1997, pp. 1, 22.

49. Note that here, as at many other points in our interviews, corporate executives mentioned using federal property to deliver campaign contributions. No one worried at all about saying this to us, even though such acts are illegal. One of the charges against Clinton and Gore is that they solicited and/or accepted money on federal property. It wouldn't surprise us if this were true, but it hardly makes them unique.

50. Clinton press conference; transcript in *New York Times*, March 8, 1997, p. 9.

51. In one instance, a company sold necklace making kits, consisting of beads and thread, for as much as $3,000, defrauding 15,000 people of $38 million. The company contributed $85,000 to the Democratic National Committee and managed to have eight of its top people photographed with President Clinton, using these photos to imply that the president endorsed the company (*New York Times*, August 25, 1997, pp. A1, 15).

52. *New York Times*, March 23, 1997, p. A1.

53. *New York Times*, April 3, 1997, p. A1.

◆ CHAPTER 3:   ACCESS

1. *New York Times*, January 29, 1997, p. B6.

2. The money is then reported as having arrived in cash from "small contributors"; typically, contributors do not need to be identified for contributions below some minimum threshold ($50, $100, or $200).

3. *New York Times*, July 10, 1997, p. A16.

4. Janet M. Grenzke, "PACs and the Congressional Supermarket: The Cur-

rency Is Complex," *American Journal of Political Science* 33 (1989): 1–24; James B. Kau and Paul H. Rubin, *Congressmen, Constituents, and Contributors* (Boston: Martinus Nijhoff, 1982); Alan Neustadtl, "Interest-Group PACsmanship: An Analysis of Campaign Contributions, Issue Visibility, and Legislative Impact," *Social Forces* 69 (1991): 549–564.

5. William Greider, *Who Will Tell the People? The Betrayal of American Democracy* (New York: Simon & Schuster, 1992), p. 259.

6. Moreover, politicians would agree.

7. *National Journal*, April 28, 1990, p. 1052.

8. The way campaign finance practices have been changing, we hope this has not changed by the time you, gentle reader, see this book; we also hope we aren't embarrassed by a subsequent disclosure that some donor and politician have already teamed up to do this and found a way to cover their tracks.

9. Martin Schram, *Speaking Freely* (Washington, D.C.: Center for Responsive Politics, 1995).

10. *New York Times*, June 6, 1986, pp. D1–D2.

11. Chalmers Johnson, *MITI and the Japanese Miracle: The Growth of Industrial Policy, 1925–1975* (Stanford, Calif.: Stanford University Press, 1982).

12. U.S. Code, *Statutes at Large*, vol. 100, 1986, Public Law 99–514, pp. 2149–2150, sec. 204.

13. Given what we know about this tax bill, what are we to make of the claims in Jeffrey Birnbaum and Alan Murray's highly praised *Showdown at Gucci Gulch: Lawmakers, Lobbyists, and the Unlikely Triumph of Tax Reform* (New York: Random House, 1987, p. 4)? According to them, the 1986 tax reform bill was opposed by corporate lobbyists, who had expected it to fail: "It was too bold, they thought, too radical. It proposed wiping out a multitude of special-interest tax breaks in return for sharp cuts in tax rates. That would be a boon to the great mass of people who pay their taxes each year without taking advantage of these deductions, exclusions, and credits. But it would be a disaster for the many business interests and high-income individuals who have come to depend on tax favors from Congress."

14. For this and the remainder of the information on the minimum wage bill, see *National Journal*, October 26, 1996, pp. 2289–2292.

15. This provision had been inserted by Senator Don Nickles of Oklahoma in an earlier tax bill.

16. *National Journal*, October 26, 1996, pp. 2289–2292.

17. *New York Times*, December 12, 1995.

18. *New York Times*, June 29, 1997, p. 19.

19. *New York Times*, July 5, 1997, p. 1.

20. *New York Times*, October 2, 1996.

21. See the excellent coverage by Nina Bernstein in the *New York Times*, May 4, 1997, pp. 1, 26.

22. The other half of the U.S. "industrial policy" is Department of Defense expenditures.

23. Donald L. Barlett and James R. Steele, "The Great Tax Giveaway," a special section of the *Philadelphia Inquirer* including articles that originally appeared April 10–16 and September 25–26, 1988, p. 4.

24. Barlett and Steele, "Great Tax Giveaway," p. 22.

25. Hey, if you're gonna screw people, why not go all the way? Material in this paragraph comes from the *Boston Globe*, June 6, 1997, pp. A1 and B6.

26. *New York Times*, February 25, 1997, p. A14.

27. Barlett and Steele, "Great Tax Giveaway," pp. 44, 5.

28. *New York Times*, May 1, 1997, p. B1.

29. Philip M. Stern, *The Best Congress Money Can Buy* (New York: Pantheon, 1988), p. 13.

30. Assuming that the individual makes a $100 campaign contribution to reduce his or her taxes by $10,000, while the corporation contributes $200,000 through its PAC to get a tax loophole worth $20 million. Considering how little the individual is contributing, he or she would presumably give it all to one member, while the corporate PAC would have to contribute to a minimum of 20 people, even if it gave the maximum contribution per candidate (and would probably in fact contribute to 150 or more candidates).

31. G. William Domhoff, *The Powers That Be: Processes of Ruling-Class Domination in America* (New York: Random House, 1979), pp. 27–28.

32. Stern, *The Best Congress*, p. 40.

33. *New York Times*, June 6, 1986, pp. D1–D2.

34. *New York Times*, July 12, 1989.

35. Fred Block, "The Ruling Class Does Not Rule," *Socialist Revolution* 7 (1977): 6–28; Nicos Poulantzas, "The Problem of the Capitalist State," *New Left Review* 58 (November–December 1969): 67–78.

36. This and subsequent quotations about Dole's actions are from the *New York Times*, September 23, 1996, p. A13.

37. New York Times March 4, 1996 p. A15.

38. The company's employees, and their families, are probably among the people suffering the most from the plant's pollution, but the company is unlikely to mention this.

39. The study was probably done by an "expert" the company, or industry trade association, hired.

40. Note that these are our words, not an actual quote. We have, and wish we could use, some terrific examples, but we cannot without violating our promise of confidentiality to our respondents. This generic quote lacks the flavor of the originals, but because our examples are company-specific there is no way to present them while still preserving our informants' anonymity.

41. Phone conversation by Denise Scott with Rob Everts, head of advertising for New England division of Neighbor to Neighbor, November 18, 1991.

42. *Standard Directory of Advertising 1990*, vol. I (New York: National Register Publishing Company, 1991), p. 180.

43. Once again, note the routine assumption that money will be delivered in a government office; if Clinton or Gore violated this rule, it's no wonder they weren't very concerned.

44. Almost the only interviews that were less pleasant and friendly were those with corporate officials who do not ordinarily engage in lobbying, either because they were too high up (they supervised the operations, but had never themselves been participants) or too low down (we somehow ended up interviewing a PAC manager who was not involved in contacts with members).

45. Denise Scott, "The Power of Women's Connections: A Study of Women and Men in Corporate–Government Affairs." Ph.D. diss., University of Massachusetts at Amherst, 1996; Denise Scott, "Shattering the Instrumental-Expressive Myth: The Power of Women's Networks in Corporate-Government Affairs, *Gender & Society* 10, no. 3 (1996): 232–247.

46. Brooks Jackson, *Honest Graft: Big Money and the American Political Process* (New York: Knopf, 1988), p. 105.

47. *New York Times*, March 8, 1997, p. 9.

48. *New York Times*, July 19, 1997.

49. National Committee to Preserve Social Security and Medicare, "Myths & Facts About the Social Security Notch" (Washington D.C., no date), p. 2.

50. *Washington Post*, March 25, 1988, p. A23.

51. Timothy Noah, "Notch Babies," *New Republic*, December 1, 1986, p. 18.

52. *Los Angeles Times*, July 25, 1991, p. A5.

53. *New York Times*, January 13, 1988.

54. Bob Rosenblatt, "The Notchies March On," *New Choices for the Best Years*, February 1989, p. 12.

55. At least people used to talk in these terms; we assume these views are less common in recent years.

56. Thus the fledgling Labor party has a T-shirt that reads, "The bosses have two parties; it's time we had one of our own."

57. Though even here, many pieces of key legislation pass by overwhelming bipartisan majorities: President Clinton is hardly a liberal, and many Republicans voted to raise the minimum wage.

58. *Business Week*, October 28, 1996, p. 46.

59. *New York Times*, April 14, 1995, p. A12.

60. *New York Times*, June 9, 1997, p. A20.

61. David Vogel, *Fluctuating Fortunes: The Political Power of Business in America* (New York: Basic Books, 1989); Thomas L. Gais, Mark A. Peterson, and Jack L. Walker, "Interest Groups, Iron Triangles, and Representative Institutions in American National Government," *British Journal of Political Science* 14 (1984): 161–186.

62. Courage in this case means a willingness to stand up for granting special privileges to a multibillion-dollar corporation.

63. Domhoff, *The Powers That Be*; Block, "The Ruling Class Does Not Rule"; Poulantzas, "The Problem of the Capitalist State."

64. James L. Sundquist, *The Decline and Resurgence of Congress* (Washington, D.C.: Brookings Institution, 1981); Walter Dean Burnham, *The Current Crisis in American Politics* (New York: Oxford University Press, 1982).

65. Vogel, *Fluctuating Fortunes*, p. 149.

66. Clearly, this would also have been true of a President Bob Dole; the fact that two such figures could be pitted against each other is itself a statement about the changing nature of the presidency, the degree to which it has become centrally involved in this kind of access process.

67. Karl Marx, *Capital: A Critique of Political Economy*, vol. I (New York: Vintage Books, 1867/1977), p. 381.

68. These are discussed in Chapter 5.

69. Ten years later, Waxman is still there.

70. Senators expect larger contributions; from a large corporation, $250 to a senate race would be something of an insult and might make it harder rather than easier to gain access.

71. Robin Lakoff, *Language and Women's Place* (New York: Harper & Row, 1975), p. 24.

72. Similarly, while the term "lobbyist" is still used, many one-time lobbyists are now "Washington representatives."

73. Our use of the term "access" is thus an attempt to present the world in the terms preferred by corporate PAC officials themselves. While this chapter argues that they actually want more than access, we have tried to make this part of our argument rather than a presupposition.

74. This behavior is the focus of Chapter 5, on corporate ideological donations and activities.

75. *New York Times*, October 18, 1997, p. A10. See also *New York Times*, December 11, 1997, p. A35, reporting that Clinton's total vetoes have eliminated $491 million out of $800 billion in spending, again less than one one-thousandth of the total.

76. *New York Times*, October 22, 1997, p. A20. In Most cases, in order to get their provision accepted, lobbyists will simply need to make arrangements with the president's representatives.

77. Michael Schwartz, ed., *The Structure of Power in America: The Corporate Elite as a Ruling Class* (New York: Holmes & Meier, 1987); Beth Mintz and Michael Schwartz, *The Power Structure of American Business* (Chicago: University of Chicago Press, 1985); Davita Silfen Glassberg, *The Power of Collective Purse Strings: The Effect of Bank Hegemony on Corporations and the State* (Berkeley: University of California Press, 1989).

78. The United States spends over $3,000 per person; Switzerland is the only other country in the world that spends more than $2,000, and its expenditures are more than $1,000 per person under the U.S. figure.

79. U.S. Department of Health and Human Services, *Health United States 1994* (Washington, D.C.: Government Printing Office, 1994), pp. 30, 93, 94, 220.

80. *New York Times*, December 10, 1995.

81. *New York Times*, July 17, 1997, pp. A1, 21.

◆ CHAPTER 4:   SOFT MONEY AND THE PAY-PER-VIEW PRESIDENCY

1. The legal limit is set per election; these are the amounts for candidates who face a primary as well as a general election. A candidate who faced only one election (typically, someone who ran in the primary and lost) could receive only $1,000 from an individual, and $5,000 from a PAC.

2. The point is, of course, legally contested. A ruling banning soft money would have certainly conformed to the spirit of the law, which clearly did not intend to permit the practice; a ban on soft money would certainly have been far more legally defensible than the FEC's SUN–PAC decision that—in total violation of both the letter and spirit of the law—permitted corporations to raise PAC money from managers, not just shareholders.

3. Bill Clinton, Letter to FEC, June 4, 1997; Center for Responsive Politics; www.crp.org.

4. At this point, any FEC decision to ban soft money would be certain to face legal challenges; in 1979, a ruling would probably have been accepted or the challenges dismissed.

5. Public Campaign reports that the DNC relied on hard money for only 58 percent of the total cost of joint activities over the 1995-96 election cycle, a direct violation of federal election law. Public Campaign press release, July 22, 1997.

6. Anthony Corrado, "Party Soft Money." In *Campaign Finance Reform: A Sourcebook*, Anthony Corrado, Thomas E. Mann, Daniel R. Ortiz, Trevor Potter, and Frank J. Sorauf, (Washington, D.C.: The Brookings Institute, 1997).

7. The $150 million figure is based on a report by the Annenberg Center at the University of Pennsylvania, reported in the *New York Times* September 17, 1997, p. A26. Although the AFL–CIO ads were effective in shaping the political agenda, Democrats won in only 15 of the 44 districts targeted by the AFL–CIO. The ads were, of course, targeted to districts with potentially vulnerable antilabor representatives. By some standards, winning one-third of those races is remarkable, given how heavily the odds are stacked against challengers: The question is how many races the Democrats would have won without the labor ads.

8. *New York Times*, July 8, 1997, p. A10.

9. *New York Times*, July 8, 1997, p. A10.

10. For quotations in this and the following paragraph, see *Washington Post*, April 13, 1997, pp. A1, A18.

11. All quotes and examples in this paragraph are from the *Washington Post*, October 9, 1996, p. A1, 12.

12. The typical pattern for the development of campaign finance loopholes is that a new practice is introduced by one party, the other party objects to it, the practice remains effectively unregulated, and soon both parties are using it full blast.

13. Jennifer Keen and John Daly, *Beyond the Limits: Soft Money in the 1996 Elections* (Center for Responsive Politics, 1997, www.crp.org).

14. *New York Times*, September 13, 1992, p. A38.

15. *Boston Globe*, February 10, 1997, pp. A1, 7.

16. You'd care about the "small" contributors, the ones who'd kick in "only" a thousand dollars? That's (one of the reasons) why you aren't a successful politician.

17. See, for example, *Boston Globe*, June 9, 1997.

18. *New York Times*, September 13, 1992, p. A38.

19. *Washington Post*, May 30, 1997, p. A22.

20. Occupations are listed for 1,988 Republican donors, but not for the other 5,895; for 327 of the Democratic donors, but not for the other 1,139. Source: FEC records.

21. The components of this (in millions) are: corporations, $140.2; business associations, $9.7; business individual contributors, $22.3 (counting only business contributors from the 100 largest individual contributors); as opposed to labor unions, $9.2; and working-class individuals, $.005 (including *all* working-class individuals, none of whom gave enough to be among the top 5,000 contributors).

22. *Fortune*, April 29, 1996.

23. The money for one Super Bowl ad would by itself be enough to qualify a corporation as the 9th-largest corporate soft money donor.

24. *Washington Post*, June 6, 1997, p. A15.

25. Of the total difference of 16,425, 15,683 are in the under $1,000 grouping, with another 748 accounted for by the $1,001 to $10,000 range; for all larger donors the numbers are almost exactly equal. The Democrats have a few more large donors.

26. *New York Times*, March 26, 1997, p. A1.

27. Contributors may well have persuaded themselves these policies would be for the good of all and would eventually trickle down to the rest of the population.

28. Quoted in *Boston Globe*, July 13, 1997, p. A30.

29. Quoted in *Boston Globe*, July 13, 1997, p. A30.

30. *New York Times*, April 17, 1997, p. A1, D22.

31. *New York Times*, September 17, 1997, p. A26.

32. *New York Times*, March 26, 1997, p. A1.

33. *New York Times*, March 8, 1997, p. 9.

34. *Boston Globe*, January 25, 1997, p. A6.

35. *New York Times*, August 12, 1997, pp. A1, 18.

36. *New York Times*, August 12, 1997, p. A18.

37. Landow denied the remarks were intended as a threat, insisting they were simply an observation and analysis. We think it's perfectly possible that the remarks were *both* a reasonable analysis—the tribe obviously wasn't going to succeed on its own—*and* a threat.

38. So far: The amount of soft money is increasing and many of the donations are given in crude influence-buying forms

39. See *USA Today*, March 28, 1997; Associated Press, January 29, 1997; and *Wall Street Journal*, February 6, 1997.

40. Seagram also faces a challenging legal–political environment. Sales of hard liquor have been declining, while sales of wine and beer have increased. For many years the distillers have not advertised hard liquor on television, but this has been a "voluntary" decision on their part, *not* something that is legally binding. Seagram decided to begin advertising hard liquor on television. This has been widely understood as a slick maneuver: Seagram can win *either* if it is permitted to advertise hard liquor, *or* if Congress imposes limits on advertising wine and beer. Seagram's soft money contribution is far less than it would spend on a television advertising campaign, but it is one vital element in this new cultural-political strategy.

41. *Washington Post*, September 30, 1996, pp. A1, A12.

42. *New York Times*, September 18, 1997, p. A30.

43. The defense of the government relations' head would probably be: That's so much money they wouldn't be willing to take it for fear of a public reaction. The CEO's response would be: That's your job, to find a way to do this without attracting attention; be creative.

44. *Business Week*, July 14, 1997, p. 28.

45. Robert Kuttner, "Why Congress Should Stub out the Tobacco Deal," *Business Week* August 25, 1997, p. 28.

46. Admittedly, it would be tough to speak out in favor of the rewards and benefits of cigarette smoking.

◆ CHAPTER 5: IDEOLOGY AND POLITICAL SHIFTS

1. Quoted in Maxwell Glen, "At the Wire, Corporate PACs Come Through for the GOP," *National Journal*, February 3, 1979, p. 174.

2. Thomas Ferguson and Joel Rogers, eds., *The Hidden Election: Politics and Economics in the 1980 Presidential Election* (New York: Pantheon, 1981), p. 42.

3. William E. Simon, *A Time for Truth* (New York: Reader's Digest Press, 1978), pp. 197, 198.

4. Simon, *A Time for Truth*, p. 228.

5. Note that here (and elsewhere) ideological PAC officials focus on members of

Congress using campaign finance to enrich themselves. Of course, in fact, top corporate executives make vastly more than members of Congress and most members could earn more if they left public office. But ideological PAC officials are extremely concerned about members enriching themselves.

6. Simon, *A Time for Truth*, p. 228.

7. Irving Kristol, *Two Cheers for Capitalism* (New York: Basic Books, 1978), p. 140.

8. Jerry Himmelstein wrote an excellent set of comments on a previous draft of our chapter, made many of the points presented here, and suggested that we read Kristol and Simon. Himmelstein's comments and book, *To the Right: The Transformation of American Conservatism* (Berkeley: University of California Press, 1990), profoundly shaped the character of this chapter.

9. Social movements were able to put these issues on the national agenda and to win advances, but they were never powerful enough to *control* the outcomes, and many of the Nixon era initiatives were intended to co-opt movements, providing the appearance of change but within a framework that limited their ability to accomplish their aims. Nonetheless, they represented real advances, and were enacted only because of the power of these movements.

10. David Vogel, *Fluctuating Fortunes: The Political Power of Business in America* (New York: Basic Books, 1989), p. 59.

11. Leonard Silk and David Vogel, *Ethics and Profits* (New York: Simon & Schuster, 1976), pp. 44, 45, 72.

12. Dan Clawson and Mary Ann Clawson, "Reagan or Business: Foundations of the New Conservatism," In *The Structure of Power in America: The Corporate Elite as a Ruling Class*, ed. Michael Schwartz (New York: Holmes & Meier, 1987), p. 204. As another example, consider the risks business runs if it is careless about the way it handles hazardous materials on railroads: "Lawrence M. Mann, an attorney who represents the Railway Labor Executives' Association, said that because of the agency's small staff and the paltry fines it charges, the railroads are under scant pressure to follow regulations. 'If I'm a manager of a railroad,' he said, 'I know they won't see my car but once a year, and even if they do see it and find a defect, they give me a chance to correct it—and even if I don't correct it, the fine will only average $27.'" (Kirk Victor, "Trouble on Wheels," *National Journal*, May 26, 1990, p. 162).

13. Clawson and Clawson, "Reagan or Business," pp. 206–207.

14. David Vogel, "Business's 'New Class' Struggle," *The Nation*, December 15, 1979, pp. 609ff.

15. *Business Week*, October 12, 1974, p. 120.

16. Thomas Byrne Edsall, *The New Politics of Inequality* (New York: Norton, 1984), p. 125.

17. Edsall, *New Politics of Inequality*, p. 111.

18. Donald Kendall, quoted in Phyllis S. McGrath, *Redefining Corporate-Federal Relations* (New York: The Conference Board Division of Management Research, 1979), p. 55.

19. See also Edward Handler and John R. Mulkern, *Business in Politics: Strategies of Corporate Political Action Committees* (Lexington, Mass.: Lexington Books, 1982); Michael J. Malbin, *Parties, Interest Groups, and Campaign Finance Laws* (Washington, D.C.: American Enterprise Institute, 1980).

20. Glen, "At the Wire, Corporate PACs Come Through for the GOP," p. 176. Not all of this change can be attributed to the effects of the letters circulating within the business community. Corporate campaign strategies always tend to follow this pattern. Access-oriented donations to incumbents can be made equally well at any point, while ideological donations aren't made until late in the campaign when it is possible to judge which races are likely to be close and to involve significant political differences between the two candidates. Therefore, late money always tends to be more ideological.

21. In many cases, open seats are the key races in deciding the ideological composition of Congress, but donations to these races do not require a PAC to oppose a powerful incumbent. Moreover, some open-seat races have foregone conclusions, because they are run in districts traditionally controlled by one party. Donations to these candidates may then reflect an access strategy.

22. James Weinstein, *The Corporate Ideal in the Liberal State: 1900–1918* (Boston: Beacon, 1968), p. xii.

23. See G. William Domhoff, *The Higher Circles: The Governing Class in America* (New York: Random House, 1970).

24. Throughout the entire period from 1976 to 1996, in no election did even a single corporation give as much as 30 percent of its money to Democratic challengers, and only rarely did one corporation give as much as 10 percent.

25. The exception was 1986, when corporate PACs gave 3.5 percent of their money to Democratic challengers, almost all of this going to Senate candidates who held other offices of concern to corporations. (The Senate challengers were serving as governors or members of the House).

26. For this purpose we include only the largest corporate PACs. For each year, we sorted corporate PACs from the largest to the smallest, then included enough PACs to account for 60 percent of the money for that year. This means that the number of PACs being considered differs from election to election, but a fixed dollar cutoff also encounters problems because of the rapid increase in the amounts contributed over this period.

27. Clawson and Clawson, "Reagan or Business," p. 209.

28. Tie-ting Su, Alan Neustadtl, and Dan Clawson, "Business and the Conservative Shift: Corporate PAC Contributions, 1976–1986," *Social Science Quarterly* 76 (1995): 20–40; Alan Neustadtl and Dan Clawson, "Corporate Political Groupings: Does Ideology Unify Business Political Behavior?" *American Sociological Review* 53 (1988): 172–190; Tie-ting Su, Dan Clawson, and Alan Neustadtl, "Corporate PACs and Conservative Realignment: A Comparison of 1980 and 1984," *Social Science Research* 22 (1993): 33–71, 1993; Tie-ting Su, Dan Clawson, and Alan Neustadtl, "The Coalescence of Corporate Conservatism from 1976 to 1980: The Roots of the Reagan Revolution," *Research in Politics and Society* 4 (1992): 135–160; Dan Clawson and Tie-ting Su, "Was 1980 Special? A Comparison of 1980 and 1986 Corporate PAC Contributions," *Sociological Quarterly* 31 (1990): 371–387.

29. Two groups had 5 members, one had 6, one had 8, and one had 9.

30. Significantly, this one corporation was United Technologies, the company whose government relations officer wrote an analysis urging more ideological PAC contributions. That analysis was sent to all members of the Business Roundtable in 1978 by Donald Kendall, CEO of Pepsico and chair of the Roundtable.

31. Quoted in Thomas Byrne Edsall, "Coelho Mixes Democratic Fund-raising, Political Matchmaking," *Washington Post*, December 1, 1985, p. 17.

32. Quoted in Edsall, "Coelho mixes Democratic fund-raising, political matchmaking," p. 18. See also Brooks Jackson, *Honest Graft: Big Money and the American Political Process* (New York: Knopf, 1988); and Thomas Byrne Edsall, "The Reagan Legacy." In *The Reagan Legacy,* ed. Sidney Blumenthal and Thomas Byrne Edsall (New York: Pantheon, 1988), pp. 3–50.

33. The fact that these three, and other leading Democratic figures, could be seen as "too liberal" is itself testimony to the shifting political terrain. Walter Mondale ran on a platform of reducing the deficit and balancing the budget. Gary Hart was openly hostile to labor and redistributive policies. Mike Dukakis was governor of a liberal state, but twice attacked public higher education. Jesse Jackson was the only major liberal figure in national Democratic policies in the 1980s, and he was thoroughly marginalized, not only by his race but by his politics as well.

34. Walter Dean Burnham, "Realignment Lives: The 1994 Earthquake and Its Implications." In *The Clinton Presidency: First Appraisals,* Colin Campbell and Bert A. Rockman, ed. (Chatham, N.J.: Chatham House Publishers, 1996), p. 363.

35. Burnham "Realignment Lives," pp. 365–367.

36. Charles O. Jones, "Foreword." In *Midterm: The Elections of 1994 in Context,* Philip A. Klinkner, ed. (Boulder, Colo.: Westview Press, 1996), p. ix.

37. Thomas Ferguson, "GOP Money Talked: Did Voters Listen?" *The Nation,* December 26, 1994, p. 792.

38. See Michael J. Webber and G. William Domhoff, "Myth and Reality in Business Support for Democrats and Republicans in the 1936 Presidential Election," *American Political Science Review* 90 (December 1996): 824–833.

39. See note 26 for a discussion of the basis of these numbers.

40. In 1994 Democratic open-seat candidates received 3.4 percent of the corporate money; in 1996, 3.9 percent. Democratic challengers received 0.5 percent in 1994, and 1.0 percent in 1996.

41. One way to read these data would be that incumbents of the party out of power receive 22 percent of corporate money, incumbents of the party in power receive 46 percent, and Republicans receive a 10 percent bonus on top of this for their ideology.

42. See William F. Grover's brilliantly titled, *The President as Prisoner* (Albany: State University of New York Press, 1989).

43. A partial listing would include almost everything ever written by Domhoff, but especially *The Higher Circles, The Powers That Be* (New York: Random House, 1979), and *The Power Elite and the State: How Policy Is Made in America* (New York: Aldine Gruyter, 1990); Beth Mintz and Michael Schwartz, *The Power Structure of American Business* (Chicago: University of Chicago Press, 1985); Mark Mizruchi, *The Structure of Corporate Political Action: Interfirm Relations and Their Consequences* (Cambridge: Harvard University Press, 1992); Lawrence H. Shoup and William Minter, *Imperial Braintrust: The Council on Foreign Relations and United States Foreign Policy* (New York: Monthly Review Press, 1977); Joseph G. Peschek, *Policy-Planning Organizations: Elite Agendas and America's Rightward Turn* (Philadelphia: Temple University Press, 1987); Edsall, *The New Politics of Inequality;* and this book, we hope, also contributes to that literature.

44. See, for examples, Clawson and Su, "Was 1980 Special?"; Su, Neustadtl, and Clawson, "Business and the Conservative Shift"; Su, Clawson, and Neustadtl, "Corporate PACs and Conservative Realignment."

45. The real interest rate (Aaa Corporate Bonds [Moody's] minus inflation rate percent [change in CPI-U, all items]) was calculated from data in the *Economic Report of the President*, February 1996 (Washington, D.C.: U.S. Government Printing Office), Tables B-59 and B-69 (pp. 347, 360).

46. And in all but two years were over one million. This and the remaining data in this paragraph come from U.S. Bureau of the Census, *Statistical Abstract of the United States, 1995* (Washington, D.C.: Government Printing Office, 1995), Table 694, p. 442.

47. U.S. Census Bureau, "Historical Income Tables: Families," Table F-2, April 1997 (www.census.gov). Income data comparing the richest and poorest also make startlingly clear the sharp character of the 1980 break. Consider the income received by the top 5 percent of the population in relation to that received by the bottom 40 percent. If this ratio were 1.0, it would mean that the top 5 percent received as much income as the bottom 40 percent; put another way, the average person in the top 5 percent received as much income as 8 people in the bottom 40 percent. If the ratio is below 1.0, income is more equally distributed (at a ratio of 0.5, the person in the top group would have "only" as much income as 4 people at the bottom); if the ratio is above 1.0, income is even more unequal. From 1968 to 1981, this ratio stayed within a very narrow band, from a low of .836 to a high of .914. In 1981, as the new policies were being enacted, the ratio was .862; in the next year, the level of inequality jumped more than it had at any time in the preceding 15 years, and the rich-to-poor income ratio continued to rise thereafter, going above 1.0 in 1985, never again falling below that level, and reaching 1.4 in 1993.

48. An alternative argument is conceivable, but far-fetched: Clinton (and perhaps Bush) were extreme liberals, and the post-1994 period marked a sharp shift by returning the nation to the sensible policies of Ronald Reagan. Some of the comments by Newt Gingrich and the House class of 1994 appear to embrace that analysis (though most of the time even they know better), but it would be extremely difficult to develop evidence to support this position.

49. *Wall Street Journal*, March 14, 1997, p. A18.

50. *New York Times*, August 23, 1997, pp. 1, 9.

51. Tricia Welsh, "CEOs: Greenspan in a Landslide," *Fortune*, March 18, 1996, p. 43; see also, Mark Weller, "The 1980 Policy Shift," manuscript, 1996—21 percent of the CEOs believed the Fed chair was more important.

52. A power that is evident to business, but generally concealed from the public.

◆ CHAPTER 6: PACS RUNNING IN PACKS

1. Robert A. Dahl, "A Critique of the Ruling Elite Model," *American Political Science Review*, 52 (1958): 465.

2. Dennis S. Ippolito and Thomas G. Walker, *Political Parties, Interest Groups, and Public Policy* (Englewood Cliffs, N.J.: Prentice-Hall, 1980), p. 282.

3. Theodore J. Eismeier and Philip H. Pollock III, *Business, Money, and the Rise of Corporate PACs in American Elections* (New York: Quorum Books, 1988), p. 6.

4. Alan Neustadtl, Denise Scott, and Dan Clawson, "Class Struggle in Cam-

paign Finance? Political Action Committee Contributions in the 1984 Elections," *Sociological Forum* 6 (1991): 219–238.

5. Dan Clawson, Alan Neustadtl, and James Bearden, "The Logic of Business Unity: Corporate Contributions to the 1980 Congressional Elections," *American Sociological Review* 51 (1986): pp. 797–811. See also Dan Clawson and Tie-ting Su, "Was 1980 Special? A Comparison of 1980 and 1986 Corporate PAC Contributions," *Sociological Quarterly* 31 (1990): 371–387.

6. Michael Schwartz, ed., *The Structure of Power in America: The Corporate Elite as a Ruling Class* (New York: Holmes & Meier, 1987).

7. Elizabeth Drew, *Whatever It Takes: The Real Struggle for Political Power in America* (New York: Viking, 1997), pp. 19–20.

8. Dan Clawson and Alan Neustadtl, "Interlocks, PACs, and Corporate Conservatism," *American Journal of Sociology* 94 (1989): 749–773; Mark Mizruchi and Thomas Koenig, "Economic Sources of Corporate Political Consensus: An Examination of Interindustry Relations," *American Sociological Review* 51 (1986): 482–491; Mark Mizruchi, "Similarity of Political Behavior Among Large American Corporations," *American Journal of Sociology* 95 (1989): 401–424.

9. Mark S. Mizruchi, *The American Corporate Network* (Beverly Hills, Calif.: Sage, 1982); Beth Mintz and Michael Schwartz, *The Power Structure of American Business* (Chicago: University of Chicago Press, 1985).

10. Gayle Rubin, "The Traffic in Women: Notes on the Political Economy of Sex." In *Toward an Anthropology of Women*, ed. Rayna Rapp Reiter (New York: Monthly Review Press, 1975), pp. 159–210.

11. Michael Useem, *The Inner Circle: Large Corporations and the Rise of Business Political Activity in the U.S. and U.K.* (New York: Oxford University Press, 1984).

12. G. William Domhoff, *The Higher Circles: The Governing Class in America* (New York: Random House, 1970); Laurence H. Shoup and William Minter, *Imperial Braintrust: The Council on Foreign Relations and United States Foreign Policy* (New York: Monthly Review Press, 1977); J. Allen Whitt, *Urban Elites and Mass Transportation* (Princeton: Princeton University Press, 1982).

13. Tricia Welsh, "CEOs: Greenspan by a Landslide," *Fortune*, March 18, 1996, p. 45.

14. Note once again, however, that even liberals are perfectly willing to help corporations, to work with them and be helpful until it comes to the final vote.

15. David Vogel, *Fluctuating Fortunes: The Political Power of Business in America* (New York: Basic Books, 1989), pp. 154–155.

16. Census Bureau, *Consumer Population Survey*, March 1996, revised September 1996, on-line (www.census.gov), Tables F-1, F-5, Table E; Thomas Byrne Edsall and Mary Edsall, *Chain Reaction: The Impact of Race, Rights, and Taxes on American Politics* (New York: Norton, 1991), p. 23.

17. Wealth consists of the total value of everything a person owns, minus the value of everything the person owes. On the positive side a person would have such credits as all the money in his or her checking and savings accounts, the book value of the car, and the resale value of the house. On the negative side, a person's debits would be the size of the mortgage(s) on the house, what is owed on credit cards, the balance on car payments, the total of any student loans, and anything else he or she owed. It is perfectly possible, therefore, to have no *net* wealth; in fact, to have a

negative net wealth. That simply means that if a person cashed in all their assets, they couldn't pay all their debts. For many people this is a more or less permanent condition of life. Others go through such a period at some time in their lives, for example, while paying off student loans.

18. *New York Times*, March 13, 1996, pp. D1, D7.

19. Edward N. Wolff, "How the Pie Is Sliced: America's Growing Concentration of Wealth," *American Prospect* 22 (Summer 1995): 58–64.

20. Erik Olin Wright, *Class Structure and Income Determination* (New York: Academic Press, 1979), chap. 1.

21. *Fortune*, April 29, 1996.

22. One-hundredth of one percent is enough to include the board of directors and top officers of the 500 largest industrials and 500 largest service companies, with spaces left over for several thousand top lawyers, foundation executives, consulting firms, and accountants. Even if we multiply this number by ten, we still include only one-tenth of one percent of the U.S. population.

23. Obviously, the elected government has the *potential* to make more important decisions. If some U.S. president decides to launch a first-strike nuclear attack, the importance of the government will, at least for a while, vastly overshadow the decisions of corporations.

24. David R. Simon and D. Stanley Eitzen, *Elite Deviance* (Boston: Allyn and Bacon, 1990), p. 10.

25. *New York Times*, July 21, 1991, p. 14.

26. On average, corporations contribute only .009 percent of their pretax net income to charity, a smaller proportion than that given by ordinary individuals, despite the fact that corporations are public institutions with enormous incomes.

27. This process, however, also demonstrated that *some* elements of the government are important to business, not just to voters; the Republican closedown dramatically inconvenienced many businesses.

28. Mark Dowie, "Pinto Madness," *Mother Jones*, September–October, 1977, pp. 18–32. This article is the basis for the account that follows.

29. When corporate decisions are challenged by unions, environmentalists, or public interest groups, executives frequently argue that they had no choice, that the constraints of the market required a particular course of action. On the other hand, these same executives justify their stratospheric pay on the basis that they are constantly required to make tough decisions, and that the company's success depends on the choices they make.

30. Dowie, "Pinto Madness," p. 22.

31. Ralph Nader, *Unsafe at Any Speed* (New York: Pocket Books, 1966).

32. Frequently, even when a regulation is imposed, it leaves control in the hands of business. For example, instead of the government testing new drugs, the pharmaceutical companies test them and report their results to the government body that is supposed to regulate them. A similar procedure is followed to determine whether new cars meet emission standards.

33. Ford based its estimate of the value of a human life on a handy government study by the National Highway Traffic Safety Administration. Dowie, Pinto Madness," p. 28.

34. U.S. Bureau of the Census, *Statistical Abstract of the United States 1996* (Washington, DC: Government Printing Office, 1996), Table 908, p. 574.

35. Such as Afghanistan, Bangladesh, Ethiopia, India, Kenya, Madagascar, Mozambique, Nepal, Pakistan, Sri Lanka, Tanzania, or Zaire. Put another way, total U.S. advertising expenditures were the same as the gross national products of Algeria, Bangladesh, Bulgaria, Egypt, El Salvador, Ethiopia, and Tanzania *combined*—countries whose combined population is greater than that of the United States.

36. U.S. Bureau of the Census, *Statistical Abstract of the United States 1995* (Washington, DC: Government Printing Office, 1995), Table 229, p. 151.

37. Average television viewing is 29 hours and 40 minutes a week; 15 to 20 percent of this time is occupied by commercials.

38. Quoted in *Boston Globe*, July 15, 1997, p. E5. The rest of this paragraph is based on or quoted in this same article.

39. The most surefire way to limit undue corporate influence on Congress and the government would be to limit overall business power, including corporate control of the economy. While we would support such initiatives, they are extremely unlikely to occur at this time.

◆ CHAPTER 7: SCANDAL OR SYSTEM?

1. "They Promised Campaign Reform: Let's Make Them Keep Their Promise" (Washington, D.C.: Public Campaign, 1997, www.publiccampaign.org), p. 1.

2. *New York Times*, September 24, 1997, p. A1.

3. *Washington Post*, February 9, 1997, p. A1.

4. *Boston Globe*, July 9, 1997, p. A1.

5. *New York Times*, September 10, 1997, p. A20.

6. *New York Times*, November 8, 1997, p. A12.

7. Another former law partner of HRC, Webster Hubbell, who had pleaded guilty to stealing funds from the Rose law firm in Little Rock, after resigning from his assistant attorney generalship in the Clinton administration, was retained briefly and paid an estimated $250,000 by the Riadys.

8. *New York Times*, September 19, 1997, p. A26. Campane was assigned to assist the Senate investigating committee.

9. Only one person, Dan Quayle's former national security adviser, claims to have heard a direct fundraising pitch at a Clinton coffee; others who attended the event dispute his account. See Chapter 4.

10. *Chicago Sun Times* reported in "Fat Cat Hotel," (Washington, D.C.: Center for Public Integrity, 1996, www.publicintegrity.org), p. 1.

11. *New York Times*, September 10, 1997, pp. A1, A20.

12. *New York Times*, September 10, 1997, p. A20.

13. Quoted in *Washington Post*, June 27, 1997, p. A8; Gore claims the memo did not apply to the president and vice president (*Washington Post*, March 4, 1997, p. A9).

14. He defended the calls as "entirely legal, regardless of where they were made from in the White House and regardless of whether they were for federal campaign funds or for non-federal campaign" purposes. *Boston Globe*, September 27, 1997 p. A10.

15. *The Nation*, March 24, 1997, p. 3.

16. See *New York Times*, September 10, 1997, pp. A1, A21; *Boston Globe*, September 9, 1997, p. A14.

17. Clinton, apparently, made only two phone calls, both from the residential section of the White House, which is not covered by the law in question.

18. *New York Times*, October 21, 1997, p. A20.

19. *New York Times*, December 3, 1997, pp. A1, A30.

20. And that for at least two reasons. First, the prosecutor wouldn't have been appointed unless there were significant evidence of misconduct. Second, this result is almost built in by the dynamic of the situation: If the prosecutor finds violations, this certifies the prosecutor's importance; if there are no violations, the tendency will be to conclude that the prosecutor was not needed—was, in fact, a waste.

21. *Boston Globe*, July 9, 1997, p. A14.

22. *Boston Globe*, July 24, 1997, pp. A1, A10.

23. *Boston Globe*, July 4, 1997, p. A8.

24. *New York Times*, September 24, 1997, p. A24. However, the individual making this charge is a former executive director of the Democratic National Committee, not exactly a neutral source.

25. *Boston Globe*, July 5, 1997, pp. A1, A12.

26. *Washington Post*, October 24, 1996, p. A16.

27. Of course, since this is an FEC staff recommendation, the likelihood is that nothing will ever happen due to a stalemate among the commissioners. *New York Times*, December 18, 1997, pp. A1, A24.

28. Peter H. Stone, "The Green Wave," *National Journal*, November 9, 1996, pp. 2410–2414; *New York Times*, January 27, 1996.

29. Jane Mayer, "Inside the Money Machine," *New Yorker*, February 3, 1997, pp. 32–37; *New York Times*, January 27, 1997; *Boston Globe*, February 21, 1997.

30. *Washington Post*, February 25, 1997, p. A4, and February 27, 1997, p. A17.

31. *Boston Globe*, March 23, 1997; *Washington Post*, February 27, 1997, p. A17.

32. *New York Times*, July 27, 1997, p. E14.

33. *Boston Globe*, July 5, 1997, pp. A1, 12.

34. *New York Times*, March 9, 1997, p. 22.

35. *New York Times*, March 9, 1997, pp. 1, 22.

36. *Slate* (on-line magazine), May 19, 1997.

37. *Boston Globe*, July 5, 1997, pp. A1, A12.

38. *Slate* (on-line magazine), May 19, 1997.

39. David Corn, "Donkey Droppings," *Salon*, December 4, 1996, www.salon.com.

40. *American Prospect*, July–August 1997, p. 11.

41. *Washington Post*, October 12, 1996, p. A21.

42. *Boston Globe*, July 6, 1997, p. A14.

43. *Boston Globe*, January 5, 1997, pp. A1, 8.

44. "Global Connections:Pacs and Soft Money Contributions from Foreign Owned Subsidiaries, 1995–96" (Washington, D.C.: Center for Responsive Politics, 1997, www.crp.org).

45. Data from *Information Please: The 1990 Almanac* (Boston: Houghton Mifflin Company), 234–235.

46. *New York Times*, March 31, 1997, pp. A1, 11.

47. *New York Times*, March 31, 1997, p. A1.

48. Robert Dreyfuss, "The New China Lobby," *American Prospect* 30 (January–February 1997): 30–37.

49. Dreyfuss, "New China Lobby," 1997.

50. Eighteen Asian American groups and individuals filed a complaint with the United States Civil Rights Commission, contending that there is widespread bias against Asians. They were responding to the fact that virtually every Asian American contributor was forced to answer a host of questions or else have their contribution returned and reporters notified of their refusal to provide the requested information (*New York Times*, September 12, 1997, p. A30).

51. G. William Domhoff, *Who Rules America?* (Englewood Cliffs, N.J.: Prentice-Hall, 1967), p. 153.

52. Eliza Newlin Carney, "Now or Never," *National Journal*, September 6,1997, p. 1740.

53. Douglas Phelps, "Setting Limits," *Boston Review*, April–May 1997.

54. The argument is that this amount is so small as to unreasonably limit a person's ability to "speak" (through their campaign contributions) for their views.

55. Political scientist Thomas Gais (*Improper Influence: Campaign Finance Law, Political Interest Groups, and the Problem of Equality*, [Ann Arbor: University of Michigan Press, 1996]) supports eliminating contribution limits, arguing that groups with less money, such as environmental or women's organizations, rely on large donors for start-up and survival. We have two responses: First, an environmental (or women's) group dependent on a few rich donors is likely to support a form of environmentalism that accepts the status quo. Second, less regulation generally means more domination by business. As Chapter 4 argued, the labor–business gap for (unregulated) soft money is much larger than that for (regulated) PAC money.

56. David Donnelly, Janice Fine, and Ellen S. Miller, "Going Public," *Boston Review*, April–May 1997.

57. Participation figures from Kenneth R. Mayer, "Campaign Finance Reform in the States: A Report to the Governor's Blue Ribbon Commission on Campaign Finance Reform," Kenneth R. Mayer, 1997, www.polisci.wisc.edu/kmayer/commission.pdf. State population from *Statistical Abstract of the United States: 1995* (Washington, D.C.: U.S. Government Printing Office, 1995), Table 27, p. 28.

58. See "Slush Funding," *The Nation*, March 31, 1997, p. 7; Committee for the Study of the American Electorate, "Use of Media Principal Reason Campaign Costs Skyrocket," at tap.epn.org/csae/media.html; Anthony Corrado, "Recent Innovations." In *Campaign Finance Reform: A Sourcebook*, Anthony Corrado, Thomas E. Mann, Daniel R. Ortiz, Trevor Potter, and Frank J. Sorauf, (Washington, D.C.: The Brookings Institute, 1997).

59. Robert L. Borosage and Ruy Teixeira, "The Politics of Money," *The Nation* October 21, 1996, pp. 21–23.

60. This is the quintessential liberal dilemma, which occurs in most areas of government policy, not just campaign finance reform. Liberalism leaves the private sector free to control itself and operate as it wishes (with tremendous inequalities and power differences), then attempts to correct the worst consequences of the free market through various kinds of government programs. But even when the government programs move in the right direction, they are always minimal, with far too little power to do more than frustrate the basic direction of the private sector. Often, of course, the programs are corrupted even before they can be implemented, so they serve ends very different from those publicly proclaimed.

61. Steven Lukes, "Political Ritual and Social Integration," *Sociology* 9 (1975): 301.

62. Philip Stern, *The Best Congress Money Can Buy* (New York: Pantheon, 1988).

63. See Dan Clawson, *Bureaucracy and the Labor Process: The Transformation of U.S. Industry, 1860–1920* (New York: Monthly Review Press, 1980), for an argument that this is not necessarily the most efficient way to organize production and that this form of organization developed to maximize profits and control.

64. Some of the people who might not agree with this are the owners and executives of major corporations, many of whom apparently feel that democracy must be kept under control and that those with extra money and power are entitled to extra consideration.

65. David Magleby and Candice J. Nelson, *The Money Chase: Congressional Campaign Finance Reform* (Washington, D.C.: Brookings Institution, 1990), p. 38.

66. David C. Huckabee, "Reelection Rates of House Incumbents: 1790–1994," Congressional Research Service Report for Congress, (Bethesda, Md.: Penny Hill Press).

67. Huckabee, "Reelection Rates of House Incumbents: 1790–1988. "In 1842 the rate was 24 percent. From 1790 to 1896, the rate never reached 70 percent. Since 1896 the rate has been below 70 percent only four times: in 1910 (68.0 percent), 1912 (64.4 percent), 1914 (68.7 percent), and 1922 (69.9 percent). The term-limitation movement is an understandable product of this lack of turnover, an implicit admission that an incumbent who is allowed to run is virtually unbeatable. Rather than creating a competitive system, term-limitation amendments simply attempt to ensure that open-seat selection occurs not just once in a generation but once in a decade.

68. Magleby and Nelson, *Money Chase*; Gary C. Jacobson, *Money in Congressional Elections* (New Haven: Yale University Press, 1980).

69. Magleby and Nelson, *Money Chase*, p. 140.

70. *New York Times*, July 4, 1986.

71. Michael Lewis, "The President's Man, and His Secrets," *New York Times Magazine*, September 21, 1997, p. 63.

72. Interested readers can find more detail, and up-to-the-minute reports, at Public Campaign's website (www.publiccampaign.org).

73. "Senate's Struggle to Pass Limits Only Opens Uphill Battle," *Congressional Quarterly*, May 25, 1991, p. 1352.

74. Free or discounted air time is part of the CMCR proposal, but we would prefer candidates simply be given enough money to run strong campaigns. Providing free television time distorts candidate choices, encouraging television and implicitly discouraging face-to-face activities.

75. As a final, more ideological, inducement to stay with public financing, the rules would be structured so that candidates who raised large sums through private financing had to take responsibility for permanently raising the level of public subsidy. The amount of public subsidy available to candidates at the next election would be based on the average amount spent by candidates in the previous election, adjusted for inflation. Thus, if candidates chose to take private financing so they could raise more than the normal amount, their opponent would be given the equivalent amount, they would each have spent more than the average, and this would raise the average subsidy for all candidates in the subsequent election.

76. *New York Times*, September 27, 1997, p. A8.

77. This and all figures in this paragraph from U.S. Bureau of the Census, *Statistical Abstract of the United States: 1996* (Washington, D.C.: U.S. Government Printing Office), Table 513, p. 331.

78. An increase in corporate taxes does not increase (or decrease) the resources in American society (at least in the shortrun), it just redistributes who pays the money—but as we have argued, exactly the same point applies to our public financing proposal.

79. *Congressional Quarterly*, "Senate's Struggle," p. 1353.

80. Jack W. Germond and Jules Witcover, "Money May Be Democrats' Headache," *National Journal*, July 13, 1991, p. 1762.

81. Brooks Jackson, *Broken Promise: Why the Federal Election Commission Failed* (New York: Priority Press, a Twentieth Century Fund Paper, 1990).

82. *New York Times*, September 19, 1997, p. A27.

83. *New York Times*, October 19, 1997, pp. 1, 22; *National Journal*, October 4, 1997, pp. 1964-1965.

84. *New York Times*, September 26 and 27, 1997.

85. Perhaps the following year Congress could entertain proposals to restore slavery, if people "choose" to sell themselves.

86. If the amount per candidate were set lower, this would in practice help incumbents, since they start out with an advantage and a challenger needs to be able to spend a substantial sum to make it a race.

87. In campaigns today, the cost of raising money is typically 20 to 30 percent of total spending. (Magleby and Nelson, *Money Chase*, p. 172.) With public finance there would be no fundraising costs.

88. Quoted in Larry J. Sabato, *Paying for Elections: The Campaign Finance Thicket* (New York: Norton, 1989), p. 60.

89. Public Campaign, "Clean Money Campaign Reform: The States Take the Lead," July 1997.

90. Princeton Survey Research Associates, "Money and Politics Survey: Summary and Overview," 1997.

91. *New York Times*, April 8, 1997, p. A14.

92. Letter to the Editor (from Robert J. Blendon and John M. Benson), *Boston Globe*, March 31, 1997, p. A14.

93. The Gallup poll has consistently found more people favoring than opposing public financing, with the single exception of December 1982 (when a very small majority opposed it). Their question explicitly ties public financing to a ban on all private contributions. The American Medical Association conducted a series of polls with a question that makes no mention of banning private contributions; they consistently found a substantial majority opposed to public finance. Given the way the issue has generally been posed to the public, we are impressed that a reasonably fair question (the Gallup poll version) demonstrates consistent public support for public funding. See Magleby and Nelson, *Money Chase*, p. 75.

94. G. William Domhoff, *The Powers That Be: Processes of Ruling Class Domination in America* (New York: Random House, 1978).

95. Perhaps one appropriate response is to aim for a "minor" change of our own—return corporations to a situation where they can solicit only stockholders,

not managers. Or require that the sponsors of loopholes be publicly identified, and also that the corporations the amendment will benefit be identified by name, with the projected dollar value of the benefit.

96. Cited in Michael Waldman, "Quid Pro Whoa," *New Republic*, March 18, 1990, p. 23.

97. Business is more responsible than any other group for these thousands of special deals, but even business recognizes the process is enormously inefficient. The company that fights for one special break for itself (which it usually sees as only reasonable) probably also denounces the system as a whole, laying the blame at every door but its own.

98. G. William Domhoff, *Fat Cats and Democrats: The Role of the Big Rich in the Party of the Common Man* (Englewood Cliffs, N.J.: Prentice-Hall, 1972); Walter Dean Burnham, *The Current Crisis in American Politics* (New York: Oxford University Press, 1982); Thomas Byrne Edsall, *The New Politics of Inequality* (New York: Norton, 1984).

99. Corporate campaigns against unions are based on essentially this principle. The real aim of union-busting tactics in organizing drives is to demonstrate that if workers insist on fighting for respect and dignity, the corporation will do everything in its power to make their lives miserable. The aim is to persuade the undecided that they can't make the company stop its tactics, so the only way they can achieve peace is by defeating the union. See Rick Fantasia, *Cultures of Solidarity: Consciousness, Action, and Contemporary American Workers* (Berkeley: University of California Press, 1988).

INDEX

Abdnor, James, 36
Abscam, 64
Academy of Social Insurance, 90
access: to Congress, viewed as a right, 77;
  to constituents by members of
  Congress, 52; costs of gaining, 93;
  defined, 38; as euphemism for
  lobbying, 101; to executive branch
  through soft money, 6; at fundraisers,
  56–61; as goal of corporate donors, 8;
  obtaining, and shaping solutions, 13,
  79–82; overt selling of, 53, 203; for
  respectful hearing, 63. *See also* access
  donors; access process
access donors: basic orientation of, 38;
  bribery and, 64–66; buying votes and,
  64–66; concern of, with company, 92;
  contribution decisions of, 40, 42, 99;
  contributions to liberals by, 186;
  criticism of ideological donors by, 145–
  146; criticized by business leaders, 140;
  criticized by ideological donors, 146;
  dominance of, 39, 43, 146; donations to
  opposition members by, 40; mail
  contributions by, 56, 60–61; minor
  wording changes as aim of, 67–68;
  political party and, 43–45; ratings and,
  42–43; and regret of action, 40. *See also*
  access process; corporate PACs;
  ideological donors; lobbyists and
  lobbying
access process: aims of, 5, 7–8, 63;
  cooperation of all members of
  Congress with, 91, 230; defending
  provisions against challenges to, 82–84;
  to delay regulations, 102, 191–193;
  facilitated by prior contributions, 78;
  friendship as part of, 84–87 impact of,
  102–107; misconceptions about,
  summarized, 63–64; as only one form

of business power, 23, 28, 89, 96; as
  relationship of trust, 88; in sidetracking
  social movements, 102; soft money
  and, 128–132; steps in, 77. *See also*
  lobbyists and lobbying; loopholes
acid rain, 8–9
advertising, 124, 194–195, 253n. 35
affirmative action, 165
AFL–CIO, 42–43, 109–110, 233, 245n. 7
Alexander, Lamar, 4
AlliedSignal, 125
American Automobile Manufacturers, 53
American Civil Liberties Union (ACLU),
  226
American Enterprise Institute, 148
American Hospital Association, 117
American Income Life Insurance, 122
American Medical Association (AMA), 145,
  257n. 93
American Occupational Therapy
  Association, 117
American Physical Therapy Association,
  117
American Red Cross, 10
American Sunroof Corporation, 133
American Trucking Association, 117
Americans for Constitutional Action
  (ACA), 43
Americans for Democratic Action (ADA),
  42–43
Americans for Tax Reform, 110
Andreas, Dwayne, 10
Anheuser-Busch, 116
Anschutz, Philip, 78–79
Archer Daniels Midland, 10
Armey, Dick, 55
Arneson, Paul, 133
Arthur, Chester, 131
Asian campaign contributions: and civil
  rights law suit, 255n. 50; as focus of